CHINA'S CRISIS

Studies of the East Asian Institute

Columbia University

ALSO BY ANDREW J. NATHAN

Modern China, 1840–1972: An Introduction to Sources and Research Aids (1973)

Peking Politics, 1918–1923: Factionalism and the Failure of Constitutionalism (1976)

Chinese Democracy (1985)

Popular Culture in Late Imperial China (co-edited with David Johnson and Evelyn S. Rawski) (1985)

Human Rights in Contemporary China (with R. Randle Edwards and Louis Henkin) (1986)

Andrew J. Nathan

CHINA'S CRISIS
Dilemmas of Reform and Prospects for Democracy

Columbia University Press
NEW YORK

Columbia University Press
New York   Oxford
Copyright © 1990 Columbia University Press
All rights reserved

Library of Congress Cataloging-in-Publication Data

Nathan, Andrew J. (Andrew James)
China's crisis : dilemmas of reform and prospects for democracy /
Andrew J. Nathan.
p.   cm.—(Studies of the East Asian Institute)
Includes bibliographical references.
ISBN 0-231-07284-8 (alk. paper)
1. China—Politics and government—1976–
2. Taiwan—Politics and government—1988–
I. Title. II. Series.
DS779.26.N38   1990   951.05—dc20   89-71266
                                          CIP

Printed in the United States of America

c 10 9 8 7 6 5 4 3 2 1

To Roxane

Grateful acknowledgment is made to the following for permission to reprint from previously published materials:

The China Quarterly: abridged version of "A Factionalism Model for CCP Politics," *China Quarterly* 53 (January-March 1973), pp. 34–66.

The Asia Society: abridged version of "Change and Continuity in Chinese Policy," pp. 1–24 of a China Council briefing paper entitled "Change and Continuity in Chinese Policy: An Exchange of Views," distributed in February 1978.

Professor N.T. Wang and Pergamon Press, Inc.: abridged version of "Political Risk in China," *China-International Business: An Information and Research Series*, Volume 1, No. 2, 1981, pp. 143–195.

Zhishifenzi magazine: English version of "Americans Look at China: The New Optimism and Some Historical Perspectives," *Zhishifenzi*, 1:3 (April 1985), pp. 10–14.

The Asia Society and Westview Press: "Politics: Reform at the Crossroad," in Anthony J. Kane, ed., *China Briefing 1989* (Boulder, Colo.: Westview, 1989), pp. 7–25.

The Mansfield Center, University of Montana, and Westview Press: condensed version of "Life, Liberty, and the Pursuit of Happiness in the Chinese Context," address at the 1989 Mansfield Conference, scheduled for publication in revised form in Philip West, ed., *Rising Expectations in China and Human Rights* (Boulder, Colo.: Westview, forthcoming).

Professor Yangsun Chou, *Asian Survey*, and University of California Press: Yangsun Chou and Andrew J. Nathan, "Democratizing Transition in Taiwan," *Asian Survey* 27:3 (March 1987), pp. 277–299. © 1987 by The Regents of the University of California.

Professor Stephan Haggard: "The Effect of Taiwan's Political Reform on Taiwan-Mainland Relations," forthcoming in Stephan Haggard and Tun-jen Cheng, eds., *Democratizing Transition in Taiwan* (Cambridge, Mass.: Harvard Council on East Asian Studies, forthcoming); also published in *Issues and Studies*. (Taipei)

Problems of Communism: "Chinese Democracy in 1989: Change and Continuity," *Problems of Communism*, 38:5 (September-October 1989), pp. 16–29.

Chapter 5 was first published as two articles in Chinese in the *Lien-he pao* (Taipei), January 27, 1988, and March 24, 1988.

Chapters 10 and 11 are to be published in Chinese in *Zhishifenzi*, Autumn 1989 and Winter 1989–90 issues.

CONTENTS

PREFACE

China has been searching for a political form for nearly a century. No other country's modern experience has been as painful and bloody. In 1989 China reached a new crisis. The sources, dynamics, and potential of that crisis for changing China are the subjects of this book.

The first and two last chapters deal directly with the 1989 Democracy Movement. The other essays record an observer's struggle to understand China's recent development as it was occurring, and offer an analysis of the forces that shaped the events of 1989. The essays share several themes—factionalism and its tendency to block change, the gap between rhetoric and policy, China's attraction to and fear of the West, the struggle of democrats inside and outside the party against the strictures of Deng Xiaoping's four principles, and the paradoxical effects of Deng's reforms in creating ideas that collided with these principles as he understood them. Two articles on Taiwan's political reforms are included to illuminate the similarities and differences between the two political experiences and to explore the impact of Taiwan and mainland China on each other's political development.

The essays were written beginning in 1973, and except for the introduction and conclusion were first published elsewhere. Most of them were not widely circulated; some were published only in Chinese. They contain their share of misjudgments and false notes. But I have presented them as originally written, except for abridgements and minor editorial improvements that do not change the substance of the argument, to show how a fairly consistent approach explained unfolding events. I have added a small amount of material at the end of some chapters to amplify their connection to recent events.

China's crisis was not resolved by the repression of June 1989;

the forces that created it are still shaping the nation's future. To the extent that these articles identified such forces as they were developing, I hope they will help readers understand events yet to come.

NOTE ON ROMANIZATION. I use the pinyin Romanization when writing about mainland China and modified Wade-Giles when writing about Taiwan, because each is familiar in that context.

CHINA'S CRISIS

ONE

Setting the Scene: Confessions of a China Specialist

A week or so after the Chinese army crushed the 1989 Democracy Movement in Beijing, a friend phoned and asked if I remembered "A Tragedy That Might Happen in the Year 2000," a short story that was published about the time Deng Xiaoping's reforms were starting ten years earlier. It was printed in one of the mimeographed "people's periodicals" of Democracy Wall in 1979, and warned people not to place too much trust in the permanence of the reforms so long as they were based in the will of one man and not in institutions that assured popular control of the government.

Set more than twenty years in the future, the story foretold how a group of conservative leaders would carry out a coup shortly after Deng's death. As the year 2000 starts, the new leaders launch a purge of Deng's followers, whom they charge with having formed a "counter-revolutionary group that schemed to split the motherland." The fallen leaders, who appear drugged, admit their guilt at show trials. A reshuffled Politburo (the top organ of Party power) announces that one of the conspirators' worst crimes was to attack the sacred memory of Chairman Mao and his Great Proletarian Cultural Revolution. The Politburo enacts regulations to recentralize political and economic power, aiming to rein in enterprises given too much independence during the reforms. The government reverses its close cultural and economic ties with the West and carries the purge deeper into society, calling for "the thorough extirpation of the influence of rotten Western bourgeois capitalism."[1]

Perhaps the author, Su Ming, had been a bit too optimistic in predicting that the reforms would last twenty years rather than ten, and as it turned out Deng participated in the coup against his

1

own reforms. But in other respects Su's story was prophetic. It foretold the reversal of economic decentralization, the strengthening of the police, the revival of old purge and thought-control techniques, the rewriting of history and manipulation of law, and the repudiation of Western influence which accompanied the repression of the second Democracy Movement in June 1989.

Su's story seemed important to me at the time especially because it warned against the limits that Deng wanted to set on reform. Deng said reform must not challenge "four basic principles"—socialism, dictatorship of the proletariat, Marxism-Leninism-Mao Zedong Thought, and party leadership. The core of the principles was the Chinese Communist Party's monopoly of power. Deng claimed that without the exclusive and unquestioned leadership of his own party, a country as large, fractious, and backward as China would crumble into chaos. These four principles were to confine the party's reform efforts and the strivings of China's democratic activists like an iron maiden for the next ten years.

Deng remained loyal to the four principles in June 1989. Although the May-June demonstrations were peaceful and did not seek to overthrow communism or the ruling party, Deng labeled them a "counter-revolutionary rebellion" because of their demand for independent political organizations and a free press. These demands threatened the Leninist principle of one-party dictatorship. To advocate political freedom, even without opposing communism, amounted in Deng's eyes to "wanting to overthrow our state and the Party."[2] His us-or-them mentality decreed that any call for limitation of the ruling party's power was equivalent to an attack on the political system as such. As Premier Li Peng stated a few days after declaring martial law, "If we were going to retreat any further, we might as well have handed China over to those people."[3]

Su Ming had foreseen that the reforms were hostage to a coup so long as they gave the people only economic freedoms and not political power that they could use to defend their gains. He was among a minority of Democracy Wall writers who argued that the reform program should therefore establish institutions of competitive democracy and a free press, guaranteeing their irreversibility by giving them a popular base. The collision between these views and Deng's led to Deng's decision in March 1979 to crush the democracy movement, which he had initially welcomed because of

2

its support for him. A number of the democratic leaders were arrested, of whom Wei Jingsheng became the best-known in the West.

Su Ming, however, was never identified by the police. He had written under a pseudonym and was unknown even to his colleagues among the democracy activists. The investigation into his case remained active, but he continued to serve in a trusted position in a central party organ. He was now in the United States, and my friend offered me a chance to meet him.

In the days before meeting Su Ming, I reflected on how much I had learned from a number of Chinese I had met in recent years, often after having written about them on the basis of documentary sources.

There was Hu Ping. I had first heard of him when he was a Beijing University graduate student who won a hard-fought election contest for a seat in the county-level people's congress in 1980, when China held its first, experimental multi-candidate elections at the county level. By competing on a platform of freedom of speech, Hu Ping became so controversial that the university could not find him a job after awarding him an M.A., and he was kept in "cold storage" on campus.[4]

In 1987 Hu Ping arrived at Harvard to study for his Ph.D. in Western political thought, and I arranged to meet him in New York. I encountered a small man with a delicate face, round shoulders, and alert eyes. He wore two-tone plastic glasses and a quick smile that revealed prominent front teeth. Hu told me about his poverty-stricken childhood in Sichuan in the 1950s as the son of an executed counterrevolutionary, his first encounter with political discrimination at the age of 15 when he was denied admission to the Communist Youth League because of his "bad class background," and his loyalty to Mao and sense of despair when denied entry to the revolutionary ranks of Red Guards in the early days of the cultural revolution. He spoke of his relish in the free debates that took place at the height of the cultural revolution, of being sent to a remote village to live among the peasants with other young people, and of his awakening there to the fact that the Chinese system was wasting its people's lives. Once he had the enforced leisure to think, he was struck by the contradiction between Mao's call for independent thinking and the reality of the repression that was stricter than ever in the early 1970s. That was when he formed his commitment to freedom of speech.[5]

After a year Hu gave up his academic work to accept the elected post of chairman of the Chinese Alliance for Democracy (or China Spring, as it is also known), a New York-based organization founded in 1982. CAD calls for dropping Deng Xiaoping's four basic principles from the Chinese constitution and the adoption of a private enterprise economy and competitive politics. Although it has never explicitly opposed socialism or advocated the overthrow of the Chinese Communist Party, it was labeled a "reactionary organization" by the Chinese government in 1987. The organization has only about 1000 members, but it exercises considerable influence among the 40,000 or so Chinese students and visiting scholars in this country. Hu gave CAD a philosophical turn, publishing a series of 200 aphorisms in the monthly *China Spring*. Some of the most interesting explored the narrow differences between political cowardice and courage, idealism and selfishness, passivity and action. Others were straightforwardly political, for example, "I willingly support a government that I can oppose, but I firmly oppose a government that I can only support"[6]

In 1989, the Chinese government accused China Spring of being one of the major "black hands" behind the student movement, and raised its rank of opprobrium from reactionary to "counterrevolutionary." The government charged that China Spring's activity in Beijing showed that the "good hearted" students of Tiananmen Square were being manipulated by "an extremely small, extremely small number" of people with sinister aims. In fact, this was far from the case, as I describe in chapter 5.

Then there was Cao (pronounced Tsao) Siyuan, who came to New York in December 1988. I wondered whether this might be the same Mr. Cao whose work on constitutional reform I cited a couple of years earlier in a footnote,[7] so I brought to our meeting a photocopy of that article. The Mr. Cao who appeared was an energetic person of about 40 with disordered hair and a humorous smile, peering through thick, small lenses. His ample body was wrapped in the kind of sturdy blue suit that Soviet travelers used to have tailored for their trips to the West. I asked why he wasn't wearing an overcoat on such a cold day. He replied, "I never get too cold, only too hot."

Cao pulled from his briefcase a sheaf of documents in English that included translations of several of his articles calling for enhancements in the role of the National People's Congress, descriptions of the Stone Institute of Social Development, of which he was director, a 24–page resume listing 150 publications, 62 lectures, and 16 press profiles since 1985, and an article from the *China Youth Daily* describing him as China's first "lobbyist" because of his work in encouraging the National People's Congress to adopt a bankruptcy law. He was indeed the author of "Ten Proposals for Revising the Constitution." He asked for a photocopy of the English translation of his essay that I had cited, and stowed it in his briefcase.

Cao told me that the Stone Institute was private and nongovernmental, suppported by the independent Stone Group Corporation, the most successful of a number of non-state-owned computer enterprises in Beijing's version of Silicon Valley. I had heard of this new company and its brash institute, but suspected they were somehow still controlled by the Party. Cao denied that this was the case, but acknowledged that all the institute's researchers were party members, including himself. I asked about his beliefs as a Marxist.

"Marxism is a science," he answered. "It grows and changes and is not dogmatic."

"What scientific truth does it reveal?" I asked.

"That the economic base determines the superstructure."

Is it a scientific truth that capitalism will inevitably collapse as predicted by Marx? "Marx was writing about the society of his time."

What do you understand by the concept of socialism, I persisted. "Marx never said what socialism has to be. He never said socialism forbids this or that. The main thing is that socialism means development of the productive forces."

"In that case," I asked, feeling that I was closing the trap, "which is more socialist, Deng's China or Reagan's America?"

"Which is closer to my chair," Mr. Cao replied, "The table over there or that one on the other side? You see, things have many aspects. My chair may be closer to that table in one aspect and to the other table in another aspect."

There was a moment of silence as I contemplated this virtuoso display of saying nothing with many words. My interlocutor must have honed this skill in years of "political study" sessions. At last we both laughed. I asked him how he had come to join the party. "It's only by joining the Chinese Communist Party that one can work for political change in China," he told me. "The Communist Party is not going to lose its dominance any time soon. For now, it is the only party with the power to rule."

The Chinese Communist Party has always enforced its control of society by placing its members throughout every institution, including those that were nominally independent. My conversation with Cao Siyuan made me realize that this process of infiltration had become mutual. Society was beginning penetrate the party. For the sake of reform the party found it useful to cultivate the fiction of an increasingly independent society. For their part independent people found it useful to join the party and to get party sponsorship for their initiatives. Each side pretended to play the other's game, and each thought it was winning. Without being challenged, Deng Xiaoping's notion of party leadership was growing hollow from within in the late 1980s.

Conservative leaders tried to correct the flabbiness of their organizational instrument with campaigns in 1983 and 1987 against "spiritual pollution" and "bourgeois liberalization." But the campaigns lacked strong leadership from Deng's aides, Hu Yaobang and Zhao Ziyang, who were in charge of the party apparatus. Their commitments seemed to lie elsewhere, as I discuss in chapter 10. In any case, a person like Cao gave the conservatives no "pigtail to grasp," in the Chinese phrase. His central goal apparently was to enlarge the role of the National People's Congress so that it could replace the CCP as the supreme organ of power, a system he disarmingly called "socialist parliamentary democracy." He also proposed that the phrase "the interests of the people" be used instead of the four basic principles as the highest constitutional doctrine of the PRC. Such arguments could not be faulted because the supreme organ of state power is exactly what what the Chinese constitution says the NPC is, and the interests of the people are what the CCP claims to serve.

But in the crisis of May–June 1989, Cao went a step too far when he assisted members of the National People's Congress Standing Committee in trying to convene a meeting to overturn Premier Li Peng's declaration of martial law. The meeting was blocked, and Cao was one of the first intellectuals arrested after the military crackdown.

In chapter 7 I tell about a third intellectual I met after writing about him, Wang Ruoshui, whose essays on the Marxist concept of alienation I puzzled over in 1983, and whom I met in the spring of

1989. Wang's birdlike, wary look seemed to show the cost of years of intra-party struggle—most of it on the losing end: he had been dismissed as deputy editor of the *People's Daily* in 1983 and expelled from the party in 1987 for advocating theories that the party's ideological authority, Hu Qiaomu, deemed conducive to bourgeois liberalization. Yet what impressed and at first puzzled me was Wang's stubborn fealty to Marxism. When he spoke, he seemed to hold private conference with the spirit of the dead philosopher before answering each riddle posed by a skeptical audience. As he buttressed each point with direct quotations from the classics and stringent analyses of their logic, his gladiatorial polemic seemed to belie his physical frailty.

Somehow the net effect of each staunchly Marxist argument was to undermine the Marxism that was defined as orthodox in China. For example Wang argued in a talk at Columbia, "It's true that Marx spoke of the proletarian dictatorship. But this meant only that the proletariat would have a complete hold on power, not that it would behave in a dictatorial manner. In fact, there should not necessarily be only one party to represent the proletariat in power."

Wang also presented the case for Marxist humanism and turned it into a sharp critique of the communism of Mao and Deng. "In Marx, proletarian dictatorship was only a means to an end, human freedom. Marx said that in communism, the development of the freedom of each will be the condition for the development of the freedom of all. Engels said that this is the key sentence of all Marxism. Yet in China, not only hasn't it been propagated; some people have even labeled it erroneous. After the revolution we propagated the idea of the collective, the sacrifice of the individual to the collective. Some people used the idea of the collective to force individuals to sacrifice their own individuality to the interests of a small group who claim to represent the collective. This is what I call an alienated collective. The most precious thing in Marx was his insight into human development. His starting point was the liberation of mankind. His goal was to get rid of all the alienations which make man unfree."[8]

What Wang said made so much sense to me as a non-Marxist that I wondered reflexively why he bothered to cast himself as a Marxist at all. But as soon as I asked myself the question I know it was misplaced.

Like many of his generation, Wang came to Marxism in the midst of personal and national crises in the late 1940s. In a memoir published some years ago in Hong Kong he recalled how his sense of depression "dissolved into the great collective cause and turned into positive resistance and struggle" once he had discovered Marxism. After the victory of the revolution, like many of his generation, he discovered that "reality was not as perfect and flawless" as he had imagined. Organizational life was oppressive. And he suffered a series of political repressions. But he concluded that "what a philosopher should seek is wisdom, and wisdom brings pain as well as happiness."[9] Why shouldn't he continue to see himself as a Marxist?

Wang rejects the cynical assumption that lay behind my unvoiced question. For Wang, it is not Marxism that has betrayed China, but the Chinese Communist Party that has betrayed Marxism by turning it into a dead ideology that most party members parrot for ulterior purposes. "I am no longer recognized as a CCP member," he says, "but I still view myself as a Marxist. Only I don't agree with 'them' as to what Marxism is. The people being criticized in China today are precisely the ones who are upholding Marxism. This is a good thing, because it shows that Marxism still has some critical value."

Yan Jiaqi was another thinker I had read about before meeting him. I first noticed his political science-fiction story called "Religion, Reason, and Practice" published in the official *Guangming Daily* in 1978. At that time party theorists were working themselves free of Maoism by carrying out what was called a "debate on practice as the sole criterion of truth." Yan's article told the story of a trip through time in which the author visits three "courts of truth."

The first is the "court of religion" in Rome in 1633, where Yan witnesses an interrogation of Galileo by the Inquisition. The traveler from the twentieth century knows that Galileo is right even though he is forced to recant, and in a transparent reference to Maoism he comments that "in the face of religion's rampant reactionary force, truth was throttled by religion, and science bowed before theology." Next, Yan travels through time to the "court of reason," Voltaire's home in Ferney, France, in the year 1755. He meets Voltaire, Diderot, and Montesquieu. In another obvious reference to the Chinese political system, the philosophes tell their visitor that it is not religion but Louis XV's autocracy that has made France poverty-stricken and turbulent. Montesqueieu informs Yan that only the separation of powers will solve France's political problems. Within a few years Yan would be openly advocating separation of powers for China. Last, Yan travels forward to 1994, where he finds the "court of practice" in Beijing, an ultramodern city of skyscrapers, moving sidewalks, automatic doors, and supermarkets. Modernization has been achieved because dogma has been vanquished, science reigns, and practice is now the sole criterion of truth.[10]

In the years following this debut, Yan published scores of articles to flesh out his vision of political modernization. He advocated separation of powers both among central government organs and between central and local governments, an end to lifetime tenure in office for political leaders, constitutional definition of the scope of individual autonomy, the vesting of true political supremacy in the National People's Congress, and the abolition of limits on political discussion. He wrote a study of political leadership which probed the sensitive issue of political succession. He and his wife, Gao Gao, wrote the first honest Chinese history of the cultural revolution.[11] In 1985, when the Chinese Academy of Social Sciences experimented with allowing researchers to elect their own institute directors, Yan was elected director of the Institute of Political Science, becoming at age 43 the youngest institute director in the Academy.

When I met Yan at his institute in Beijing in 1987, I was struck by his lack of what the Chinese call *jiazi*, "frame" or air of self-importance. The reception room was small and a bit disordered, and the two or three associates who joined Yan seemed notably at ease. The angular, casual-looking Yan was lacking most of his upper teeth. He said he had been waiting three months for bridge.

The Hong Kong press was reporting that Yan had been invited to serve in the Political Structure Reform Office of the party center. This office was drafting proposals for Zhao Ziyang—then Premier and acting party secretary—to present to the Thirteenth Party Congress in October 1987. If Zhao had indeed turned to Yan for advice, it might be a signal that Zhao's program would be relatively radical. Yan politely turned my question on the rumor aside, an indication that it was true. When the party congress opened in October, Zhao enjoyed a victory in the distribution of seats to his pro-reform allies in the new Politburo. But his proposal for political restructuring was limited to measures of administrative streamlining. Zhao even took the trouble to affirm that "We shall never abandon [the special features of our system] and introduce a

Western system of separation of the three powers and of different parties ruling the country in turn."[12] Most of Yan's advice had apparently been rejected.

The limits continued to be set by Deng, Yan said in a talk the following spring at Columbia University. But he insisted that progress toward rule of law was inevitable because of the lessons learned about arbitrary power during the cultural revolution and because personal freedom was growing as part of the economic reform.

Yan's optimism was challenged during the events of May and June 1989, in which he played a major role. After the students started their hunger strike, Yan emerged in the lead of a loose organization called the Association of Intellectual Circles in the Capital, which worked tirelessly to press the government to meet the students' demands while urging the students to end the hunger strike. The student leaders were receptive to the appeal, although the hunger strike continued anyway after the student group split. But, for reasons which I explore in chapter 10, the government was obdurate against the group's plea that it recognize the constitutionality of the independent student union. On May 17 Yan and a group of his colleagues issued a sharply worded statement attacking "China's uncrowned Emperor" as "a senile, muddle-headed dictator" and demanding his resignation.[13]

On the night of the military crackdown two weeks later Yan learned that there was a warrant out for his arrest. He and his wife took a few items of clothing and fled, leaving their 15–year old son in sympathetic hands. Yan surfaced some days later in Hong Kong and then again in Paris, where he joined with student leader Uerkesh Daolet (Wu'erkaixi) to announce the formation of a Chinese Democratic Front to unite opposition forces abroad. When Yan visited New York again a few months later, his hopeful attitude was unchanged. Democracy would still come peacefully to China, he insisted. Within ten years or so the country would have a new constitution, freedom of speech, a directly elected and effectual people's congress, and a depoliticized military. The Chinese Communist Party would be competing on an equal basis with a legal democratic opposition. Yan's optimism and moderation were typical of the Chinese intellectuals, yet curious in light of the violence the government had used against them. I explore the reasons for this moderation in chapter 10.

These conversations with Chinese intellectuals were a valuable source of insight into the growing crisis of Deng Xiaoping's regime.

Hu Ping, Cao Siyuan, Wang Ruoshui, and Yan Jiaqi were better known than most intellectuals I met, but their attitudes were typical. The intellectuals, of course, did not represent all Chinese, but their defection would send a signal to other social classes and would deprive the regime of the support of an essential group.

Such honest conversations with PRC citizens were a relatively new experience for me. My generation of graduate students were trained in the 1960s to study the country without going there or meeting any PRC citizens except refugees. We sifted through the documents of a closed society as if they were the shards of a dead civilization. When I finally walked across the footbridge from Hong Kong's Lo Wu railway station into Guangdong Province in 1973, and my group passed some soldiers with baggy green uniforms and peaked caps with Mao buttons, I felt we were stepping through the looking glass from the real world into a propaganda poster.

And in a way we were. For foreigners at least, the China of Mao's late years was a stage show. People lived in terror of uttering a wrong word. Everything they said to visitors and much that they said among themselves was rehearsed. During that first trip, a group of senior professors who briefed us at Fudan University in Shanghai under the watchful eyes of young propaganda officers said that the school had been a revisionist stronghold before the cultural revolution, that they had all benefited from being sent down to the countryside to learn from the peasants at May 7 cadre schools, and that they were collectively rewriting all of their earlier scholarly work, which was trash. They said these things with conviction.

As late as 1983 Chinese displayed caution even in private conversations outside of China. The political study and political campaign systems were still functioning at home. Academics traveling abroad were given briefings on how to answer sensitive questions. Visitors criticized their own society to the extent it was being criticized in the official press and expressed themselves in favor of reforms that were being discussed in the official press. I found that it was discourteous to ask a visitor whether he or she was a member of the Chinese Communist Party because party members were supposed to keep their membership secret. Chinese guests would look outside an office door to see if there were other Chinese there; they would lower their voices in Chinese restaurants. But perhaps they were still less afraid of being reported by someone else than of the report they would have to give on themselves when they returned home, and less constrained by fear than by the unfamiliarity of being asked to speak their minds.

Sometime around 1984 these inhibitions began to fall away. Chinese began to talk openly and critically, not only in private but even in public, not only abroad but sometimes in their own country.

No single event seems to explain this change. Several deep forces were at work. Economic reform had progressed to the point where citizens were slipping the bonds of the control system. This had been based on monolithic control of the individual by his work unit and of the work unit by the party. Now in the countryside, the party legalized long-term contracts to rent land to the peasants, completing the dismantling of the commune system and its replacement by household agriculture. In factories, the government authorized managers to retain a portion of their profits and to pay bonuses to workers; political activities were ignored because they were time-consuming and irritated the workers. In cities and small towns small private enterprises (some of them ostensibly collectively owned) had grown so numerous that the party could do no more than occasionally inspect their financial and political books. At about this time also, the number of Chinese students and scholars in the United States grew to nearly 20,000, most of them coming here at their own initiative.[14] All these developments reduced the party's ability to punish people for speaking their minds.

Among intellectuals, a long, painful process of introspection about their behavior under the Maoist dictatorship seemed to have reached a point where many were determined no longer to sacrifice their self-respect for political security. Liu Binyan, the prominent journalist, published a report on two ordinary men who had each spent a lifetime protesting Mao's excesses at great personal cost. He called the article "The Second Kind of Loyalty" to contrast their fealty to principle to others' service to the official line. A dramatist, Wu Zuguang, stood up at a writers' congress to recall what his family had suffered under Mao and to urge that such things never happen again, but he told the audience that his wife was so frightened of the consequences of his speaking up that she had threatened to disrupt the meeting if he said anything to offend the leaders. Wang Ruoshui refused to follow the party tradition of self-criticism when his views were attacked by high officials, and instead published passionate rebuttals, some of them outside the pale of party control in Hong Kong. Another controversial party theorist, Li Honglin, issued an unrepentant collection of his articles with a series of notes indicating how each had been criticized and why the criticisms were wrong.[15]

All four of the writers I have just mentioned were party members. The change that occurred in 1984 was not a rebellion of society against party control, but a change that originated within the party. The general secretary, Hu Yaobang, had encouraged the change of atmosphere. As head of the party's Organization Department in 1977–78, he rehabilitated millions of party and non-party members who had been unjustly persecuted during the cultural revolution. As vice-president of the Central Party School, he authorized publications and meetings to begin the process of ideological deMaoification which was necessary to prepare the way for reform. He promised intellectuals there would be no more political punishment for academic and theoretical debate—no more "seizing of pigtails, wielding of clubs, putting on of caps, and building up of dossiers." In 1984 disciplinarians in the party tried to restore ideological control through a campaign against "spiritual pollution." As usual in campaigns of this sort, party intellectuals were called upon to *biaotai*, or express pro forma support, but this time many refused, and no one punished them for it. This was probably the final event that persuaded many intellectuals that it was safe to speak frankly.

For years, to say that a person "said things against his heart" (*shuo weixinhua*) was meant as an exculpation; the person had bowed to irresistible political force. Now this was a criticism. One of the senior leaders, Bo Yibo, even published a memoir in *People's Daily* regretting that he had joined in the attack on another leader at a party meeting in 1959. "When I review it today," Bo said, "there were still some words contrary to my convictions (*weixin de hua*) in my speech at that time. This is something for which I cannot excuse myself and for this I still have a guilty conscience."[16] As far as I know, Bo was the only party leader to admit publicly to a guilty conscience for anything that had happened in the years since 1949.

The friend who was going to introduce me to Su Ming told me that Su worked closely for some time with Hu Yaobang. I was curious to ask Su Ming about Hu Yaobang's motives for loosening ideological controls. He was a thin, anxious-looking man who asked that I keep his identity confidential.

"Hu was much more democratic than most people realize," Su

told me. "He often talked on the phone with people like Wang Ruoshui or attended meetings with them. He sympathized with a lot of their ideas and sometimes used to suggest topics for leading theoreticians to write about. He sponsored the secret Conference for the Discussion of Guidelines for Theoretical Work that took place from January through April of 1979, when Yan Jiaqi and others like him presented their new ideas on the nature of socialism, political reform, the mistakes of the Mao era, and other such controversial topics. What looked like a loss of control over ideology in the 1980s was actually a process of intellectual exploration guided by Hu. His main concern was to find ways to prevent another cultural revolution. He told us, 'Right now, the CCP is more corrupt than the KMT was when we made the revolution.' "

rei (Hu Yaobang)

"During the cultural revolution," Su Ming continued, "Hu was locked up at the Youth League headquarters for several years [he was head of the Youth League] and then sent to the countryside to labor. His wife and children were treated as counterrevolutionaries. Later he was brought back to Beijing. He had plenty of time for reflection and met often with young people and friends from the 1950s. After a lot of thought he concluded that the cultural revolution had happened because of the overconcentration of power in the party. To guarantee it would never happen again, the party had to be democratized. Hu Yaobang often spoke of a revitalization of the party. He was a Chinese Gorbachev long before Gorbachev came to power."

But didn't this put Hu in contradiction with Deng's four principles? I asked. In a way, it did, Su Ming said. The two men understood the four basic principles differently, and over the years Deng came to disapprove of what Hu was doing. Hu Yaobang saw himself as a Marxist, but he understood Marxism as a developing science that provided an approach to problems rather than a set of solutions. He accepted socialism as a goal, but admitted he had no idea what it would be like. As for party leadership, he saw no contradiction between it and his vision of the ideal communist party, which would be open and democratic within, and subject to electoral competition and press criticism without. He did not envision democratic processes as a threat to the party's control, but as strengthening party rule by keeping the party healthy and popular.

But the loosening of control infuriated the senior generation of leaders. In January 1987, after Hu had responded leniently to student demonstrations, Deng and the other elderly leaders dropped

14

him from the leadership and purged a number of the party intellectuals he had protected. According to Su Ming, Hu accepted his fate
quietly because he was a strong believer in "party character."

If Hu was not willing to split the party while he lived, he did so
involuntarily after his death. It was during his funeral services that
the great demonstrations of April 1989 started, over the students'
demand that the party withdraw its criticism of him for having
failed to suppress the student movement of 1986. Deng's former
partner in power came back to haunt the supreme leader like
Banquo's ghost. The Tiananmen Square demonstrations were as
much the expression of a struggle within the party over its style of
rule as they were an explosion of popular discontent over its performance. The forces that Hu had fostered within the party linked
with the non-party students and intellectuals to create a movement
that threatened Deng's concept of the regime.

China scholars had been tracking the emerging crisis for several
years. Its immediate causes were the blockage of economic reform
since the mid-1980s, with consequent growing inflation and corruption; the widening rift between the regime and the intellectuals;
and the deterioration of the Communist Party's control network
throughout society. Its signs included worsening social mores, rising crime rates, frequent strikes and demonstrations by students,
workers, and peasants, as well as open disaffection of intellectuals
at home and abroad. A minority of specialists saw these strains as
normal responses to the pressures of a changing society. But most
of us felt we were witnessing a true crisis of the regime. One
observer described Chinese society as suffering from normlessness;
another described the country as a boiling pot with the leaders
perched precariously on a rattling lid.

The essays in this volume illustrate some of the rewards as well
as a few of the pitfalls of China scholarship in providing a guide to
unfolding events. The theme of factionalism, which is the subject
of chapter 2 and recurs in chapters 3, 6, 10, and 11, has always
been important for understanding Chinese politics and is likely to
be no less so in the post-Deng years. Published in 1973 when Western scholars had virtually no access to China, chapter 2 is theoretical and somewhat speculative, but still provides a capsule history
of the regime's first two decades as well as a way of understanding
Chinese politics that remains relevant. No one has explained why
the Chinese leadership is so persistently factionalized or why factionalism seems to wax and wane as a form of political conflict.

But given that factionalism is a fact of Chinese politics, the essay suggests how this fact explains some of the otherwise baffling features that characterize the game of politics in Beijing.

Chapter 3, written in 1981, asked whether political instability might threaten the interests of foreign firms trading or investing in China. Factionalism and a deep Chinese ambivalence about relations with the West were the themes that informed the analysis, leading to the conclusion that prospects for Western businesses in China were less rosy than they were commonly thought to be. The essay sketched six possible scenarios for the future. The two to which I assigned the highest probabilities turned out to describe fairly well the events that came to pass, with scenario A taking place during most of the 1980s and scenario C roughly anticipating the events of 1989. Today issues of national identity and foreign power remain central to Chinese ambivalence about reform. Sensitivities about foreign economic and cultural relations and their political and social consequences were among the major issues that came to a head in the crisis of 1989, and they will continue to shape China's relations with the West after Deng.

The two essays in Part II were previously published in Chinese. Chapter 3 aimed to explain to Chinese readers why some Americans in the mid-1980s were heralding the arrival of capitalism in China, when most Chinese felt that the hand of the state was still heavy on their economy and society. Chapter 4 explored for a Taiwan audience some of the complexities of American policy-making toward China as these related to human rights issues, and analyzed the changing state of mind toward their home government of mainland Chinese students and intellectuals in the U.S. Americans are less optimistic about China today and more critical on human rights issues, but we need to remain aware of how our interpretations of China are colored by our attitudes about ourselves and by the passions of our domestic politics.

Part III brings the analysis to the crucial year of 1988, when forces of social change and intellectual freedom created by the successes of Deng's reforms brought the crisis nearly to a head. Tensions were exacerbated by Deng's mishandling of price reform, which engendered a spurt of inflation and a widespread sense that reform had reached a dead end. Chapter 6, written before the Democracy Movement erupted, identified the forces that would soon give rise to it; chapter 7 amplifies the analysis by evaluating the successes and failures of reform in a longer time perspective and dwelling on the relations between the regime and the intellectuals.

While mainland China struggled with the legacies of Maoism, the Kuomintang regime on Taiwan led its society through a period of rapid economic growth, and in 1986 launched a political reform which interacted with mainland reform in several ways. The Taiwan political reform was partly a response to the challenge of the mainland's new "peaceful reunification diplomacy;" in turn it posed a challenge to the government in Beijing by demonstrating that a culturally Chinese political system was capable of substantial democratization, and that democratization might even be conducive to economic growth. Political reform in Taiwan made reunification on Beijing's terms a more remote possibility than ever. The two essays in part IV explore these themes. They show that it is useful to study events on both sides of the Taiwan Strait together in order better to understand both. Chapter 11 returns in part to the subject of Taiwan to analyze mainland and Taiwan reform in comparative perspective.

Chapters 10 and 11 deal with the 1989 Democracy Movement itself. The first discusses the demands of the democrats and asks why their goals and tactics were so moderate both before and after the June 4 massacre. Chapter 11 sums up the themes of the book in an analysis of the prospects for Chinese democracy.

Although the essays collected in this book identified the emerging crisis that led to the spring 1989 demonstrations, I did not anticipate the explosive quality of those events. No one in the West, and so far as I know no one in China, expected that the demonstrations would grow to such a huge scale or that the regime would use so much force and pay such a high price to put them down. As events developed, China seemed to slip back behind the looking glass into a world of mythic courage and mythic folly. China specialists like other Americans were dizzied by events that were not just half a world away, but seemingly in another political dimension.

In retrospect, three dynamics explain the size and speed of the civic explosion. First, the succession struggle within the party immobilized the regime, so that it could not respond decisively to the demonstrations in the early weeks when they could have been suppressed with threats, a little force, or compromise. Zhao Ziyang, who succeeded Hu Yaobang as party secretary after Hu was demoted in 1987, tolerated the demonstrations when they started in mid-April, then disappeared for a scheduled official visit to North Korea, and upon his return seems to have seen an opportunity to turn the demonstrations to his political advantage. I analyze his role in more detail in chapter 10.

After Zhao's return from Korea, the showdown with the students was postponed again by Mikhail Gorbachev's summit visit. Gorbachev brought the international press, giving the students an opportunity to embarrass the regime and further delaying the crackdown. The students increased their demands, and the regime's apparent weakness emboldened more people to come into the streets. A remark by Zhao to Gorbachev that all major decisions were made by Deng revealed the conflict among the leaders. These developments hardened the resolve of the party elders to use force despite Zhao's resistance. Without his intending it, Gorbachev's visit removed any slight remaining possibility of a peaceful solution to the crisis.

The second dynamic was that the intensity of the mass movement fed on itself, combining with paralysis at the top to create a carnival of unaccountability for the masses of Beijing. Although Deng signaled his intention to crush the movement on April 26 with an editorial in *People's Daily* labeling it a "turbulence," most Beijing residents seemed to feel that the movement was so popular that the government could not conceivably use force. Once an estimated 150,000 people had demonstrated safely on April 27 in the presence of police and troops, hundreds of thousands more felt it was safe to join in. Demonstrating gave vent to resentments that had been building for some time. Once the catharsis started, people discovered in themselves a depth of anger that surprised them, because they had learned to suppress it for their own good. The anger was so strong that when troops moved from their holding positions into the heart of the city on the night of June 3, hundreds if not thousands of citizens faced them weaponless and were killed.

Third, the panic of the ill-prepared troops who were sent to face the angry people of Beijing, and the panic of the men who sent them, caused the violence to escalate. Chinese troops are not trained or armed for crowd control. According to some Beijing residents, the troops who were sent in on June 3 were isolated and indoctrinated for weeks beforehand. In the streets they encountered resistance and some threats to their lives. They responded with fury. Indeed, this may have been the intent of the politicians who sent them into combat. They did not attempt to use teargas, fire hoses, or rubber bullets; instead, some reports said, dumdum bullets were used. Demonstrators were allowed to withdraw from the southern part of Tiananmen Square with few or no casualties on the night of June 3–4, but in other parts of the Square and many other places in the city troops shot thousands of unarmed citizens over the course of several days.[17] There has been no public inquiry into, or acknowledgement of, the excessive use of force. The roundup of activists since June 4 suggests that the government's aim is not just to reestablish public order but to extirpate opposition.

Four flaws in the American understanding of China weakened China specialists' grasp of these events.[18] Unfortunately, two of them are irremediable. We knew the importance of the web of personal relationships among the Chinese party leaders, and appreciated how influential the internal politics of the Chinese military could be in political crises. Both were decisive factors in 1989. But these are the two most tightly guarded subjects in a very secretive country. Even the U.S. government's intelligence specialists seemed to know little about them.

Two other flaws in some China specialists' insight could have been avoided: the failure to distinguish between pronouncements and performance in China's reforms, and the assumption that Stalinist conservatism was dead because the Chinese leadership turned a liberal face to the West. As government in-and-outers, business consultants, or academic entrepreneurs, some scholars acquired a vested interest in seeing the reforms succeed, which made it harder to give the signs of trouble the weight they deserved. For others, a focus on policy studies and bureaucratic politics drew attention away from civil society, where Chinese bureaucrats themselves were often out of touch with what was happening.

The scholars who most readily avoided misjudgment seem to have been those who studied the workings of the party organization and propaganda apparatus and knew how it could manipulate and coordinate information across a vast front of seemingly unrelated activities; those few who did field work in the Chinese villages, where things are always much worse than the government claims; those who studied the Maoist era or earlier historical periods in some depth and were sensitive to continuities in political culture; and those who maintained contact with dissidents in China or abroad. But such sources of information did not offer any easy key to the truth either. Each of them was as partial and biased in its own way as information based on visits to model villages or audiences with Deng Xiaoping.

As the China studies enterprise in this country has grown steadily larger and each generation of students is better trained, the quality of our insight into China has improved. The performance of American China specialists in understanding the events of 1989 was generally good. To the extent that it was partially flawed, the only corrective is more of the same: more study of language and history, more field work, more scholarly exchange, and more intimate contact with China.

The challenge of understanding China will only grow larger as the country enters a new period of dramatic change. The years to come should show whether the events of 1989 signified another failure in China's long search for democracy, or, as I suggest in chapter 11, conceivably the beginning of success.

PART I

Factionalism and the Limits of Reform

TWO

A Factionalism Model for CCP Politics

U ntil the Cultural Revolution, the predominant Western view of contemporary Chinese elite conflict was that it consisted of discussion (*taolun*) within a basically consensual Politburo among shifting "opinion groups" with no organized force behind them.[1] The purges and accusations which began in 1965 and apparently still continue have shaken this interpretation, and a number of scholars have advanced new analyses. Of these new views, perhaps the most systematic—and at the same time the one which represents the least change from the pre-Cultural Revolution opinion group model—is the "policy making under Mao" interpretation, which sees conflict as essentially a bureaucratic decision-making process dominated by Mao.[2] Deviating further from the unorganized opinion group model are interpretations which explain political alignments and policy advocacy in terms of leaders' attachments to various bureaucratic "interest groups."

I believe that a factionalism model, which I will delineate here, can be applied to Chinese Communist Party (CCP) elite politics. The model is not intended to explain everything about CCP politics, but it can clarify how the Chinese leaders organize themselves to carry out conflict, how they mobilize resources for the struggle, under what formal or informal rules the conflict is carried out, and what sanctions are visited upon the losers. The model deals only with what might broadly be called organizational constraints on political behavior, and not with the other sets of constraints—e.g., ideological and cultural—which provide additional rules of the game. It has to be said at the outset that the available data on CCP elite conflict are not adequate to prove or disprove the model decisively. But if the model passes an initial test of fitting available data, it can be used to suggest ways of understanding and interpreting the situation that the data are too slim to confirm.

23

The Structure of Factions

The starting point is a kind of human behavior which I shall call the "clientelist tie"—a nonascriptive two-person relationship founded on exchange, in which well-understood rights and obligations are established between the two parties.[3] Such ties include patron-client relations, godfather-parent relations, some types of trader-customer relations, and so forth. Clientelist ties in a given society combine to form complex networks which serve many functions, including social insurance and the mobilization and wielding of influence (i.e., political conflict).

What happens when political conflict is organized primarily through clientelist ties rather than through formal organizations, corporate lineage units, or mass or class movements? I would argue that there are three possibilities. First, the individual seeking to engage in political conflict may do so by cashing in on his personal ties to operate as a power broker. The second possibility, which occurs in a setting of electoral competition, has been called the "clientelist party," "vertical group," or "machine"—a mass political organization which buys electoral support with particularistic rewards distributed through a leader-follower network of clientelist ties.

The third possibility occurs in an oligarchic or relatively small-scale setting when an individual leader mobilizes some portion of his network of primary, secondary, tertiary ties, and so on,[4] for the purpose of engaging in politics. A machine or clientelist party consists of a great many layers of personnel, but this third type of clientelist political structure consists of only one or a few layers. I call such a structure a faction.[5]

The Structural Characteristics of Factions[6]

Because it is based upon personal exchange ties, the faction enjoys considerable flexibility: the leader sees the opportunity for political gain, separately recruits each member into the faction, and directs the activities of each member for the overall good of the faction. On the other hand, this characteristic tends to set limits to the number of levels to which the faction can extend without becoming corporatized and to the degree to which large factions can engage in finely coordinated activities.

Since it is founded upon exchange relationships, a faction depends for its growth and continuity upon the ability of the leader to secure and distribute rewards to his followers. It tends to expand and contract with success or failure, and may even be dissolved when removed from power. But it can always be reconstituted when it regains the capability to reward its members. When the enemy is overthrown, the faction may return to full activity unchanged in form and flexibility. Since the set of clientelist ties on which it is founded forms a unique configuration centered on the leader, the faction can never be taken over as a whole by a successor. The unique combination of personnel and strategic political positions held by the faction cannot be completely reconstructed once the leader is lost.

Complex factions are most likely to develop, and are likely to develop to the largest size, within bureaucratic formal organization. The hierarchy and established communications and authority flow of the existing organization provides a kind of trellis upon which the complex faction is able to extend its own informal, personal loyalties and relations. There is a tendency for vertical cleavages to develop within the complex faction, running up to the level directly under the highest leader. The conflict between the two major entities within a faction is kept under tight rein by the faction leader. After his retirement or death, however, the two entities become two new complex factions.

Internal cleavages tend to be increased by the fruits of victory. First, the path to victory inevitably involves reaching opportunistic alliances with factional leaders who are incorporated as allies within the faction but are not reliable. Second, the increased scale and numerical force of the faction as it grows enhances the tendency mentioned earlier for divergent interests to emerge among component subleaders and subfactions. Even if loyalty prevents an open revolt against the leader, it permits political clashes and struggles among his subordinates. Third, if the faction comes near to or achieves victory in a conflict arena as a whole, the unifying factor of a common enemy ceases to exist, while divisive factors such as struggle over spoils and efforts by smaller, enemy factions to buy over component units increase in salience. Fourth, the growth of the faction tends to deprive the leader himself of direct control over component units, weakens his position vis-à-vis subordinates, and thus hastens his political retirement and the consequent open split of the faction. In short, division and decline is the almost inevitable result of success. The only way to avoid such disintegration is to refuse to expand beyond the borders of an internally unified and easily defended factional base.

Finally, the faction is limited in the amount and kinds of power it can wield and generate. A faction is limited in size, follower commitment, and stability by the principles of its own organization. Certain other types of conflict structure, for example highly organized political parties or armies, can, by virtue of their complex, functionally specialized organization, their clear boundaries, and their high degree of control over participants, engage in feats of mobilization, indoctrination, and co-ordination which are beyond the capacities of factions.

The Characteristics of Factional Politics

Factions, I have argued, have less potential for power than formal organizations because of the limitations on their extent, coordination, and control of followers implied by their basis in the clientelist tie, their one-to-one communications structure, and their tendency toward breakdown. It follows from this that the several factions in a given factional arena will tend, over time, to enjoy relative power equality; for no faction will be able to achieve and maintain overwhelmingly superior power. A faction engaging in conflict with other factions must therefore operate on the assumption that it will not be able decisively and finally to eliminate its rivals. The faction which holds power today can expect to be out of power and vulnerable tomorrow. Politicians in a factional system are "condemned to live together."[7] This enables us to posit that the following modes of conflict will be typical of factional systems.

1. Since the impulse to crush one's rivals decisively is stymied by the limited nature of power, a code of civility arises which circumscribes the nature of political conflict. Factions relatively seldom kill, jail or even confiscate the property of their opponents within the system (the killing and jailing of persons felt to present a threat to the system is another matter; see point 12).

2. Since factions are incapable of building sufficient power to rid the political system of rival factions, they have little incentive to

try to do so. For any given faction, the most important and usually most immediate concern is to protect its own base of power while opposing accretions of power to rival factions. Initiatives to increase its own power and position are of secondary importance. Defensive political strategies therefore predominate over political initiatives in frequency and importance.

3. When a faction does take a political initiative (which it does only on those rare occasions when it feels that its power base is secure and its rivals are relatively off balance), it relies upon secret preparation and surprise offensive. This minimizes the ability of rivals to prepare their defensive moves in advance and provides the aggressive faction a momentum which carries it further than would otherwise be the case before the defensive moves of rivals stop its progress.

4. In the face of such an initiative, the defensive orientation of the other factions in the system tends to encourage them to unite against the initiative. Thus factional political systems tend to block the emergence of strong leaders. The strong leader constitutes a threat to the other factions' opportunities for power, and they band together long enough to topple him from power. In many political systems this leads to governmental instability.

5. Since the political life of a factional system consists of occasional initiatives by constituent factions, followed by defensive alliances against the initiator, any given faction is obliged to enter into a series of constantly shifting defensive alliances. Factional alliances cannot remain stable. Today's enemy may have to be tomorrow's ally.

6. It is therefore impossible for factions to make ideological agreement a primary condition for alliance with other factions. As I argue below, factions operate within a broad ideological consensus (point 13) while exaggerating the small differences that remain among them (point 10). The struggle for office and influence is unremitting, immediate, and never decisively resolved. In order to stay in the game, factions must often cooperate with those with whom they have recently disagreed. Although factional alignments do not cross major ideological boundaries, within those boundaries they are not determined by doctrinal differences.

7. When decisions (resolutions of conflict, policy decisions) are made by the factional system as a whole, they are made by consensus among the factions. To attempt to take action without having first achieved such a consensus would take the ruling coalition

beyond the limits of its power: the decision could never be enforced. Furthermore, the effort to enforce a decision would hasten the formation of an opposition coalition to topple the ruling group from power. Decision by consensus also has the advantage that action is taken in the company of one's rivals, so that responsibility cannot be pinned on any single faction.

8. There is a typical cycle of consensus formation and decline which characterizes factional systems. The cycle begins with a political crisis. As the factions contemplate the crisis, "the limits of what every party (or every clique or individual) may be capable of attaining" becomes clear to all, and after a lapse of time the crisis becomes "ripe." "Imperious necessity . . . make[s] the . . . groups disregard their positions of principle" which had blocked consensus, and action becomes possible.[8]

As a result of the consensus among the factions on the need for action, a faction or factional alliance achieves office and receives a mandate to act. The victorious faction takes culturally appropriate actions to test and solidify the support the other factions have been obliged to give it. The leader may refuse to take office until the other factions have publicly committed themselves to him; he may try to associate the leaders of other factions in the action he proposes to take; he may allow, or encourage, the crisis to worsen. Ultimately, however, he acts.

The third phase is the decline of the factional consensus. The actions taken by the faction in power inevitably have implications for the relative strength of all the factions in the system. While the actions carry the system through the crisis which had produced the consensus, they benefit some factions—usually the one in power and its allies—more than others. The other factions act to block the effort of the leading faction to strengthen itself, and the factional consensus deteriorates. The factions return to mutual squabbling.

The period of factional conflict often lasts a long while as the factions maneuver for political resources, alliances, and a favorable moment and pretext for precipitating a new crisis. Eventually a faction feels it is in a good position to take a political initiative, to precipitate a test of strength with its major opponent. In many factional systems, this takes the form of asking the most obstructive opposition factions to form a government in the expectation that they will fail. Whatever its form, the test of strength initiates a new crisis which begins another cycle.

A second set of propositions is based upon the fact that factions consist of a series of clientelist ties. The resources with which the faction carries out political conflict are not corporate, shared resources, but the personal resources of the individual members— their personal prestige, official positions and their own further clientelist ties.

9. To weaken their rivals, factions try to discredit opposition faction members, dislodge them from their posts, and buy away their allies. This leads to a politics of personality in which rumor, character assassination, bribery, and deception are used. Passions of jealousy and revenge are aroused, opportunism and corruption are fostered, and urgent short-term political goals require the compromise of principles. These, in short, are the "comic opera" politics or "pure politics" so characteristic of factional systems.

10. A further characteristic of factional political conflict may be called doctrinalism, i.e., the couching of factional struggle for power in terms of abstract issues of ideology, honor, and face. Factions adopt rigid and minutely defined ideological positions, exaggerate small differences on abstract questions, and stress the purity of their own motives. Yet the issues which arouse such fierce and elaborate debate appear upon close examination to be those with strategic implications for factional power. Although the real distance between cliques in ideology and program is small (points 12 and 13), and although no faction is likely to be able to carry out an innovative political program, grand policies and sweeping programs are articulated and debated, with small points attracting the most passionate and lengthy discussion.

Such debate serves several purposes. First, it distinguishes one faction from another, providing a rationale for the continued struggle among such otherwise similar entities. Second, it provides an opportunity to discredit other politicians and to justify oneself on abstract or ideological grounds. Third, the broad programs often include inconspicuous provisions of true strategic political importance. The struggle which is couched in abstract terms is really over the advantages of a policy to one side or the other.

A third set of propositions concerns the size and shape of the factional system as a whole and the way it relates to its political environment.

11. Any factional arena is composed of a limited and not very large number of factions. This is so because in an area with a very great number of factions, it will be in the interests of the factions

29

to amalgamate, in order to defend against other factions doing the same thing. The incentives to amalgamate cease to be stronger than those to engage in conflict only when the total number of factions has been reduced the point where most of the constituent factions enjoy enough strength to launch political initiatives and defend themselves, while further amalgamation would simply bring in more followers to share the rewards of the faction without decisively affecting its ability to survive. It is doubtful whether more than a score or two of factions can exist in a given factional system or arena. (The limitations on the number of members in a faction, and on the number of factions in a system, form a logical circle with the initial assumption of a oligarchic or small-scale arena.)

12. I have already established that the members of the small factional elite act within a code of civility which limits the severity of the sanctions they employ, and under tactical constraints that require alliances with former enemies and opposition to former allies. This closely knit elite is further united by one overriding shared interest: that the resources over which they are struggling should be allocated among themselves and in accordance with the rules of conflict they are following, rather than to some force from outside the system which pays no attention to those rules and whose victory would end the political existence of the factions. The result is a sharp difference between the modes of intra-elite conflict described in points 1 to 10 and the drastic steps which may be taken by the united factional elite to resist external enemies or to destroy counter-elites who challenge the legitimacy of the factional system. When for example, foreign conquest, rebellion, or a military coup threaten to overthrow a factional regime, the factions unite behind a suitable leader long enough to preserve the system, before returning to politics as usual. If the threat to the system comes from within, from a factional leader attempting to break the rules, the efforts of the other factions are directed toward defeating that attempt and reestablishing the stability of the system.

13. Within the factional elite, it is taboo to question the principle of legitimacy upon which the factions base their claim to a role in the larger society. Thus, for example, a factional parliament, regime, or party may play the role, in the larger society, of a central or local government, on the basis of a constitutional or charismatic claim to legitimacy. No matter how much the vicissitudes of struggle oblige the factions to trample in fact upon constitutional principles, or to disobey in fact their symbolic leader, these must never

be openly questioned or flouted since that would encourage other forces in the larger society to "throw the rascals out." Thus politicians in factional systems compete in expressions of fealty to the constitution or leader and rationalize every action and every position in terms of their fidelity to it or him. Care is taken to assure the constitutional or charismatic continuity of the regime.

14. Issues which arise within the elite are resolved only slowly and with difficulty. The consensus which is necessary for action is difficult to achieve because every decision is more advantageous to some factions than to others. Only the cycle of crisis and consensus brings action, but it is short-term action to meet the immediate emergency, and may in any case be followed by contradictory decisions after the next cycle of conflict. The resulting failure of policy to move clearly in any one direction is what was called, in the French Third and Fourth Republics, immobilism.

15. The immobilism of factional systems, the lack of extreme sanctions employed in their struggles, and their tendency to defend their existence against rival elites or external threats mean that they are in a certain sense extremely stable. It does not seem to be true, as some observers have suggested, that factional systems have an inherent tendency to break down.[9] In the absence of outside pressures (in which I include those from social forces within the society), no force within the factional system is capable of amassing enough power to overthrow it. Thus, only continued factionalism can be predicted on the basis of the fact that a system is already factional.

There will, of course, be other causes acting upon a factional system which also affect the outcome. Personal, cultural and technical resources for more complex organizations may be present to a greater or lesser degree; so may leaders' political vision and the will to move beyond the factional form of organization; and so may the challenge of changing social conditions. Members of factional systems may abandon factions for other forms of organization (often clientelist political parties). But if they do so, it will not be because of any dynamic of the factional system itself. More often than not, factional systems under challenge from within or without respond by trying to reassert their equilibrium rather than by changing their internal structure.

CCP Political History Interpreted in Terms of
the Factionalism Model

CCP Political History Interpreted in Terms of
the Factionalism Model

The Chinese Communist Party and its army have formed throughout their history a single institutional system with a single elite
performing simultaneously the functions of political and military
leadership. While the institution as a whole was striving toward
power in the Chinese revolution, its elite was from the beginning
frequently racked with internal conflict. The doctrinalism of these
debates, the lack of extreme intra-Party sanctions, the inability of
Mao to exclude his opponents and their views from the Party all
hint at the operation of factions. This suspicion is encouraged by
the charges aired during the Cultural Revolution that Mao's enemies had built personal followings and opposed him throughout
the history of the Party. As the party/army grew, I would argue,
each major leader played upon his personal network of clientelist
ties to cultivate a personal faction, seeding his followers in important posts and using them and their resources of office, prestige,
and personal connections to further his own standing in the movement and the adoption of the policies he thought it should follow.
Since the CCP as a whole existed in a condition of strong threat
from the Kuomintang and the Japanese, it could not have survived
if it had not limited its internal rivalries to factional forms.

With Liberation in 1949, the organizational substructure beneath the elite increased in size and complexity, and the resources
of power available for control by elite factions increased. However,
the central elite itself, I hypothesize, remained factional in its internal divisions. Factionalism would have been superseded (i) if intra-
elite conflict had ceased, which it clearly did not; (ii) if a member
of the elite had mobilized the institutional means (as did Stalin) or
the personal charisma to earn the sole power to resolve conflict,
which also clearly did not occur; (iii) if the Party had split into
permanently hostile segments which moved beyond the rules and
resources of factional conflict toward the goal of mutual extirpation, which obviously did not occur; or (iv) if the Party had established procedural rules (e.g., voting in the Central Committee) which
all its elite members accepted as the sole legitimate way to resolve
controversy, and whose decisions were accepted as binding by all.
This final alternative—the institutionalization of the Party as a
conflict-resolving mechanism—may have seemed for a time to have

occurred, but as the 1950s wore on the evidence accumulated that, on the contrary, factionalism continued.

The factional conflicts were for the most part deeply hidden. Only occasionally, as in the purge of Gao Gang and Rao Shushi in 1954 and the purge of Peng Dehuai in 1959, did factionalism erupt into public view. But the 1950s and early 1960s were full of circumstantial evidence of factional conflict. This evidence included the regularly shifting policy lines (the alternation of radical and moderate policies in agriculture, foreign policy, cultural affairs, and the like), the often simultaneous issuing of contradictory policy signals, and the resulting failure of the system to move consistently in any single policy direction after the initial establishment of order and the destruction of the landlord class and other opposition elements.

There is no reason to suppose that Liu Shaoqi and Mao Zedong were consistently on opposite sides of these issues during these years; quite possibly in the shifting alliances of elite factions they sometimes found themselves on the same side of an issue. But in 1959 in the aftermath of the Great Leap they found themselves opposing one another. Most factional leaders were unified in the wish to subtract from Mao's too dominant power. The bargain which was struck called for greater power to pass into the hands of Liu Shaoqi and his followers and allies, and for Mao to move into a weaker position.

During 1959–62, Mao's power was weak, and within the small world of the elite he was subjected to persistent, damaging attack by followers of one of his rivals, Peng Zhen. At the same time, his charisma was exploited by the regime to strengthen its legitimacy, harmed by the Great Leap; the cult of Mao was launched even while—and perhaps all the more willingly because—Mao was himself in eclipse. The new Minister of Defense, Lin Biao, in an effort to solidify the control over the PLA of his own faction, initiated a program to study the thoughts of Mao within the Army. Whether he was already then allied with Mao or simply turned to the Mao-study campaign as a convenient means of consolidating his personal influence against rival factions in the PLA is unclear. In any case, the campaign made Lin a natural ally for Mao in the latter's counterattack on his rivals which began in 1962.

Mao's counterattack of 1962–64, carried out with the help of Lin Biao, was still within the rules of factional strife. It included the socialist education campaign, the learn-from-the-PLA campaign, the extension of PLA influence throughout the country, the escalation of the cult of Mao, and the pressure for attacks on intellectual cadres in the Party. Mao's strategy was to use his national prestige, which his opponents had been obliged to enhance for the sake of the regime itself, and his alliance with Lin Biao, to undermine the personal power of his rivals, founded in the Party and cultural apparatuses. The rivals responded in typical factional fashion by stymying, blocking, and evading Mao's initiatives.

If Mao had continued to attack his rivals in the factional tradition of the party, he would eventually have precipitated another of the periodic elite crises, a realignment of factions, and a redistribution of power which might have improved his position. But Mao decided to break the rules, to mobilize new sources of power from outside the elite. We may speculate that his goal was no longer merely an improved position for his faction in the elite, but an end to factionalism and its associated policy oscillations, and an institutionalization of the Party as an instrument of Maoist will, capable of outliving Mao himself. Lacking the organized intra-Party power base of Stalin, Mao prepared to mobilize student power to drive his rivals out of office. The students were an attractive choice because of their historical role as official-topplers in modern China, because of Mao's faith in the revolutionary qualities of youth, and because of their suppressed tensions which were capable of exploding into a passionate political movement upon orders from a respected authority.

If the essence of the Cultural Revolution was a student-based Maoist attack on the factional Party elite, then its decisive period was the year in which the battle was fought over mobilizing versus demobilizing the students. This year (August 1966 to September 1967), saw a series of efforts by the factional elite to resist Mao's extra-Party offensive, demobilize the Red Guards, and restore the factional conflict system, if not the factional alignments, of the first fifteen years of the regime. The ultimate reason for the victory of Mao's rivals was that Mao had no direct organizational link to the Red Guards, and was obliged to employ means under the control of the Party center (the authority of the Party center, the hierarchy of Party committees, the official press) to call the Red Guards into existence and to direct their activities. Even as he reached outside the factional system for his instrument of power, he remained dependent upon the party for the means of wielding the instrument.

The defeat of the Red Guards, I would argue, settled the fate of

Mao's effort to end factionalism at the party center. Key factions at the center—perhaps an example was the faction of Zhou Enlai—had supported Mao long enough to enable him to launch the successive Red Guard outbursts. Now such swing factions feared further Red Guard activism, either because they were ready to consolidate their own positions or because they felt that future attacks would be directed at them. Mao could no longer divide and conquer. Although the Cultural Revolution was to continue in name and with occasional outbreaks of violence, after September 1967 there was no longer any hope of using the Red Guards to cleanse the party center of factionalism.

Some Problems and Implications of the Model

The factionalism model assumes a situation where politicians rely exclusively on clientelist ties to structure political action—a condition which must be set if a relatively coherent and comprehensible model is to be constructed, but which is not likely to be fully satisfied by many actual cases. A given political system is more likely to be a mixed than a pure type, both at a given moment in time, and, even more emphatically, through time, as forms of political organization change. Systems are usually mixed, but models are pure: the correspondence is seldom perfect. A model remains useful to the extent that it provides a relatively accurate diagram of the predominant dynamics of a system at a given point in time.

Particularly important in any fuller explanation of CCP elite politics would be the interplay between organizational and ideological constraints. There is certainly no contradiction between commitment to Maoist ideology and participation in factions. Although "faction" as such is deplored, factions may simply be conceived as ways of coordinating the efforts of like-minded colleagues to achieve goals in which they believe. As the model argues, factional struggle occurs within the context of a broad ideological consensus on goals and methods. It would therefore be a mistake to identify the factionalism model with a crude power struggle theory, if the latter assumes that leaders are cynical in their ideological statements. But it would be equally foolish to believe that in China alone men's perspectives on ideological and policy issues are not influenced by their individual political vantage points. The occasional impression that this is so may be the result of our

35

knowing so much more about the issues than about the vantage points.

Factionalism Today

Chinese politics has continued to display many characteristics of factionalism. The last years of Mao's life were marked by Byzantine court politics during which the reclusive, sickly ruler recalled Deng Xiaoping from internal exile and then had him purged again. In his final year of life Mao chose a relatively unknown provincial official, Hua Guofeng, as his successor. As soon as Mao died, Hua joined a coup against Mao's wife and other officials who had been close to Mao, promptly labeled the "Gang of Four." Over Hua's resistance a coalition of older officials insisted on bringing Deng back to office. Deng then began to purge Hua's allies (see chapter 3). Afterward, Deng continued to outmaneuver Hua and soon demoted him into political obscurity. Deng's coalition then split and resplit several times. The men he chose to succeed him in office, Hu Yaobang and Zhao Ziyang, were successively purged during the events that led up to and were part of the crisis of 1989.

Factionalism did not prevent the Deng regime from carrying out far-reaching economic reforms. In terms of the factionalism model, one could argue that the stagnation of the late Mao years presented such a threat to the regime's survival that all the leadership groups agreed on the need for reform. Some of the reforms, once started, went further than the leaders intended. For example, once peasants were assigned the responsibility for cultivating specific plots of land, they did away with most of the structure of the rural communes. Until the mid-1980s, each success generated support for new experiments. As the frontier of reform moved forward, so did the focus of factional conflict over it, as described in the following chapter and in chapter 6. But by 1988 the regime seemed mired in the kind of immobilism described in the model, creating a perception of stagnation which was one of the causes of the mass movement of 1989.

Factionalism is not the sole key to the events of the 1980s, and sometimes perhaps not the best key. At times the system functioned more as a personal dictatorship, with Deng's thinking, personality, and political skills best explaining how the reform process was managed, why it went no further than it did, and why the succession problem proved so difficult to solve. At other times the history of the 1980s seems to have been written as the struggle of a Leninist party or a Stalinist bureaucracy to preserve its privileges in the face of rising social forces that had been freed from the constraints of the Maoist system and demanded a share of influence in politics.

A shortcoming of the factionalism model is its inability to explain how factional modes of conflict interact with other modes, or why and at what times factionalism emerges as the main way of organizing elite conflict. Nor does the theory go beyond analyzing the workings of a factionalized system to explain what causes it to become that way or why—other than through its own tendency to persist once in place—such a system is so hard to outgrow.

The events of 1989 can be interpreted as another instance of a force outside the factional system, in this case students, intellectuals, and urban society in general, erupting into the political arena in an attempt to end the factions' monopoly of politics, and of the factions closing ranks to protect their joint position. The difference from events two decades earlier was that under Mao the students were mobilized from above, full of faith in the leadership; this time, they mobilized spontaneously out of a lack of faith. As argued in chapter 10, Zhao Ziyang, like Mao, was willing to go outside the system to use social forces to end the leadership paralysis. But like Mao he failed to do so.

As a consequence the political system is even more factionalized than before, which bodes ill for the regime's ability to solve its problems. However, I suggest in the concluding chapter that under circumstances where the population demands democracy, the needs of factional struggle may lead some groups of leaders to turn again to society for outside support, which may set in motion a process of democratic transition.

THREE

Political Risk in China

The death of Mao Zedong and the rise of Deng Xiaoping have brought striking changes in China's foreign economic relations and important opportunities for foreign businesses. China has decided to learn from the West by importing technology and equipment. To pay for these, exports are being promoted, including traditional manufactures but also breaking new ground with oil and tourism. Foreign investment is welcome, including joint ventures with up to 100 percent foreign equity.

At the beginning of the 1980s, the economic context is promising. After a rocky start in 1977–78, over-ambitious modernization plans were revised in late 1978 and the government announced three years of "readjustment." The readjustment policy seems to be producing good results. According to an official report on 1979 economic performance, agricultural output value increased 7.3 percent over 1978, industrial output value 8.5 percent, and total agricultural and industrial output 8.2 percent. Exports were up 26 percent, imports 30 percent.[1]

Projections for the growth of China's economy and the role of foreign enterprises are encouraging. The National Council on U.S.-China Trade forecasts that China's exports will grow an average of 17 percent a year and imports 18 percent a year from 1979 to 1985, to reach a total trade figure of $63 billion in 1985 (compared with some $20 billion in 1978). Thanks to such factors as the tourist trade and oil exports, China can buy some $40 billion worth of Western technology "while keeping its debt service ratio no higher than 15 percent."[2]

But confidence in China's economic prospects is counterbalanced by widespread concern with political risk. A poll of international bankers in June 1979, ranked China 27th in "country risk" behind Hong Kong, Singapore, and Korea, mainly for political reasons.[3] In the same vein, a recent CIA report observed: "Plans for long-term modernization depend on whether the present leadership can consolidate its hold on power and implement its current and contemplated economic priorities. Success in this endeavor is by no means assured."[4] And in Tokyo, the *Japan Times* noted "serious concern . . . about the potential risks in lending . . . money to a socialist country that has a history of violent political changes."[5]

International political risk insurers have recognized the anxiety about China's political future. National Union Fire Insurance Company of Pittsburgh (a member of the American International Group, Inc.) and Lloyd's of London offer political risk insurance for China, "based on the possibility that political upheaval in China—another Cultural Revolution, for example—could bring about the repudiation of the billions of dollars of contracts now being negotiated in Peking with United States companies."[6] U.S. Government OPIC (Overseas Private Investment Corporation) insurance to cover inconvertibility, expropriation, and loss due to war, revolution, or insurrection is likely to become available in 1980.[7]

The Chinese leaders have tried to reassure foreign businessmen. Vice Premier Deng Xiaoping told an American delegation on June 5, 1979:

> Another question which some people are concerned with overseas is whether or not there will be more turbulence in the political situation in China. I would like to assure you that you need have no worries in this regard. We in China have suffered too much from political turbulence and we have gained a very deep impression from this experience; deeper than any similar experience you may have had. There is now a situation of political tranquility and stability.[8]

Vice Premier Yu Qiuli pledged in Tokyo on April 10, 1980:

> [T]he Chinese government will not confiscate or requisition the assets belonging to foreign investors in accordance with the joint ventures law. If China should find it necessary to requisition them under very particular circumstances, it will give the foreign investors reasonable compensation.[9]

The Chinese People's Insurance Company now offers political risk insurance against losses due to wars and riots, or government requisition, confiscation or restrictions.[10]

Foreign analysts often accept Chinese claims for the stability of their new course and the leadership coalition that supports it. Few have analyzed in detail the likelihood of various favorable and less favorable scenarios for the 1980s or have distinguished the specific factors in the Chinese political mix that bear on the fate of foreign businesses. A realistic look at these factors seems in order as foreign business ties with China intensify.

Conceptually, measuring risk is quite different from foretelling the future: risk is a distribution of currently existing (and supposedly knowable) probabilities, while the future is anybody's guess. But the exercise of evaluating political risk is uncomfortably akin to trying to make predictions. No doubt it is a sensation common to political risk analysts for all countries, but it is especially discomfiting in the case of China, where less is known about politics than in most other places. China specialists have foreseen virtually no important political event since the founding of the People's Republic in 1949—not the Great Leap Forward, not the Cultural Revolution, not the purge of the Gang of Four, and not one of Deng Xiaoping's two purges and two rehabilitations. It seems that the risk of writing about China is even higher than that of doing business there. Nonetheless, in order to be brief and clear I will not hedge my arguments with all the qualifications and disclaimers they logically require.

Six Scenarios

I have conceived here six "scenarios" and three "factors." The scenarios are possible futures for China in the 1980s: the "expected" one, which most businessmen seem to anticipate, and five alternatives, to each of which I assign a probability (see table 3.1, below). The bulk of the chapter is devoted to explaining my reasons for assigning these probabilities in terms of three domestic political factors—elite factionalism, policy debates, and social and bureaucratic forces—that I believe will among them primarily determine China's political evolution in this decade.

I have reduced a potentially infinite range of future events to six scenarios by several expedients. First, each scenario is defined in terms of outcomes relevant to China's foreign economic policy. Various combinations of other events might coexist with a given foreign economic policy, but for the purposes of this business-oriented analysis, it would be wasted effort to create a separate scenario for each combination. Second, each scenario is couched in fairly general terms. Any number of particular events will fulfill a given scenario so long as they conform to the overall characterization of that scenario. For example, none of the scenarios specifies whether or not Deng Xiaoping survives the 1980s—in any case, the issue is the survival of a "Dengist" leadership, whether it consists of Deng or his followers. Third, three scenarios are explicitly excluded because—for reasons I will give—I consider each to have a probability approaching zero.

With six probabilities totalling 100 percent, I seem to imply that no other developments are possible. Of course, unpredicted things may happen. It would be realistic to assign a probability to the unforeseen—perhaps a large one. But this would be analytically vacuous. It makes better sense to admit that if something unforeseen occurs, the analysis was at fault for failing to include it as a scenario—rather than claim vindication by pointing to some residual category of "other scenarios" to which one had assigned a probability.

By the same token, however, this analysis can claim some accuracy if any of the six scenarios does occur. For, as stated earlier, an assessment of risk is not the same thing as a prediction. If a set of future events are assigned probabilities totalling 1.00 and the least likely of the events occurs, the risk analysis has not been falsified. Nicholas Schweitzer put it well when describing a CIA experiment in probabilistic political analysis:

> [T]here have been times of great uncertainty during our reporting periods when the assessed probability of certain hostilities rose, only to fall back again later. Does this mean that the high probability of the event was somehow in error? Rather, it would seem to mean that at the time the event could very well have occurred if other factors had coincided. The evaluation cannot really be considered "wrong."[11]

Scenario A is the "Expected Future." It foresees Deng Xiaoping's continuation in office or an orderly succession of his followers. The government continues the foreign economic policies Deng has laid down (allowing for reasonable adjustments to changing circumstances). Foreign trade grows along the lines predicted by Western projections described earlier. Tax and other laws are promulgated; they satisfy prospective foreign investors and increasing numbers of joint ventures are established. Most do reasonably well. Offshore oil development proceeds on schedule, with the continued participation of foreign firms. Tourism grows; hotels are built; internal air routes expand. China uses all normal forms of international credit, including concessionary credits and government-to-government development aid. Growing social constituencies form behind the new policies. The bureaucracy, assured of the nation's direction, becomes increasingly efficient in processing decisions required to conduct business relations with the West. By the end of the 1980s, China is still a highly centralized, Communist Party-controlled society, but the standard of living is rising. Some of the social and political problems of "developed communism" familiar in Eastern Europe are evident but well under control.

This is the path of development most Western businessmen seem to expect and on which many of their investments appear to be premised. It requires permissive international conditions (no serious war, no break with the West), reasonable skill in economic management, and an absence of catastrophically damaging weather. The conditioning factors fall outside the range of our analysis. But based on the domestic political factors to be analyzed below, I assign this scenario a probability of only 30 percent.

Scenario B is "Another Cultural Revolution." An anti-foreign faction claiming loyalty to Mao's memory emerges as a dominant group or strong minority in the leadership. It criticizes the foreign economic policies listed in scenario A as betrayals of Maoism that subvert socialism and tie China to dependency on the capitalist West. It finds a mass response from those who have not benefited from the new policies, especially unemployed and underemployed young people. Bureaucrats whose careers have not prospered under Deng (perhaps those who first rose in the Cultural Revolution) join the movement. There is widespread civil disorder. Joint ventures are confiscated, contracts abrogated. China turns inward.

This scenario might be sparked by a collapse of the world market, a major war in Korea or Southeast Asia, poor economic results under Deng or conspicuously growing economic inequality. Businessmen seem to view it as the most likely of the alternative scenarios. I will argue that it is one of the most unlikely, with a probability of 5 percent.

Scenario C is "A Factional Shift to the Left." This would be stimulated by the same factors as scenario B (world depression, war, economic stagnation in China, or gross economic inequality). It would also lead to similar (perhaps less extreme) foreign economic policies: a rejection in theory of the opening to the West and a relatively anti-foreign, more self-reliant model of development. It differs from scenario B because it is limited to a factional shift at the top and a purge of Deng or his successors by a new coalition of leaders. It calls for no mass uprising and the policy reversals would probably be less severe. I will argue that this is one of the most likely of the six scenarios, although I estimate its chances at no more than 30 percent.

Scenario D, "A Change of Mind," is scenario C without the purge. Deng remains in power or hands over power peacefully to his followers, but the leadership becomes disenchanted with current foreign economic policies and switches to a more isolationist development policy that significantly reduces opportunities for Western businessmen. Obvious causes for such a shift would be poor economic performance or Soviet success in tipping the balance of power against the West. Either development would lead to a reappraisal of the utility of Western ties in developing China and assuring Chinese security. While Westerners might assume that economic disappointments can be remedied by opening even further to the West (scenario F), scenario D assumes that the practical limits of the outward-looking economic strategy have already been approximately reached and that room for adjustment lies in the isolationist direction. I will argue that this scenario is neither highly probable nor out of the question. I assign it a probability of 10 percent.

Scenario E, "Immobilism," joins B and C in assuming the existence of leadership factions for whom foreign economic policy is a matter of disagreement. But this scenario does not envision the fall of the Dengist faction. It foresees simply the survival among the leadership of strong anti-Dengist factions, perhaps unclearly seen in the West but known to the Chinese bureaucracy. The consequence of mixed signals at the top would be bureaucratic inaction at the middle and below, where the fate of most foreign-related projects is determined. Economic or international-security reverses could encourage both factional debate and bureaucratic malaise, as could unpleasant incidents involving tourists or resident foreign technicians. However generated, immobilism could lead to a slow strangulation for foreign businesses—an outcome not always classified as political risk but one that I argue has a fair chance (20 percent) of occurring in China.

The final scenario is "A Shift to the Right." Scenario F envisions

Deng and his successors, or an alternate leadership group, adopting significantly more internationalist policies than those now in force. Both the desire of a Communist Party leadership to do so and its ability to overcome opposition are doubtful. I assign this scenario a probability of only 5 percent.

Three additional scenarios that businessmen sometimes ask about are so improbable that I exclude them from further analysis. The "Fall of the Regime" means a loss of power by the Communist Party (as opposed to a shift in power from one party faction to another). The Communist Party is an elite organization of some 38 million. Although it was paralyzed in the Cultural Revolution, it has re-emerged in the last ten years as strong as ever. Its internal discipline and control over society are being strengthened further under Deng, as I will discuss below. The party dominates all institutions of society, including the army, the government ministries, the press, and the universities. It reaches down to the communes and neighborhood committees. It has no significant organized opposition. Any political change that occurs in the 1980s will occur within and through, not against, the Party.

This analysis can be extended to address the possibility of a military coup. The party does "control the gun," in the Chinese phrase. The institutional power of the army reached a high point during the Cultural Revolution, but was whittled down by 1973 to a point at which Mao could suddenly transfer all eleven military region commanders. (Again in February, 1980, seven regional commanders were shifted on central government orders.) At the higher levels the military and party leaderships are intertwined: all top leaders in the army are believed to be party members, and the great bulk of party leaders have had long army careers. Thus, although individual military leaders are politically influential, the army leaders do not form a coherent interest group; instead, political disputes and factions cut across army-civilian lines. Each new power group in past purges has had both civilian and military members, and this would be true of any new power group in the 1980s. If a factional coup and purge (scenarios B and C) occur, they will not be distinctively "military." A junior officers' coup is also impossible. The army is penetrated at all levels both by a commissars' hierarchy loyal to the party and by a network of party cells. Moreover, the massive size of the Chinese army precludes effective horizontal organization of the middle and lower officer corps.

Finally, political risk analysis usually asks about potential ethnic or nationalities strife, and in China there is superficial reason to consider this a factor. China has 55 officially recognized national minorities, ranging in population from a few hundred to roughly 10 million. The largest of these groups occupy strategically crucial areas such as Tibet, Xinjiang, and Inner Mongolia (Nei Menggu). The Chinese press now charges that much was done to alienate these minorities during the 1960s and 1970s and has called for policies to repair the damage. But the minorities are located peripherally to most foreign economic activity; their power in the central government is almost nil; and their ability to threaten government territorial control is slight. Large-scale disorder in these regions is unlikey and if it occurs will hardly affect foreign economic policy or its implementation.

In sum, the table portrays a China susceptible to political change in the 1980s. Only two of the scenarios, A and F, are entirely optimistic for foreign businesses, and their total probability is only 35 percent. The other scenarios, with probability of 65 percent, portend more or less severe political risk. Catastrophic loss is unlikely (scenario B, 5 percent). But partial or full reversal, or paralysis of the current policy appear quite likely (scenarios C, D, and E, totalling 60 percent). Of course, it matters greatly whether such reversal is full and quick or partial and slow, since losses for a given business may vary significantly in magnitude. To understand more fully both the range of possibilities comprehended within each scenario, and the thinking that lies behind the assignment of probability to them, one must analyze the three domestic factors that will affect the evolution of China's politics in the 1980s.

The First Factor: Leadership Stability versus Factionalism

In assuring foreigners of China's political stability, the Chinese leaders point to the decisions of the Central Committee's Fifth Plenum of February 1980. Xu Dixin, a highly placed economist, told an economic seminar in Hong Kong in March that "the decision of the fifth plenary session shows that China is absolutely firm in its resolve to accomplish the four modernizations before the end of the century under the leadership of the Central Committee and under the premise of stability and unity. As far as politics is concerned, I do not think that there is any risk."[12] Similar assurances can be heard privately from many Chinese. Their viewpoint echoes

Table 3.1 Scenarios for China in the 1980s

Name and Characteristics	*Probability*
A. The Expected Future	.30
Orderly succession—continued outward-looking economic policies—public and bureaucratic support	
B. Another Cultural Revolution	.05
Anti-foreign faction emerges—Maoist slogans revived—widespread civil disorder—foreign ties heavily reduced	
C. A Factional Shift to the Left	.30
Purge of Deng group—opposition hoists Maoist banner—partial or full reversal of Deng program	
D. A Change of Mind	.10
Deng group remains, but re-evaluates outward-looking strategy—reduction of foreign economic ties	
E. Immobilism	.20
Continued factionalism at top—bureaucratic paralysis—difficulties for foreign businessmen	
F. A Shift to the Right	.05
Intensification of outward-looking strategy—further opening to the West—either under Deng or alternative leaders	
TOTAL	1.00

Excluded Scenarios:	
Fall of the Regime	.00
Military Coup	.00
Nationalities Strife	.00

the Fifth Plenum's official communiqué, which states that its decisions are "in line with the arduous work required for modernization and will also ensure long-term continuity of the Party's line, principles and policies and long-term stability of the collective leadership of the party."[13]

What are the decisions of the Fifth Plenum and why are they considered so crucial? To understand this requires a glance at events since Deng Xiaoping's reemergence on the political scene in July 1977. His restoration to power was delayed nine months beyond Mao's death and the purge of the Gang of Four because there remained opposition to Deng in the Politburo. But once in office, Deng gradually shifted the balance of power. In December 1978, at the Third Plenum, he turned the spearhead of criticism against his opponents, notably the former chief of Mao's palace guard, Wang Dongxing, who was attacked both at the meeting and in wall posters on the streets. Wang and three others were deprived of some administrative duties and the plenum promoted four of Deng's supporters to the Politburo. In 1979, three new pro-Deng vice-premiers took office, and at the Fourth Plenum, in September 1979, twelve more of Deng's allies were added to the Central Committee. One of them was elected to the Politburo. The Fifth Plenum culminated this consolidation of power. Four of Deng's rivals (the so-called "small gang of four") were demoted. Besides Wang Dongxing, they were Chen Xilian, Wu De, and Ji Dengkui. Two men closely associated with Deng, Zhao Ziyang and Hu Yaobang, were promoted to the Politburo Standing Committee, giving Deng, in effect, at least four of the seven votes there. A party secretariat was established (none had existed since the Cultural Revolution), staffed with Deng's supporters and technocrats.

The Fifth Plenum also accomplished the long-brewing posthumous rehabilitation of Liu Shaoqi, who had been tagged as "number one capitalist roader" during the Cultural Revolution. This completed the wreckage of the case compiled against Deng during the same period as the "number two capitalist roader," and it signaled that China would not be bound by Mao Zedong's theories and acts. It also helped to revitalize the theme of intra-party discipline with which Liu had been closely identified.

Beyond the Fifth Plenum, it is clear that Deng has a program to assure an orderly political succession and the continuation of his policies. "People of my age should really be concerned about arranging for what comes after," he has said. "By that I mean we must find good and reliable successors, so that once the succession takes place, new turmoil will not break out again."[14] The first step is to forge a smoothly functioning collective leadership consisting largely of the younger men he has brought to the top—especially Zhao Ziyang, 61, and Hu Yaobang, 65. Hu runs the party secretariat, while Zhao, a vice premier, is "in charge of the day-to-day work of the Cabinet."[15] The second step is to obtain the orderly, gradual resignations from their multiple posts of such party elders as Ye Jianying (chairman of the National Peoples' Congress and party

47

vice-chairman, age 82), Li Xiannian (vice-premier and a party vice-chairman, age 75), and Chen Yun (vice-premier and party vice-chairman, age 80). To set an example, Deng (age 76) has announced that he will resign as vice premier this summer, retaining his position as party vice chairman.[16]

If Deng's plans succeed, China's political future will resemble scenario A—"The Expected Future"—or scenario D or one version of F. Yet I assign these scenarios a total probability of only 45 percent. The other three scenarios, with an aggregate probability of 55 percent, envisage factional strife. Why this slightly pessimistic evaluation of Deng's chances to assure an orderly succession?

Factionalism has long been a feature of Chinese politics.[17] It bedeviled the dynasties, especially in their later, weaker phases. In the twentieth century, no political party or government seemed able to eliminate it. Under Mao and Liu, the Chinese Communist Party became a highly disciplined fighting organization—yet at crucial junctures party business had to be set aside while factions struggled for power. There have been eleven major "line struggles" since the party's founding—five since 1949. These were the purge of Gao Gang and Rao Shushi in 1954, the purge of Peng Dehuai in 1959, the anti-Liu/Deng struggle of the Cultural Revolution, Lin Biao's fall in 1971, and the post-Mao purge of 1976. And this does not count such lesser episodes as the removal of the "small gang of four" in February, 1980.

Why has factionalism been so persistent? The factions are based on personal loyalty. (Hu Yaobang, for example, has been associated with Deng Xiaoping since the early 1940s.) Their political battle is primarily over position—not because policy is unimportant but because position and power are prerequisites to effecting policy. In the search for position, factions enter shifting coalitions. (Deng Xiaoping, for example, sided with Mao against Liu Shaoqi in the mid-1950s; in the 1960s he sided with Liu against Mao. But Liu and Mao themselves had often been allied.) Such coalition politics tend to frustrate any faction that seeks to consolidate power, since one faction's consolidation of control spells the end of the other factions' chances for a turn in office. (Mao's grip on power was broken by a coalition including Liu and Deng in the later 1950s; Liu's consolidation was opposed by Mao in the mid-1960s; and in the early 1970s, China was semi-paralyzed by an unresolved factional conflict of which Deng's rises and falls from power were a symptom.)

Against this background, how much credence can be given to the claim that the leadership is now united—that this time the consolidation of power has been successful, the ruling coalition is firm, and the opposition factions have been reduced to "remnants," scattered in the party and capable of being won over to the ruling group by persuasion?[18] This is, of course, not the first time such assurances have been given. They were voiced after each of the previous purges. In the year or so preceding the Fifth Plenum itself, there were many celebrations of political stability—all of which turned out to be premature in view of the demotions that occurred at the plenum.

As this is written, it is too soon after the Fifth Plenum to expect much evidence of the persistence of traditional factional patterns to surface. However, the precedents of the past suggest two related hypotheses: that "radical" or "Maoist" groups who now seem silent may have survived to play a role in new coalition cycles in the 1980s; and that the "moderate" coalition headed by Deng may itself fracture like an image in a kaleidoscope as it grows larger.

In a paradoxical way, even the results of the Fifth Plenum are not entirely reassuring regarding China's future political stability. The plenum's emphasis on personal politics—the crimes of Lin Biao and the Gang of Four, the restoration of Liu Shaoqi's reputation, the demotion of the "small gang of four," and the appointment of "talented successors" in the Politburo and Secretariat—suggests that in China political stability is still not a matter of institutional continuity but is perceived as depending on the qualities of leading personalities. One gets an even sharper impression of this when speaking with individual Chinese, who respond to questions about political stability by remarking that one can feel secure now that Deng Xiaoping is in charge. But a system in which policy depends so much on who is in charge is inherently vulnerable to shifts in personnel, and a system in which there is no fixed procedure for making these shifts is vulnerable to factionalism. Deng's consolidation has not yet visibly transcended the old factional patterns by establishing reliable, predictable methods of handing down power or changing policy. With the death or retirement of many senior leaders all but certain in the course of the 1980s, one cannot be sure that Deng's followers will maintain their hold on power against almost inevitable challenges, among others perhaps from Hua Guofeng, whose official rank gives him powerful resources for such a conflict. Such considerations preclude assigning a dominant probability to those scenarios which envision a stable leadership. The scenarios which involve continued factionalism in the 1980s are given a probability of 55 percent.

Among the factional scenarios, however, a much higher probability is assigned to those that see the challenger factions adopting a position to the "left" of the present policy (50 percent) than to those envisioning a turn to the "right" (5 percent). To understand why this is—and to understand in more detail the likely range of policy options under either new leaders or Dengist leaders who change their minds—we must look at the debates on foreign economic policy that have occurred over the last decade and more in Beijing.

The Second Factor: Policy Disputes and Options

Whether the leadership is stable or not, so long as one or another group of Communist Party leaders rule China, the realistic policy options are largely defined by the debates that have occurred in the leadership since the early 1970s.

The extreme, polemic language of much of the foreign trade debate should not mislead us into thinking that the "leftist" position is autarkic, anti-industrial, or irrational, or that the "rightist" position verges on capitalism or abandons the idea of self-reliance. To understand the debates requires the rhetoric to be peeled to the core of real policy issues. The arguments of both "left" and "right" contain legitimate concerns and common sense. Nor are the rival positions as polarized as they seem. All parties agree on the need to enter the international marketplace and to learn from advanced foreign technology. All agree on the importance of China keeping the initiative and control in its own hands. The existence of broad common ground helps to explain why foreign economic policy in practice has been far less volatile than the verbal battles surrounding it. But within a broad consensus there has been significant disagreement over specific measures for achieving common goals and over the dangers each measure poses to China's independence and socialist values.

The Issue of Dependency. The most emotionally charged issue has been that of economic dependency. Almost all Chinese believe that the 1949 revolution liberated them from a century of neocolonialist exploitation, during which their mines were tapped for foreign benefit, their silk industry squeezed for rock bottom prices, then cast aside in favor of the competing Japanese product, and their native handicrafts destroyed by the competition of foreign manufactured goods. Lack of control over its own resources brought China both economic stagnation and political weakness. In order to become economically prosperous and politically independent, China must be "self-reliant." As Deng Xiaoping explained in 1974, "By self-reliance we mean that a country should mainly rely on the strength and wisdom of its own people, control its own economic lifelines, and make full use of its resources."[19] In 1980, he repeated, "We must rely primarily on our own sources and our own efforts."[20]

On this point, all Chinese appear to agree. They also agree that self-reliance can be helped by selectively learning from abroad ("making foreign things serve China"). The problem lies in defining the difference between an acceptable level of foreign ties and the creation of dependence on outside capital and technology. Many Chinese seem to fear that the Deng policies are drawing China back toward its former semi-colonial status as a "market where the imperialist countries dump their goods, a raw material base, a repair and assembly workshop, and an investment center."[21]

Much of the debate has focused on the export of natural resources. China is richly endowed with coal, oil, iron, antimony, tungsten, and other resources. Under Mao, however, the Chinese did not seek large foreign sales of these resources. They viewed the world commodities market as exploitatively stacked against the seller, and they believed that China's material wealth should be used as raw material for her own industries, not for those of other countries.

Deng Xiaoping's view is somewhat different. While he would not consign China to the role of a raw materials supplier to the capitalist world, he argues that oil and coal can fuel export earnings, industrialization, and eventually self-reliance at a higher level of development. He is even willing to compensate foreign mining equipment suppliers with guaranteed supplies of coal or oil. Few deals of this sort have actually been concluded. But the very idea of "mortgaging" resources raises deep opposition because it seems to imply loss of control over how much will be sold, to whom, and at what price. It also brings foreigners back into the mines where they were at the end of the nineteenth century.

Perhaps the most complicated issue has been the import of technology. Some Chinese fear that reliance on imported technology will encourage a dependent psychology of "pin[ning] our hopes on imported items and new projects" and a "belief that foreign versions are always better than ours." "If we merely import equipment without studying and absorbing the new advances in science and technology, what is advanced now may become backward four or five years later"—prolonging China's role as a technological client of the West.[22] The preferred solution is to buy one item and copy it ("importing chickens rather than eggs")—obtaining, when possible, the appropriate licenses and patents. But as one recent article pointed out, "generally speaking, foreign enterprises will not transfer the most advanced technology by granting patent licenses."

Joint ventures are seen—among other things—as a partial solution to this problem. "[S]ince the foreign investors will be directly involved in the management of joint ventures and share profits and losses with us . . . we are in a better position to obtain advanced technology and equipment through joint ventures."[23] Yet, the Chinese worry that the venture partner may provide second-rate or outdated equipment.[24] Hence, the Joint Venture Law adopted in July 1979 pointedly provided that "the technology or equipment contributed by any foreign participant as investment shall be truly advanced and appropriate to China's needs. In cases of losses caused by deception through the intentional provision of outdated equipment or technology compensation shall be paid for the losses."[25]

Even if the technology is satisfactory, many Chinese perceive joint ventures as a costly form of acquisition. "Some people . . . worry: Won't we be suffering losses by letting foreigners make profits in our country? We must treat this question from a dialectical viewpoint. . . . Although they may take away a portion of the profit, our country will enhance its material and technological foundation. In this sense, we cannot say that we are 'suffering losses.' . . . [I]t is necessary for us to pay the 'tuition.'"[26]

The issue of sovereignty. Just as the 1949 revolution signified that China was seizing its economic future in its own hands, it also meant an end to unequal treatment in the world of nations. From the mid-nineteenth century on, the Japanese, British, and Portuguese seized Chinese territory and forced China to accept unfavorable border settlements. China was deprived of the right to set her own tariffs to protect infant industries. Chinese living overseas were often denied the same privileges as other foreign residents. Perhaps most humiliating of all, under the doctrine of extraterritoriality, foreigners in China did very much as they pleased. Missionaries preached, journalists pried, researchers conducted surveys, social experimenters set up projects, adventurers and idealists meddled in politics. The Chinese government could do little to control them. An intense patriotism fueled the revolution: once China had "stood up," no infringement on its sovereignty, no matter how small, should be permitted.

This commitment to sovereignty is obvious in the broad sweep of China's foreign policy: the refusal to contemplate Taiwanese independence; the insistence that border issues with the Soviets will be settled only when the other side admits that the present borders originated in "unequal" treaties; the vigorous 1979 military response to Vietnamese nibbling at the border. When it comes to foreign trade, the principle of "equality and mutual benefit" is supposed to ensure that there is no infringement of sovereignty by either side. Yet, in the eyes of some Chinese leaders, the more complicated foreign economic relations become, the more they seem to require compromises of sovereignty.

Take the relatively innocuous question of visas. Once foreign businessmen began coming and going regularly, they pressed for long-term, multiple-entry visas. Some in the Chinese leadership—probably the public security apparatus—resisted this request, arguing that each time a foreigner enters China, his or her reliability should be restudied and a specific length of stay determined.[27]

Indeed, police and intelligence issues seem to play a large part in the resistance to increased foreign economic contacts. The precise arguments of the security men are not known, but one can imagine some of the points they make. If China buys telecommunications equipment (some of it capable of military application) it is vulnerable to electronic eavesdropping by the supplier nation. Foreign technicians working in Chinese mines gain valuable economic and technical intelligence. Technical experts who stay for long periods to help with development projects learn about Chinese technical capabilities and local society and geography.[28]

Over four million foreigners and overseas Chinese visited China in 1979, many more than in any previous year.[29] Some tourists guilelessly stroll or photograph where they shouldn't; a few may be real spies. In 1978–79, tourists and foreign journalists provided an audience for the Chinese literary underground which had previously been stunted for lack of world attention. "Even today" (after the suppression of the Democracy Wall movement), the authorities charge, "certain individuals are still carrying out secret liaison work and even making secret contacts abroad."[30] Tourism also means new problems at the borders; at a recent conference for customs workers the staff were instructed "not [to] regard normal literary and art exchanges as infiltration of feudal, capitalist and revisionist things."[31] Summing up Beijing's uneasiness about visitors, a high-ranking official warned that people who "think that when we open the door we do not distinguish between wolves and friends . . . have made a gross mistake."[32]

Some Chinese leaders feel that sovereignty is subtly undermined in another sense when they are forced to alter their existing ways of doing things in order to meet the demands of trading partners. For example, tax and patent laws are being codified and revised in order to satisfy the demands of foreigners who are unwilling to invest until these matters are cleared up. In pursuing exports, the Chinese have found that some foreign buyers insist on inspecting Chinese factories as part of their agreement to purchase processed foods or manufactured items. Food items must be registered with the American FDA which demands information from the Chinese supplier.[33] And the Chinese have come under heavy American and EEC pressure to accept voluntary textile quotas. On the import side, China must fill out the American form 629—an end-use statement—and permit on-site inspection in order to buy certain forms of high technology.[34] Other technology requires U.S. government export licenses. Such accommodations between trading partners are standard international practice, but because sovereignty has been such a sensitive issue in modern Chinese history, even the smallest accession to foreign requirements has strong critics.

Foreign financial assistance raises its own host of sovereignty issues. When China started to borrow in 1977, international capital markets were liquid. In tighter markets, international bankers will demand higher interest rates, more information, and tougher terms. They are also likely to choose among projects on the basis of their potential for earning foreign exchange and guarantees that debt retirement is a first call on income.[35] Chinese bankers seem concerned that such foreign lenders' conditions verge on interference.

"If I cannot pay," said one Chinese official, "I will not borrow. It is not necessary for the United States to look at our economy."[36] Another official stated more cautiously, "We are willing to consider using any methods used by international banks that are not detrimental to our country's sovereignty."[37] When China joined the IMF/World Bank, which requires extensive financial and economic information, updated yearly, a Chinese official noted the "IMF should consider the differences in ability by member countries to provide information, and member countries have no obligation to provide information so detailed as to reveal related confidential information."[38]

Government-to-government loans have been even more controversial. Years of ideological commentary instilled the fear that large foreign debts mean loss of control over economic decisions. The break with the Soviet Union in 1960 taught the Chinese that an aid-receiving country can resist political blackmail only at great cost. For two decades, China eschewed foreign aid. But in August 1979, China applied to Japan for a $5.5 billion loan for eight projects; in December, six of the projects were accepted and an initial $225 million commitment was made.[39] The Chinese are aware that such a loan gives Japan a large political stake.

Joint ventures—already discussed as raising issues of dependency—are also controversial in the light of sovereignty concerns. Allowing foreign capitalists to lease property in China, putting Chinese workers under foreign managerial control, allowing foreigners to repatriate profits earned with Chinese labor and materials—all recall the neocolonialist past of foreign enclaves and exploitation. The memory will be all the sharper when such ventures are located in the planned Special Economic Zones where, according to a spokesman, "a more open approach is adopted toward administration" and "we'll allow exploitation to a certain degree."[40] "Will joint investment enterprises affect China's sovereignty?" asked *Workers' Daily* in July 1979. No, it answered, because such ventures will "strengthen our material forces for defending the complete independence of our sovereignty as a socialist country" and "are governed by our law."[41] Yet concern over sovereignty must explain the long delay, vagueness, and frequent contradictions in the statements of Chinese spokesmen on such issues as the top percentage of foreign ownership, the powers of foreign managers, and the life of joint venture agreements.

The issue of economic distortion. Opponents of expanded foreign economic ties also assert that they distort the development of the economy, pushing it in unwanted directions and creating unmanageable side effects.

Foreign trade has least impact on the economy if a country sells only such materials and goods as are left over after domestic needs are fulfilled, and buys abroad only as many goods as can be paid for with available foreign exchange. This kind of residual, short-term, small-scale trade has never been controversial in China.[42] But insofar as current trade policy departs from this model, it has linkage effects on the domestic economy that raise political hackles.

Take the question of oil sales abroad. Instead of selling leftover oil, China is now entering into long-range oil sales contracts. The oil committed to foreign sales is withdrawn from domestic supply, forcing some industries to use coal even though they prefer oil. To opponents, this is a "comprador philosophy" of "selling out the natural resources of the state" and setting foreigners' needs above China's.[43] The proponents of trade answer that "where goods are in internal and external demand and are in relatively tight supply, active efforts must be made to develop production so that a portion may be squeezed out for export . . . [I]f this is properly done, there will not be considerable adverse effect on the domestic market."[44]

Another complaint is that the large-scale importation of advanced technology will require large commitments to support and ancillary services for the imported equipment. This will withdraw investment from less spectacular but equally necessary indigenous development projects, or from existing, relatively backward plants the upgrading of which would bring fast growth at low cost. The need to realize relatively quick profits from imported plants creates pressure to locate them in highly developed areas such as the Shanghai region, the Northeast, and Shanxi. Less developed provinces have argued that even though investments in their areas pay off less quickly, they provide better dispersion of industry, both for defense purposes and for longterm nationwide growth.

Tourism is an interesting case of the issue of economic distortion. Although it is highly profitable, tourism strains transport facilities and removes translators from technical work. Some Chinese ask how it is possible to invest millions in luxury hotels when available urban housing averages only 3.6 meters per person.[45]

The critics have further economic concerns. They believe work-ers' jobs are threatened by new, capital-intensive equipment. Shift-ing the laid-off workers into other jobs is not a full answer since there remains serious unemployment in Chinese cities. Thus, for-eign investment has become enmeshed in a wider debate over China's traditional "iron rice bowl." The critics also fear that the recently acknowledged Chinese inflation will be worsened by for-eign purchases. Projections by the National Council for U.S.-China Trade suggest that throughout the first half of the 1980s China will experience an annual net drain on foreign exchange reserves to make payments for loans and imports.[46] Although the projected 15 percent debt service ratio is modest by world standards, it discom-fits some Chinese leaders accustomed to even more conservative standards of fiscal management. Finally, the new development strategy entails a relative deemphasis on military modernization, a predictably controversial decision given the urgency of China's military needs.[47]

The issue of social distortion. A final set of issues concerns the foreign impact on the lives and thinking of the Chinese people. The need to turn abroad for advanced equipment has awakened the suspicions of some Chinese that socialism is not really superior to capitalism. During the "Peking Spring," dissidents argued that importing foreign science and technology was a halfway house— real modernization would require a thorough shakeup of the bu-reaucracy and the democratization of politics ("the fifth moderni-zation"). In response, the Chinese youth paper argued that "social-ism is far superior to capitalism . . . [even though] certain young people still have vague ideas on this matter." It contended that many American workers have cars only because industries are located far from residential areas in order to make them buy cars on the installment plan and go further in debt to the capitalists.[48] An extensive press campaign has been mounted to correct the over-idealization of America, urging for example that "capitalism is in its death throes"[49] and that American democracy is really a one-party system, "that is, the Democratic-Republican party under the disguise of a two-party system."[50]

A related issue is the rise of bad social habits as a consequence of exposure to foreign ways. There is more and more such exposure as foreign goods begin to be advertised in Chinese media and dis-played in Chinese stores, tourists penetrate to new cities, and Hong

57

Kong magazines and Taiwan tape cassettes turn up in Chinese black markets. "Some youngsters are imitating certain ways of living in Western capitalist society," a Chinese newspaper noted, "including wearing long hair, beards and dressing themselves in bizarre clothes.[51] "Some went out to collect pornographic pictures," said another report. "Others danced vulgar versions of rock and roll all night."[52] And according to a third report, "some people in Guangzhou Municipality recently . . . exchanged foreign currencies at rates higher than the state's quoted rates, . . . then scrambled to buy through different channels, electronic calculators, recorders, cassette tapes, television sets and other commodities in great demand and sold them at higher prices."[53]

In light of this concern with the decay of social mores, several policies are liable to come under particular attack. The recently announced policy of exporting labor—hitherto a "taboo" as the Chinese press noted—would have incalculable social effects if the number of workers sent overseas became very large.[54] The development of Special Economic Zones in Guangdong and Fujian will create enclaves of foreign-oriented affluence whose social effects may be hard to contain.[55] And, of course, there are inevitable objections to the policy of sending students abroad.

A final social distortion that concerns many Chinese is the rise of a technocratic elite that seems to accompany the import of advanced technology. The new elite learns foreign languages, travels abroad, and reads foreign business and technical periodicals. The government has decreed their exemption from most requirements for political study, and factory party committees and managers are ordered to work harmoniously with them at all costs. The technocrats' growing power and their deepening exposure to foreign cultures revives a long-standing argument over whether "science and technology have a class nature" and inevitably carry a "decadent bourgeois ideology and way of life." For at least one segment of the political leadership, the answer to this question has long been that they do.

What does the foreign economic policy debate imply for the six scenarios for China in the 1980s? First, it suggests that some of the key elements of "The Expected Future" remain intensely controversial. Second, the policies adopted by Deng's regime are not a compromise package. They reflect quite full implementation of the "outward-looking" or "open-door" position articulated in the debates. Hence the prospects of a move further to the "right" (scenario F) seem dim. Third, correlatively, any policy shift is likely to be to the "left," i.e., in the direction of narrowing economic ties to the West, particularly in the fields I have designated as vulnerable to political risk. Such a leftward shift is compatible with scenarios B ("Another Cultural Revolution"), C ("A Factional Shift to the Left"), or D ("A Change of Mind"). Also, the continuing vitality of the leftist critique lends support to scenario E ("Immobilism"). But the debate also indicates the limits of a leftward swing. Rhetoric aside, a truly autarkic policy position does not emerge in the debates.[56] Those considerable areas of foreign-related enterprise that have proven relatively uncontroversial are unlikely to be abandoned for political reasons.

The Third Factor: Social and Bureaucratic Forces

Four of the six scenarios can be evaluated largely in terms of factionalism and policy debates. The other two require a discussion of trends in the bureaucracy and in society at large. Scenario E ("Immobilism") would require not only factions at the top but also a divided bureaucracy. Scenario B ("Another Cultural Revolution") would draw on widespread social discontent.

The bureaucracy. The Chinese bureaucracy is so large and diverse that there is always some danger of confusion or delay. Recent policy shifts and experiments have intensified the problem of coordination among overlapping and competing organs whose responsibilities are not always defined. Economic powers have been shifted among the different levels of the hierarchy—central, provincial, and local—several times in past decades. In the foreign trade/ investment sphere, some of the provincial-level (e.g., Fujian and Guangdong) and even local-level units (e.g., Shenzhen) have been granted new powers to enter into some transactions without consulting higher levels. But these powers are untried and their extent unclear. Sometimes a transaction becomes more complicated than before because more levels are involved or because several levels are locked in a struggle for authority. At a given hierarchical level, there are functional organizations whose responsibilities overlap. Within a given city, foreign firms are sometimes bewildered by a host of independent local organizations.

Unanticipated bureaucratic complexity is one possible source of

59

business frustration and loss, and hence represents a kind of political risk. But the more serious problem of bureaucratic immobilism comes from the sensitivity of the bureaucracy to factional struggles at the top.

The upheavals of the last 15 years have left most Chinese organizations with precarious mixtures of rival groups. Assignment to a given unit is normally for life. When a purged cadre is rehabilitated, he returns to the office where he worked before and where those who attacked and purged him are also still working. "When some previous leading cadres resume their power," according to one Chinese newspaper,

> they call back their previous confidants, assign them to important posts and even carry out a big reshuffle of personnel so as to "change the courtiers simultaneously with the emperor." In these localities and units there are many small circles formed because of many historical reasons [former political clashes] and individual interests.[57]

Even if the factions thus perpetuated live in outward harmony, "factional activities are carried out in a covert way. A floating duck makes strokes under water."[58]

The existence of semi-repressed but virtually permanent factional disunity in Chinese organizations naturally reduces efficiency in several ways. It makes it difficult for officials to work together smoothly in mutual trust. And it creates what the Chinese call "lingering fear." This is a condition of intense bureaucratic sensitivity to signs of factionalism at the top. "Some comrades," *Red Flag* has recently pointed out,

> are obsessed with "fear" and worry that the policies will change. They are not assured although the policies are clearly laid down in the documents of the party Central Committee. They still try to make "weather" observations and look out for the "trend." . . . What are these comrades afraid of? They are afraid of committing mistakes in the line again.[59]

Given the price many cadres paid for their participation in either "right" or "left" lines over the past 20 years, it is not surprising that the coexistence in the same office of jealous rivals should create pervasive caution.

To spur the bureaucracy to action, the leadership must persuade it that policy is firm and that the factional alignment of the government is secure. Such assurance was lacking during the early 1970s. "Bureaucrats responsible for carrying out day-to-day trade operations, not wanting to be on the wrong side of the fence, became intransigent" in negotiations with foreigners.[60] By conspicuously consolidating power, Deng Xiaoping evidently hopes to overcome bureaucratic fears. The claim that the Fifth Plenum's decisions "will . . . ensure long-term continuity of the Party's line, principles and policies and long-term stability of the collective leadership of the Party" is thus directed as much to Chinese officials as to foreign businessmen.

The party leadership has persuaded at least some cadres and citizens that its policies are secure. Students and scientists who go abroad to study and officials who negotiate business deals with foreign firms are staking personal bets on the staying power of the Deng group. So far, most of these practitioners of the "Great Leap Outward" seem to be older men, intellectuals, and technocrats rehabilitated from the Cultural Revolution, sometimes of "bad class background." It will be interesting to see whether those who were on the other side in the Cultural Revolution begin to appear among the active negotiators and overseas students. If so, it will be a sign that Deng's program is taking firm hold throughout the bureaucracy.

Renewed signs of factionalism at the top would quickly reverse whatever bureaucratic responsiveness Deng's current campaign engenders. "Lingering fear" will revive immediately if bureaucrats see there are still central factions who may eventually criticize officials for implementing Deng's program. This situation could be damaging to foreign enterprises even if Deng's group remains in power, for business success depends on more than permissive policies at the top: it requires active cooperation all through the bureaucracy.

These considerations lead me to assign a 20 percent probability to the "immobilism" scenario (E). If Deng is unable to eliminate factionalism during the 1980s, this fact alone will tend to immobilize the bureaucracy and create serious politically generated losses for foreign businesses quite independent of which factional coalition emerges on top.

Social forces. One overlooked lesson of the Cultural Revolution is the strength of party and government control over Chinese society. Although this violent episode was nurtured by widespread social strains, it did not burst into violence until Mao gave the signal, and through a year of social conflict the local "mass factions" were responsive to directives from central leaders. The millions-strong Red Guard movement was easily demobilized and its members sent to the countryside once Mao gave the order. The political unity of the Center was in question during the Cultural Revolution, but not the Center's control over society.

There are no signs that government control over society will weaken in the 1980s or that forces outside the regime will be strong enough to countermand the policy of a united government. But social forces might play an important role if they are mobilized in the course of a leadership struggle.

This possibility has to be evaluated in the light of the larger package of social and economic policies of which the new foreign economic policies are a part. These broader policies offer something for most major groups in China. Peasant income will be substantially increased by higher prices for agricultural goods and lower prices for agricultural inputs. Urban workers have gained modest wage raises and bonuses, and the cities' standard of living is going up, thanks to a reemphasis on consumer goods and urban amenities. Especially strong support for the new policies comes from rehabilitated cadres, technicians, managers and intellectuals who were demoted or persecuted during the Cultural Revolution. These people have an enlarged role in the present modernization drive. Although they are not all of one mind on the specific issues connected with foreign trade, they can be counted as generally supportive of Deng's regime.

Poor economic performance could dissipate this widespread support. Peasants and urban workers expect steady, if modest, increases in income and want to be able to spend this money on housing, clothing, bicycles, and TV's. Discontent will be generated if the fruits of growth are clumsily distributed, or if inflation makes income growth an illusion, or if light industry fails to supply at least a portion of what people want to buy. But if the economic program goes reasonably well, such strains should prove transitional.

The new policies also inflict setbacks on some important groups. Middle and lower-level administrators must now cede authority to scientists, technicians, and factory managers. As the modernization program progresses, this classic "apparatchik"-"technocrat" division is likely to be intensified and may lead to conflicts of interest and viewpoint. Class tensions will also be increased because new college admission policies reduce the chances for peasants' and workers' children to get ahead in higher education just when the status and income of college-educated intellectuals and technicians is rising. Meanwhile, the 16 million or so "sent-down youth" who were posted to the countryside from 1967 to 1977 have become a "lost generation" with little chance to get ahead in the new order. Although the government has begun to allow these youths to return to the cities, it is unable to give most of them good jobs there, nor are there sufficient college places to allow them to resume their educations.

In the long run, the problem of youth and their futures will be the most serious social strain of the 1980s as it was of the 1960s. Seven million middle school graduates enter the labor force every year, and fewer than one million go on to higher education. Both rural and urban labor markets are glutted. At the beginning of 1979, there were 20 million urban unemployed; during the course of that year, five million new jobs were created, but primarily in the low-paid "collective" sector of small factories and service trades. Technological modernization of both industry and agriculture may to some extent slow the rate at which economic growth creates jobs. Population control—if it succeeds—will ameliorate the youth problem in the 1990s, not the 1980s. Meanwhile, there will be many people dissatisfied with their prospects in life. This reservoir of frustrated young people could be called up by a dissident central faction to attack the leadership whose programs had failed them.

How large and resentful this young population will be during the 1980s depends on the government's ingenuity in finding them rewarding work. Granted modest success in this endeavor, there are several reasons to think that a new cultural revolution is unlikely. First, as in the first Cultural Revolution, most other groups in society are sufficiently well served by the modernization program so that youthful rebels would form a relatively narrow constituency for a leadership group seeking to overthrow a Dengist regime. Second, almost all sectors of Chinese society—and many even in the Maoist wing of the leadership—had such bad experiences during the Cultural Revolution and saw so much damage done to China that this form of political struggle seems to be widely discredited. Young people may be wary of being used and abandoned as happened to the Red Guards in the 1960s.

In conclusion, the social resources for a second cultural revolution will be present in China in the 1980s, but the balance of social forces is weighted against the success of such an endeavor, and for this reason scenario B has a low probability.

Conclusion

China is a great, continental economy, essentially self-sufficient. Foreign trade occupies a relatively small proportion of the GNP. The country is rich in raw materials and has a complete, well-rounded industrial establishment that can produce its own equipment for self-sustaining growth. The present leadership believes that the country can modernize more quickly by using foreign trade, investment, and technology. But this does not mean that such foreign connections are seen as essential at all costs. On the contrary, China has shown in the past that economics alone cannot constrain it from breaking with foreign suppliers of capital and technology—first in the split with the Soviet Union in 1960 and again during the autarkic interlude of the Cultural Revolution. A highly self-reliant development policy has always been and continues to be a real possibility for China. And a strong tradition of anti-foreign feeling, sometimes verging on xenophobia, continues to make self-reliance an attractive possibility to some.

Thus, the question of political risk is a real one. I have suggested that six scenarios describe the forms that political risk might take in China in the 1980s. I have analyzed three sets of factors that I believe among them largely determine the probability of each of the six scenarios. It remains to draw together the argument by summarizing the reasons for the probability assigned to each of them.

Scenario A, "The Expected Future," foresees the success of the plans which Deng Xiaoping now has in train. Politically, it involves an orderly succession from Deng to his designated successors. Economically, it entails continuation of the development policies Deng has initiated, and in the foreign economic realm it means continued development of economic ties with the West through trade, technology import, and joint ventures. As the 1980s begin, Deng has achieved a degree of dominance over the Politburo and Central Committee rare in the past 30 years, has presented a clear vision of the future, and has apparently gained widespread bureaucratic and social support. His chances of success are considerable. Yet, our analysis of leadership factionalism suggests that there is a serious possibility that anti-Deng factions exist and that during the next decade, at an opportune moment, they will form coalitions to un-seat or checkmate Deng or his successors in the time-honored pat-tern of Chinese factionalism. Our analysis of policy disputes shows that in such an eventuality the movement of policy would probably be toward the left. And our analysis of the bureaucracy and society has shown that despite the attractions of Deng's program, there are forces that may oppose it. All these considerations make it impos-sible to assign "The Expected Future" a dominant chance for suc-cess. We assign it a probability of 30 percent.

Scenario B is "Another Cultural Revolution." This would entail the emergence of an opposition faction using Maoist slogans, that faction's call for a mass movement against Deng's line, and strong response from dissatisfied elements in society. I have argued that opposition factions may exist, that Maoist slogans will continue to make sense to many in China, and that a large dissatisfied youth population will be present during the 1980s; nevertheless, it is unlikely that all these elements will come together as the scenario requires. The balance of social forces would militate against the success of this strategy, and strong sentiment among both the leaders and the people would probably isolate a leadership faction that used this strategy of conflict. This scenario cannot be ex-cluded, but its probability is small—I estimate it at 5 percent.

Scenario C is "A Factional Shift to the Left." It involves a seizure of power by a faction using Maoist slogans to promote a foreign economic policy of self reliance. Our inspection of the current polit-ical scene suggests that factions do still exist and that the leftist policy options remain attractive to my Chinese. If the dynamics of Chinese politics remain what they have been, Deng's consolidation of power will stimulate factional counter-activity within the lead-ership. Since Deng's group has occupied the "right" in the Chinese policy spectrum, an opposition coalition is likely to move to the still vital left. Hence, I assign this scenario a probability equal to that of scenario A, 30 percent.

Scenario D is "A Change of Mind." This involves a policy shift to the left but without a change of leadership. This scenario would be possible if the current economic policy leads to slow growth or severe social tensions, or if events in the international arena make it difficult for China to maintain good relations with the West. The plausibility of a policy shift to the left has been demonstrated by our review of Chinese policy debates. But a policy shift without a power shift would be unusual in a factional system, since a policy's failure weakens its sponsors. So scenario D is far less likely (10 percent) than scenario C.

Scenario E, "Immobilism," envisions a factional stalemate at the top and a bureaucratic response of crippling caution. There is no reason why "lingering fear" cannot become a way of life in the bureaucracy for a decade or more; hence the urgency for Deng both of consolidating his power and of being seen to have consolidated it. Many bureaucrats can be expected to wait as long as another year or two to see whether it is entirely safe (in the case of supporters) or necessary (in the case of opponents) to work wholeheartedly for Deng's program. Any leadership dispute or purge in the interim is likely to be echoed and amplified in government offices and thus lead to frustrations and perhaps serious losses for foreign businesses. Given my estimate of the likelihood that leadership factions persist, I assign "Immobilism" a fairly solid probability of 20 percent.

Scenario F is "A Shift to the Right." I have shown that, in the ideological spectrum, few defend policies further to the right than those now in train. If a "more rightist" policy position exists, it has barely been articulated. Some of the writings of theorists and politicians associated with Deng—particularly Chen Yun, Xue Muqiao, and Zhao Ziyang—contain suggestions of a domestic development strategy involving looser planning and greater reliance on market mechanisms of coordination, but so far they have said little about foreign economic policies. One cannot exclude the possibility that, if Deng succeeds in consolidating his power and if the present program is spectacularly successful, China may experiment with even closer ties to the West. I assign this scenario a probability of 5 percent.

The businessman contemplating involvement in China can draw several general conclusions from this analysis. First, given the size and economic potential of China, the prospect of political risk is not sufficient to deter a businessman who has something of real interest to offer China. Second, however, political risk is indeed substantial; I estimate that there is an aggregate 65 percent chance of politics engendering significant difficulties for foreign businesses during the 1980s. Of course, to translate this into political risk for a given enterprise involves attention to many particulars. If the enterprise is a joint venture, or involves oil exploration or tourism

—fields I have described as relatively risky—or if it will not realize its profits potential until the end of the decade, then it runs the full proportion of risk that I have described. But if a business relationship falls into an uncontroversial area (to take the extreme case, purchase of Chinese export items), or if its profit potential can be realized in the next year or two while Deng Xiaoping is most likely to remain in power, then the quotient of risk if far less than the 65 percent given as the overall figure for the decade.

Political Risk in the 1990s

During the crackdown of 1989, the government called for maintaining the open-door policy, tried to persuade foreign businesspeople who had fled in June to return, and promised to pay all its international debts. But the regime also insisted on the need for vigilance against "an international trend that is attempting to make the socialist countries abandon the socialist road." "We must withstand this trend," wrote *People's Daily*, "otherwise socialist China will again become an appendage to international capitalism."[61] It seemed likely that doing business in China would be harder for foreign companies in the next few years. China has gained much from its opening to the West—nearly $50 billion in accumulated foreign loans and investments, and in annual trade turnover approaching $80 billion—which makes it difficult or impossible to close the door completely. Nonetheless, the sensitivities described in this essay will continue to make Chinese economic dealings with the outside world politically controversial, as they have for century.

PART II
American Views of China

FOUR

Americans Look at China: The New Optimism and Some Historical Perspectives

A mericans have greeted the Chinese Communist Party's announcement of new reforms in the urban economy (announced by the Third Plenum of the 12th Central Committee on October 20, 1984) with a surge of optimism that China is becoming more like us—an old American dream. "The big event of 1984," cheered conservative columnist William Safire in *The New York Times*, "was surely the rejection of Marxism and embrace of capitalism by the Government of a billion Chinese."[1] "China Reinvents Itself: New Capitalists Line Up to Lure U.S. Firms," headlined the *Christian Science Monitor*.[2] The most remarkable example of the new optimism was the view expressed by Maurice Stans, Secretary of Commerce in the Nixon Administration, writing in the conservative *National Review:*

> If China does continue on its new path and its success measures up to its extraordinary opportunity, will the Soviets not be forced to emulate its demonstrated success by adopting similar policies? . . . Perhaps China may, by showing how much a free economy can do for its people, point the way to the demise of rigid Marxism and the ultimate reconciliation of differences among the political systems of the world.[3]

Just as the late-nineteenth-century Chinese philosopher Kang Youwei predicted that China would lead the world to a utopian order of "Great Harmony" based on Confucianism, so Stans sees China not only as abandoning socialism for capitalism, but also as leading the way for a historic convergence of all systems on the capitalist model.

So far, this new optimism about China's course is found chiefly on the conservative side of the American ideological spectrum, although not exclusively so (for example, Safire's colleague Flora

Lewis, a liberal columnist, basically shares his view).[4] Moreover, it is encountering considerable skepticism among China specialists, who now, as often in the past, are trying to counterbalance what they see as an excessive swing in opinion on the subject of their expertise. Kenneth Lieberthal, for example, warns that because of opposition within the political elite and the bureaucracy, "there remains little chance that the current reform effort can be brought to completion," and predicts that before long China will revert to conventional Marxist economic and social policies.[5] Political scientist Alan P. L. Liu in a letter to the editor of *The New York Times* calls the idea of a Chinese abandonment of Marxism "overblown."[6]

Thus, as 1985 begins, the new optimism is only a nascent trend among one section of the opinion leaders of the press, the business world, and academia. Nor, in the absence of a public opinion poll, can one say how widely the new image of China has spread among the general public. After all, most Americans are not very interested in foreign countries and know little about them. But the new trend is still important, because opinion leaders tend to change their views more rapidly than the general public, and their opinions exert considerable influence on government policy both directly, and indirectly through their eventual effects on the attitudes of the general public.

Seen in historical perspective, the new optimism is one more episode of a kind of China fever that has shaken sections of American elite opinion from time to time. And past examples suggest that this episode, like earlier ones, is likely to yield sooner or later to another round of disappointment. For although the U.S. probably has the largest scholarly, journalistic, and governmental China-watching establishment in the world, its public attitudes on China have long been characterized more by romanticism than by analysis.

Distinctive American attitudes toward China did not take shape before the nineteenth century. In its earlier years America did not have many dealings with the Far East and tended to accept the European view of China as a well-governed realm enjoying agricultural prosperity, enlightened despotism, and religious tolerance. This flattering image derived from Enlightenment thinkers who, for their own ideological purposes, portrayed China as a utopia where the values they favored for Europe had already been put into effect. In the nineteenth century the American relationship with China began to expand. American businessmen looked to the China market for an outlet for manufactured goods; American Protestant groups made China one of the major foci of their worldwide missionary effort; and American diplomats formulated the "Open Door" policy, calling on all nations to respect China's territorial integrity.

Those Americans who dealt with China (of course, a tiny minority) put forward the idea of a "special relationship" between America and China, claiming that unlike other countries, America was a benevolent, unselfish "friend" of China. In fact, according to recent historians, American policy was no more benevolent in motive than any other country's.[7] The "Open Door" policy, despite its unselfish rhetoric, was designed to protect American access to China at a time when America lacked the military strength to compete with other powers for concessions and spheres of influence. But the idea of a special relationship became a real force in the formation of American opinion. It exerted its impact in towns and churches across the country as sermons and lectures were given about our friends, the Chinese, and about the good work that was being done for them in mission work or famine relief. When China participated in the Second World War on the side of the Allies, Americans idealized Chiang Kai-shek and his Protestant wife as staunch allies and true democrats who were trying to transplant Western values into their country.[8]

But after the victory of the CCP, China "leaned to one side." Americans soon found themselves in a bitter war with Chinese troops in Korea. Then stories came out of Chinese "brainwashing" of U.S. missionaries and prisoners of war. Americans saw these events as a betrayal of a traditional friendship. Secretary of State John Foster Dulles stated in 1950, "Our relationship with China is primarily based upon a long background of religious, cultural and humanitarian association. ... History will never judge that we have been motivated by anything other than a desire to serve what we honestly believe to be the welfare of the Chinese people."[9] The estrangement continued for two decades. When China was shaken by the Cultural Revolution, Americans could view it only as a kind of inexplicable sickness. This attitude was summed up by the title of a TV documentary: "China: The Roots of Madness."

A new phase in public attitudes began in the late 1960s. In an influential series of hearings arranged by Senator William Fulbright of the Senate Foreign Relations Committee in 1966, a parade of China specialists argued for a shift from "containment and isolation" of Communist China to a policy of "containment without isolation" as a way of beginning to come to terms with the communist regime. In October 1967 Richard Nixon wrote in *Foreign Affairs*, "We simply cannot afford to leave China forever outside the family of nations, there to nurture its fantasies, cherish its hates and threaten its neighbors."[10] Although the term "China card" was not used at this time, the idea can be traced to this period. Strategic thinkers perceived that China's break with the Soviet Union made it useful for America to develop ties with one-quarter of the world's population. In addition, the new view was shaped by America's involvement in the Vietnam War. The Fulbright witnesses tried to undercut the Johnson Administration's rationale for the war by refuting the claim that China was an expansionist power that the U.S. needed to resist by proxy in Southeast Asia. Nixon for his part put forward the view that the Chinese threat to the region was real, but that it could be stemmed only by pulling China back into the world community.

These were pragmatic rather than emotional assessments of the importance of China ties to America, but in the American political system a radical change in foreign policy requires some change in public attitudes. In 1966, leading China scholars, assisted by liberal foundations, established an organization called the National Committee on U.S.-China Relations to help form more realistic public attitudes about China. (Today, that committee continues to exert a powerful influence by arranging exchange visits of Chinese and American political and opinion leaders to each other's countries. Meanwhile, the China Council of the Asia Society has taken over the task of public education.)

A second strain of opinion which emerged at about the same time proceeded from very different assumptions but reached similar conclusions. This was a sympathetic view of Maoist China that developed as an outgrowth of opposition to the war in Vietnam. The war's critics (who eventually became a majority of Americans) took a new look both at the enemy—the so-called Asian communism of which China was supposed to be the headquarters—and at their own society, which they came to see as aggressive and imperialistic. In this self-critical mood, many Americans doubted that they had any right to impose their values on China. For example, a Quaker delegation which visited China in 1972 wrote in its report, "The American social experience of pluralism and diversity and the relatively ungoverned U.S. economy do not constitute a lens through which Americans can successfully examine the basis of

Chinese society." In this view, although the Chinese system might appear totalitarian to Westerners, it was not appropriate to voice criticisms based on Western individualism, since this was not a value that Chinese shared. Instead, the Chinese system should be evaluated in Chinese terms. Thus the Quaker delegation concluded:

> [China's] political system . . . is willingly supported, in our opinion, by the great majority of the Chinese people. From their point of view it has delivered real and enduring benefits. Past regimes failed, but the People's Republic succeeded in replacing grinding poverty with economic security, disorder with order, mass oppression with mass justice, weakness with strength, and national humiliation with national pride.[11]

Such favorable views of China under Mao came to be widely accepted among American opinion leaders in the early 1970s. When Americans gathered around their television sets to watch President Nixon's arrival in Peking in February 1972, they saw network TV correspondents framed against a background of masses of Chinese sweeping the streets clean of a light snowfall. Most of the TV correspondents praised the discipline and civic-mindedness of the Chinese people. In the aftermath of the Nixon trip, American professors, reporters, and professionals began to visit China, almost always for guided "study tours." There was a spate of "China trip" books reporting the wonders of acupuncture, the achievements of the model production brigade Dazhai, the success of the model operas in combining Chinese and Western music and dancing, the lack of inflation and crime, and the willingness of the Chinese people to "go wherever the party wants me."

To most Americans, what people say is what they think, and seeing is believing: American travelers therefore tended to accept what they were told and shown by their guides as reflecting "the real China." When Chinese professors told American visitors that being "remolded" in May Seventh Cadre Schools had been good for them, the Americans believed it. In the same spirit, they accepted may other claims: that China combined book learning with physical labor in order to meet China's practical development problems, that Chinese were able to solve problems in agriculture or oil drilling by using the "Little Red Book," and so on. Some American writers began to view Mao Zedong's theories both as a valuable new development model for the third world, and as a possible answer to some of the problems of the developed West, such as crime, social alienation, and ecological pollution.[12]

This viewpoint must be hard for people who were then living in China to comprehend today. Many Americans, even China specialists, were unfamiliar with the Marxist theory of propaganda and assumed that so many Chinese newspapers and individuals would not all say the same thing unless they believed it. And because many Americans' faith in their own country's values was shaken by the Vietnam War, they were not willing to apply their own intuition or common sense to question the credibility of what was presented to them. Moreover, the resumption of Sino-American contacts from 1971 on made many Americans feel more comfortable about our China relations than did the preceding twenty years of antagonism. Americans could bask in a renewed sense of a "special relationship" with China. China was our friend again, on a new, more equal basis.

There were, of course, a number of writers who, from varying perspectives, disagreed with the prevailing view. Anti-communist values informed a book by Ivan and Miriam London which told about the cruelty and irrationality of the Red Guards during the Cultural Revolution.[13] But many China specialists raised questions about this book's reliability, because it was based on interviews with a former Red Guard conducted in Taiwan, because of its anti-communist perspective, and because many China specialists were actually still unaware of the widespread violence of the Cultural Revolution, which the Chinese media were still denying. Similarly, a scathing attack on the whole Maoist system written by a Belgian diplomat who had lived in China for several years had a wide readership because it was so well written, but was generally discounted by China specialists because of its polemical tone.[14]

From a different perspective, a number of senior scholars like A. Doak Barnett and Lucian Pye presented an argument that might be called "technological determinism" (although they did not use this term). They contended that modernization posed certain requirements, such as the need for advanced education and the cooperation of technical experts, and that Maoism, with its anti-intellectual bias, could not fulfill these requirements. Maoist values would eventually have to be modified if China was to solve its development problems.[15] But this view was rejected by many younger China scholars and self-labeled "radical" development specialists, who argued that the modernization path of the developing countries was different from the Western model and that the Maoist pattern of development suited third-world needs.[16]

American feelings about China took a major new turn toward negativism shortly after the purge of the "Gang of Four." This was not because of any partisanship for the four leaders or because of surprise at the factional struggle itself, for a succession crisis had long been predicted. The passion behind the new negativism may have been motivated in part by the realization that in idealizing Maoism, Americans had been made fools of. We had supposed China was different from other communist countries, and it wasn't. The commentators who helped to form public opinion on China— scholars and journalists—seemed to make a silent resolution not to be taken advantage of again. Moreoever, negative feelings were fueled by revelations that became available because of improved Western access to China and gradually increasing (although hardly complete) Chinese honesty about the past.

Thus, paradoxically, skepticism and disillusionment set in just as Chinese-Western relations were undergoing substantial improvement, and just as China was moving away from some of the worst abuses of the Maoist era. The trend reached its height after normalization of relations made it possible for American newspapers to station reporters in China. The most influential books to come out of this first generation of post-Mao American resident reporters were Richard Bernstein's *From the Center of the Earth* and Fox Butterfield's *Alive in the Bitter Sea.*[17]

The nature of the criticisms made by different commentators varied. Some deplored China's backwardness or authoritarianism, while others expressed pessimism about the prospects for modernization. In any case, by the early 1980s there were few if any American writers who were willing to paint a predominantly favorable portrait of China. Even those who considered themselves pro-socialist now shifted to a critical view. Some of them simply admitted (openly or tacitly) that they had been wrong in their belief that Mao had found a new road to socialism. Others maintained their ideological consistency by criticizing Deng Xiaoping for abandoning Maoism, even though this seemed to put them in the strange position of being foreigners who claimed to tell the Chinese what Maoism really is.[18]

As we review the four great swings in American attitudes toward China since 1949, one feature of American opinion stands out: the prominence of emotional and evaluative components. China for Americans, as Harold Isaacs wrote, "is uniquely capable of arousing intense emotion."[19] Instead of viewing China from a distance, in a relatively detached and objective way as we do most other countries, Americans want to judge China, to decide on an attitude of approval or disapproval. China is by no means the country of the most strategic or economic importance to the U.S. Russian actions have more influence on the future of America; Japan is a more important trading partner; Britain shares our language; Latin America and the Middle East are probably both of greater strategic significance; India is a large, developing, strategically important Asian nation and the seat of a great civilization, like China, but also has political values much closer to ours. Yet Americans have a special kind of concern with China, delighting when China seems to accept our values (or when we can accept Chinese values) and grieving when China and America are estranged.

One reason for this may be that there is a missionary impulse inherent in the American character—a desire to see other people confirm our values by becoming more like us. This impulse may have its roots in the origins of this nation as a land of refuge for those who suffered religious persecution in Europe. Whatever its sources, accidents of history have caused this impulse to become more strongly focused on China than on any other country. Because of its weakness, China was open to foreign influence for most of the last hundred years, but it was not part of the empire of any other nation. Thus it seemed more available than any other large country to be "saved" by America—a promising field for American energy and ambition. This was the sense in which American missionaries in the nineteenth century spoke of China as a "Niagara of souls" tumbling to perdition: all of them needed salvation, and Americans could provide it. In the twentieth century, instead of religion, Americans tended to promote liberalism with equal conviction. The existence of a Western-oriented intelligentsia tempted Americans in the Kuomintang period to hope that Chinese students and scholars would be won over to our way of life. Much the same sense of missionary self-satisfaction seems to lie behind the new optimism of 1985, the feeling that China is acknowledging the superiority of our way of life after thirty-five years' rejection of it.

The emotional quality of American attitudes toward China has been encouraged by both the American and the Chinese governments. Each has skillfully played the game of "friendship diplomacy" in order to encourage people on the other side to support policies in its interests. This has encouraged Americans, and perhaps Chinese as well, to expect more from the other side than just utilitarian trade or strategic ties.

Of course, there have always been economic and strategic interests at stake. According to Michael Hunt, the "open door constituency" of missionaries, businessmen, and diplomats who in the nineteenth century promoted the idea of China's special importance and friendliness to the U.S. did so because they harbored expansionist hopes and hoped to gain the support of public opinion for a more active China policy.[20] Summing up both the cultural and practical factors, John K. Fairbank wrote that for America, Asia became the furthest reach of the frontier; American China policy "resulted partly from attitudes of mind created in us by our westward expansion across the open spaces of the American continent."[21]

Although these factors help to explain the role of emotion in American attitudes toward China, the valence of American feelings has shifted in response to other forces. One important cause, obviously, has been the general state of political relations: a warming trend tends both to support, and to require support from, favorable public attitudes. Yet this is not the only factor; public opinion has gone through several major fluctuations since the late 1960s, even though governmental relations have tended steadily to improve.

A second factor is the information and opinions that Americans derive from the Chinese themselves. Our large China-watching community remains considerably dependent upon the official Chinese press and government-controlled access to China for information. The favorable attitudes of the late Mao years to some extent simply reflected American acceptance of official Chinese claims; the shift to negative attitudes in the post-Mao years was stimulated by revelations put out by the Chinese government about abuses under Mao; and the enthusiastic response to Deng's reforms reflects the great claims made for them in official Chinese statements. Although the same claims emanating from another communist country might not have achieved so much credibility, American specialists have tended to view China in isolation rather than in comparison with other communist countries, both because of China's break with the Soviet Union and because of the linguistic and other difficulties in the way of gaining expertise on both China and other communist systems at the same time.

There is a third factor at work that is more subtle. Today, as in the past, American attitudes about China are in part a projection of American attitudes about ourselves and our own society. The 1950s and early 1960s were times of patriotism and ideological self-confidence in the United States. In intellectual circles, this was the time when the theory of "totalitarianism" was proposed, which placed communist systems like China's in the same category of oppressive, unjust, and aggressive systems as Nazi Germany or Fascist Italy. American intellectuals tended to identify with the establishment (a term that became popular then); those who wrote fundamental critiques of American values were in a distinct minority. Satisfaction with the American system expressed itself partly as strong rejection of the China of the "blue ants."

But when the Vietnam War began to undermine American self-confidence, many Americans adopted toward competing social systems what Paul Hollander has called the "benefit of the doubt" posture.[22] In this view, values that are antagonistic to those of our own society may have more to recommend them than we initially thought and should not be hastily dismissed. The political struggle over the war set large segments of the intelligentsia in opposition to the government. For them, standing the unfavorable China images of the 1950s on their heads was a useful rhetorical device to shock Americans into seeing themselves in a new light. According to this argument, it was not China but America that was aggressive; not Chinese that were unfree, but Americans; not China that was violent, but America; not China that had irrational economic policies, but America.

America's isolation from China made it easy for even those who were China specialists to analyze China on this abstract plane without suffering the contradiction of Chinese realities about which little information was available. Thus praise of Mao's China served for some as a thinly disguised critique of American society rather than as a serious analysis of China. Writers in this vein were often motivated by a high sense of moral purpose in addressing the contradictions in American society. But history has exposed the irony that they failed in their moral duty to draw attention to the crimes that were being perpetrated in the Chinese society that they were supposed to be experts on.

Both the new negativism of the late 1970s and early 1980s and the current wave of optimism reflect the slow rehealing of American culture after Vietnam. Already under Jimmy Carter, a revived sense of cultural self-confidence was revealed in the foreign policy emphasis on human rights. The era of Ronald Reagan has brought a "new American patriotism" and an economic recovery that has helped restore faith in the capitalist system. Many of the intellectuals have resumed their earlier role as defenders of the establishment rather than as members of a dissident class. Americans' willingness to judge China by our own values increased along with this rise in cultural self-confidence. At the same time Americans writing about China for the press and scholarly publications began to have access to more detailed and realistic information about China than ever before. In this sense, the negative attitudes of the early post-Mao years actually represented a new realism about China. But it was not a purely objective realism, for its emotional coloration came from a sense of disappointment.

The new optimism of the mid-eighties serves a rhetorical purpose in American politics just opposite to that served in the late 1970s by the idealization of Maoism. This was obvious in Ronald Reagan's remark, after his 1984 China trip, that "this first injection of free-market spirit has already enlivened the Chinese economy. I believe it has also made a contribution to human happiness in China and opened a way to a more just society."[23] If in the 1970s the left praised China in order to condemn capitalism, today the right praises China in order to flatter capitalism. Once again the commentators are overlooking the complicated details of Chinese reality in their eagerness to draw lessons for the public at home.

So far the opinion trend remains concentrated mainly among business circles and more conservative journalists, with relatively few academic specialists joining in. Whether the new optimism reigns for a long time, or proves a short deviation in a longer period of critical views, will depend partly on the success or failure of Deng's reforms and partly on the ability of the second Reagan administration to sustain Americans' newly recovered zeal for their own system. In any case, American elite opinion on China continues to be shaped as much by the tides of American culture as by the facts of Chinese reality. For China specialists, the task remains of helping to form a more objective and illusion-free public attitude on China as a foundation for a more stable American China policy.

FIVE

U.S. Human Rights Policy Toward China: Two Essays

A DOUBLE STANDARD?

During Mikhail Gorbachev's 1987 summit visit to the United States, the American side placed human rights issues high on the agenda. Several commentators remarked that these issues are never given the same degree of prominence in American dealings with the PRC. A *Los Angeles Times* editorial stated, "From the reopening of relations with Beijing in 1972 to the present time, successive Administrations have considered it helpful to U.S. interests to say as little as possible about the status of human rights in China." The newspaper concluded, "a double standard indeed exists."

The term "double standard" implies that policy-makers think China should be judged by different moral criteria than other countries. Certainly some American policy-makers, journalists, and scholars think this way. But this belief is not the fundamental reason why American policy toward human rights in China differs so much from policy toward the Soviet Union. The danger of the double standard theory is that it can encourage a misunderstanding of the motives of American foreign policy and of the dynamics of policy-making processes. A deeper understanding of why U.S. human rights policy toward China is weak will be more useful in guiding those who wish to make it stronger.

The human rights strand in American foreign policy is often misunderstood, even by Americans, as growing out of a missionary impulse introduced into American politics by our first Christian-fundamentalist president, Jimmy Carter. But the human rights policy was not the creation of the Carter administration. The U.S. has been promoting democracy in the rest of the world since at least the late nineteenth century. American policy-makers have long perceived the promotion of human rights and democracy abroad as a hard strategic interest leading to a safer world for America.

The Soviet Union, South Africa, and South Korea are good examples. In the Soviet Union, the long-term goal of successive administrations has been to contain Soviet expansionism until the Soviet Union gradually changed into a peaceful, status quo power. Whether correctly or not, American policy-makers believed that a more open, more democratic Soviet state would be less motivated and less able to make war. This has been the fundamental reason for the U.S. to push for changes in Soviet internal human rights practices. In the case of South Africa, by pressing for the black population to be given the rights they demand, the U.S. hopes to forestall violent revolution and a takeover by pro-Soviet forces. In South Korea, American pressure for human rights has aimed at stabilizing the pro-American regime by encouraging it to avoid political polarization with its domestic opposition.

No such urgent practical motives exist for the U.S. to make an issue of human rights in China. China is not perceived as an expansionist threat. Nor is the stability of the Chinese regime a major worry for American policy-makers. True, the evolution of China in a more democratic direction would be in the long-term American interest for several reasons. It might help lead to a peaceful solution of the Taiwan problem. And it would help assure the permanence of the cooperative economic and strategic ties between the U.S. and China. But these concerns are less urgent than the ones that motivate human rights policy toward the Soviet Union, South Africa, and Korea. Thus, human rights considerations easily receive a lower priority in the total foreign policy mix when other practical concerns appear more urgent.

This has been the case during most of the Reagan presidency. Because the Reagan Administration came to office on a platform of anti-communism and better relations with Taiwan, many people expected it to be franker in criticism of the PRC than the Carter Administration. However, precisely because of his pro-Taiwan campaign rhetoric, when Reagan came to office he found that American ties with mainland China were in danger of serious damage. The questions of arms sales to Taiwan, technology transfer, political asylum for tennis star Hu Na, and other issues made the early years of Reagan's relations with China especially difficult.

During the 1980 election campaign, Reagan's goal had been to distinguish himself from the competing candidate. But as President his aim was to preserve the foreign policy assets inherited from the previous regime. A good relationship with the PRC is always an important asset, but it was especially so in the context of the confrontational policy Reagan adopted toward the Soviet Union. Therefore, after taking office, the Administration's public statements on China emphasized the friendship between the two countries, pointed to improvements in China's human rights situation, and avoided public criticism of human rights abuses.

American foreign policy, however, is perhaps more complex and multi-stranded than that of any other major power. There is often a gap between declared policy and specific policy actions. This gap has several sources. One is the independence of various sectors of the bureaucracy in carrying out their missions. A good example of this is the annual report on human rights compiled every year for Congress by the State Department Bureau of Human Rights. Despite the Administration's stress on friendship with China, the report on China has been tough and fair every year since it was first issued in 1980.

Second, there is the confusion introduced into U.S. foreign policy by the separation of powers. Under the American system, Congress has the constitutional right to oversee foreign policy. But in the past, under the doctrine of bipartisanship, both parties in Congress generally supported the administration in its conduct of foreign policy. The Vietnam War, however, caused a breakdown in Congressional trust in the Administration's conduct of foreign policy. In recent years Congress has involved itself more and more frequently in the details of foreign policy, a trend some scholars refer to as micro-management. In the human rights field, Congress has enacted legal restrictions on the Administration's ability to give aid or to sell military equipment to regimes that do not meet certain rights standards.

Congressional committees often use their hearings not only to gather information, but also as forums to force the State Department publicly to evaluate human rights practices in certain countries and to bring the pressure of public opinion to bear on foreign governments. Congressmen traveling to foreign countries often inquire about human rights cases of concern to their constituents. Perhaps most confusing of all to foreign governments—who wonder which branch of government in the U.S. is really running foreign policy—Congress sometimes passes "sense of the Congress resolutions" or legislative amendments which lack specific provisions but simply express Congressional disapproval of the activities of foreign governments. The most recent example was a Senate resolution criticizing Chinese policy in Tibet.

Congressional micro-management is strongly responsive to public opinion. The Jackson-Vanick amendment, which prohibits the granting of Most Favored Nation trade status to nations that inhibit freedom of emigration, was adopted in response to American Jewish concerns about the denial of exit visas to Soviet Jews. Similarly, the Senate resolution on Tibet is testimony to the strength of American public concern about that part of China. There is a small "Tibet lobby," led by the Office of Tibet in New York, but the strength of public sympathy for the Tibetans seems attributable mainly to a romantic image of Tibet and the fact that in recent years tens of thousands of Americans have traveled there.

Third, not only Congress, but also the White House and the State Department are often responsive to public opinion. When Yi Xigong, the fiancé of American graduate student Lisa Wichser, was arrested in China, the U.S. government pressed inquiries about his case and he was quickly released. Hanson Huang (Huang Xian), an American lawyer of Chinese descent, was sentenced for espionage but given early parole after American expressions of concern. The State Department has been inquiring regularly about the status of Yang Wei, who had been a student in America before returning to Shanghai last winter, and whose wife, a Chinese citizen, is still in the U.S.

It is relatively easy for American citizens and even for foreigners living in America to get appointments to see State Department staff members, Congressional staff, and even members of Congress. The State Department is required to answer all inquiries from members of Congress and almost always answers direct inquiries from the general public as well. By directing an inquiry to the State Department through any of these channels an American can usually get the U.S. Embassy in Beijing or one of the U.S. consulates to request information from the Chinese government about a political or religious prisoner. Depending on the amount of public and Congressional concern and the nature of the case, the State Department will sometimes inform the Chinese government of the seriousness of public concern or ask for an early release of a prisoner on humanitarian grounds.

This kind of diplomatic intervention is most likely to occur and tends to be most vigorous when the American side has some clear excuse for taking an interest, such as the involvement of an American citizen, the relative of an American citizen, or the employee of an American firm. Thus the State Department was especially active in pressing the Chinese for the release of *New York Times* reporter John P. Burns, who is a Canadian citizen but the employee of an American newspaper, when he was detained for traveling in forbidden areas. But a strong American connection is not required so long as there is an American constituency to pressure the U.S. government about the case. The government has made inquiries to the Chinese about Wei Jingsheng because several groups in the U.S., including Amnesty International, have asked about him. Also, the Catholic Church in the U.S. is active through an organization called "Free the Fathers" in pressing the State Department to inquire about priests imprisoned in China because of their loyalty to the Vatican.

By its nature, it is difficult to get complete information about this sort of quiet diplomacy. But my impression is that in recent years the State Department has been increasingly willing not only to raise individual human rights cases with the Chinese government, but also to state publicly that it is doing so. J. Stapleton Roy, Deputy Assistant Secretary of State for East Asian and Pacific Affairs, testified recently before the Senate Foreign Relations Committee that "through official channels, we have raised a number of human rights concerns, both on questions of general principle and individual cases." Making this kind of public statement about its inquiries in China represents a subtle shift of emphasis in State Department policy, but it may prove to be a significant and long-lasting one. American public opinion is now somewhat more critical of China than it was in the early 1980s; American relations with China are now virtually free of major problems or crises, leaving more room for dialogue on human rights issues; and the improved relations of the Soviet Union with both the U.S. and China have reduced the bargaining power of China in the strategic triangle. So long as these conditions persist, the State Department will probably continue to find it relatively easy to make inquiries and expressions of concern to the Chinese government about cases that American citizens and residents are interested in.

On one human rights issue, the administration has been not easier on China than on other governments, but tougher. For three years in a row the administration has withheld its annual contribution of about $25 million to the UN Fund for Population Activities, contending that the population planning program in China, which is one of the programs the UNFPA supports, engages in coerced abortions and sterilizations.

Here is a prime example of the impact of American public opinion on foreign policy. Abortion is a major issue in American politics. The Right to Life movement endorses or opposes political candidates at almost every level of the American electoral system in almost every electoral district. The movement is large, and like other single-issue movements has influence even greater than its numbers because it effectively mobilizes its constituency to vote. The Right to Life movement was from the beginning a strong supporter of the Reagan presidency. Reagan, however, has been unable to do away with government funding for abortions or to achieve adoption of a constitutional amendment to forbid them. Criticizing the Chinese population planning program and penalizing the UNFPA were actions that provided some satisfaction to his right-to-life supporters at little political cost to him.

This analysis leads to two conclusions. First, because the human rights impulse in American foreign policy is ultimately founded on a perception of national self-interest, it is not likely to disappear as an element of American China policy even though it is sometimes de-emphasized in favor of other concerns that appear of more immediate urgency. Second, even now the American government would probably take a greater interest than it does in Chinese human rights problems if there were stronger public lobbies calling attention to them. Free the Fathers, the Office of Tibet, and the U.S. section of Amnesty International are relatively small organizations, and each deals with only a portion of the total Chinese human rights picture.

Based on the model of American Jewish leadership in publicizing human rights problems in the Soviet Union and black leadership in lobbying to change American policies on South Africa, one might expect Chinese-Americans and Chinese citizens in the United States to lead the way in forming bigger, more comprehensive lobbies on China. But so far, except for the Chinese Alliance for Democracy (China Spring), which has had some success lobbying with Congress, few in the Chinese community have been active in bringing human rights issues to the attention of the U.S. government. The reasons for this are no doubt complicated—perhaps a tradition of abstention from politics, lack of organization, patriotic pride in recent progress in the mainland, or a greater identification with Taiwan than with the mainland. Whatever the reasons, the open nature of the American political system offers the prospect that when Chinese-Americans begin to express their concerns about human rights issues in China, the U.S. government is likely to respond.

BEHIND THE YANG WEI CASE

In his September 25, 1987, interview with NBC television news anchor Tom Brokaw, then-Premier Zhao Ziyang was asked whether the party might release some of those who had been jailed for criticizing the Party's policies and leadership. "So far as I know," Zhao replied, "no one has been arrested or put into jail for that. There is no such case where people are thrown into jail because they have criticized the policies of our Party or its leaders. Of course, it is a different matter if someone violates the law." Not only did the Premier's reply ignore the cases of Wei Jingsheng, Wang Xizhe, Xu Wenli, and other political prisoners from the Democracy Wall period, but three months later his words were further contradicted when a Shanghai court sentenced Yang Wei, a Chinese student who had been studying at the University of Arizona, to two years' imprisonment for the crime of "counterrevolutionary propaganda and incitement" because he hung wall posters and distributed letters encouraging the student demonstrations of December 1986.

Of course, Yang and the other prisoners I just listed were convicted of crimes under the Chinese Criminal Law. But the law's provisions concerning counterrevolutionary activities are so vague that they permit the sentencing of people for acts that ought to be considered constitutionally protected free speech. None of the four used or advocated the use of violence. They were jailed for no other reason than that they criticized the Party's policies and leaders. By international human rights standards they are political prisoners. All of them have been adopted as "prisoners of conscience" by Amnesty International.

But there is more to the Yang Wei case than the news that Chinese human rights practices, although better than in the past, still need improvement. The case throws light on the changing climate in U.S.-China relations, among Chinese students overseas in the U.S., and in China itself.

The Shanghai court accused Yang Wei of acting on behalf of the Chinese Alliance for Democracy (China Spring), a dissident organization founded in New York in 1982. According to the organization's magazine *China Spring*, Yang Wei did not deny that he was a member of the CAD or that he had posted slogans at Fudan University in the organization's name.

Yang Wei's activities were remarkable, since from the time of the CAD's founding the Chinese government had warned students and scholars who were going abroad to avoid all contact with the organization. Chinese who became involved with the CAD have usually kept their identities secret or made up their minds not to return to China; some of them have applied for political asylum. Yang Wei was the first member to return to China and to act so openly as virtually to declare himself to the Public Security Bureau.

What happened after his arrest was also unprecedented. The CAD immediately organized a sophisticated publicity and lobbying effort to bring American pressure to bear on the Chinese government. News of Yang Wei's arrest was quickly provided to the *New York Times* and other major newspapers. With the apparent encouragement of the CAD, an organization primarily made up of Americans called the Chinese-American Association for Human Rights was formed to generate publicity and letters on the case. CAD's chairman, Wang Bingzhang, went to Capitol Hill and visited the offices of a number of sympathetic senators, including Jesse Helms and Dennis DeConcini. The two senators proposed a bill urging the Chinese government to release Yang Wei immediately. In September, the Senate Foreign Relations Commitee held hearings on human rights in China at which representatives of the State Department, Amnesty International, and Yang Wei's wife Che Shaoli—also a student in the U.S.—commented on the case. CAD then organized a wave of telephone calls to various senators' offices from Chinese students in the U.S. Finally on October 8, the Helms-DeConcini bill was adopted by a vote of 85 to 5.

The pressure of public opinion was also felt in the State Department, which repeatedly pressed the Chinese authorities for information about the case. According to press reports, even Secretary of State Shultz raised the Yang Wei case with Chinese officials during his visit to China in March. Shortly before Yang's trial, more publicity was generated by a petition to the Chinese government, signed by over a thousand Chinese students at many American universities, calling on the Chinese government to refrain from prosecuting him for the peaceful expression of his political views.

Moreover, in a daring but successful publicity move, the CAD sent one of its members on the very eve of the trial directly to Shanghai, where he generated further international publicity by appearing on the steps of the Shanghai people's court to distribute copies of an open letter demanding Yang Wei's release. The Shanghai police detained this person, Qian Da, but because he is a Taiwanese holding American permanent residency, dealing with him harshly would have created international complications. He was simply expelled from the country.

Never before had a Chinese political case aroused so much pressure in the United States. And from the beginning there were signs that the Chinese government felt the pressure. Arrested in January, Yang was not tried until December, although the Chinese Criminal Procedure Law provides for a trial within three months of detention except in "an especially major or complex case." Judging from the eventual verdict, Yang's case was "complex" mostly in terms of the problems it aroused abroad. When He Dongchang, Vice-Minister of the State Educational Commission, visited the U.S. during May-June 1987, he had to deal with angry questions on the case from groups of Chinese students with whom he met. When the trial finally took place, Yang received a two-year prison term, the lightest sentence known to have been given to a Chinese convicted of counterrevolutionary activity.

Besides the unprecedented level of American and overseas-student pressure, the Yang Wei case revealed three other trends. First, the case gives evidence of the growing strength of the CAD. In its first five years of existence the organization faced many problems—leadership splits, a shortage of money, charges that it fabricated material published in its magazine, accusations of untrustworthiness against its founder Dr. Wang, and most serious of all, accusations that it was secretly supported and directed by the Taiwan authorities. (Several members of its leadership are from Taiwan.) But recently there have been signs that the tide of opinion among Chinese students in the U.S. and Chinese-American businessmen has shifted somewhat in CAD's favor. More mainland students have submitted articles to the magazine despite the risk of doing so, and several of them have dared to publish without using pseudonyms. As a result, the quality of the magazine has improved.

Some Chinese-American businesses now advertise in *China Spring*, and this apparently has helped alleviate the organization's financial problems. Some students have begun to discount the problem of Taiwan financing for CAD, saying that even if the rumors are true, what matters is not the source of the money but what CAD does with it. The organization has begun an internal discussion about whether to upgrade from a pressure group to a political party. Most significantly, at its Third Congress, held in late December 1987 and early January 1988 in San Francisco, the CAD elected a new chairman, Hu Ping. A graduate student at Harvard, Hu Ping last year was elected chairman of the Association of Chinese Students of Political Science and International Relations in the United States. In carrying out an orderly succession in office in accordance with its own constitution, the CAD has demonstrated a greater power to survive and find supporters than many observers thought it had.

The second trend is the sharpening dissatisfaction toward the Chinese government among the approximately 19,000 Chinese students studying in the U.S. Great hopes were raised by the discussion of political reform encouraged by Deng Xiaoping during the summer and fall of 1986. The campaign against bourgeois liberalization in 1987 deeply disappointed many of the students, even though this campaign appears to have had little permanent effect on intellectual life in China.

Perhaps an equally important factor influencing overseas student attitudes has been the Party's response to the January 1987 open letter to the Chinese government, signed by 1682 Chinese students in this country, of whom 701 used their real names. The letter protested the ouster of Hu Yaobang from the post of Party General Secretary and the purge from the Party of three leading intellectuals (Fang Lizhi, Liu Binyan, and Wang Ruowang). In drafting the letter the students stressed their loyalty to the motherland and carefully avoided any linkage of their letter-signing movement with the CAD. They waited anxiously for a sign that the party leaders understood their good motives and would not punish them after they returned home. For whatever reason, the party has refused to offer such assurances publicly and has not even offered convincing assurances privately. For these and other reaons, more and more students seem to have concluded that it is hopeless to expect fundamental political change in China and personally unwise to go home. This may help explain the CAD's ability to generate a thousand protest signatures on the recent student petition on the Yang Wei case.

The growing alienation of the students and the increasing prestige of the CAD formed part of the complex background to the Yang Wei case, requiring the Chinese government to make a careful decision about how to handle it. The government's decision was to use the occasion of Yang Wei's sentence officially to label the CAD a reactionary organization for the first time. In an interview published simultaneously with the sentence, an anonymous Shanghai Public Security Bureau official warned that Chinese who participate in the CAD or contribute to its magazine will be dealt with according to law upon their return home. Perhaps as a means of emphasizing the dangerousness of the CAD, the official painted its influence in more impressive terms than any observer has done before, stressing its ability to gather information inside China, to distribute its magazine and flyers there, and to recruit supporters overseas. Another decision which may have been taken—it has been rumored but not yet publicly announced—is to reduce the number of students who will be permitted to go abroad from now on, especially to the United States.

Lying behind these events is a third and still more important trend, the growing inability of the Chinese Communist Party to enforce ideological unity at home. The Chinese students abroad are, after all, part of the Chinese intelligentsia, and they are influenced more deeply by the movement of sentiment at home than by events in their student communities abroad. The most striking symbol of the state of mind of the Chinese intellectuals is the fate of Fang Lizhi and Liu Binyan. The Party itself gave their thoughts wider circulation during 1987 than they had ever enjoyed before by compiling their most provocative speeches and talks into booklets for negative study, distributing them widely, and requiring party members to study them. After being purged from the Party, both became more popular and influential than ever.

The loss of ideological unity is not solely the result of resistance on the part of the intellectuals to the Party's pressure for conformity. Under Hu Yaobang the Party itself had come to accept the fact that if it wanted to pursue modernization and reform it would have to respect the independence of the intellectuals more than it had under Mao. Despite the resistance of some of the senior conservative leaders, Zhao Ziyang has continued to pursue this policy. It formed the final part of the "complex" background of the Yang Wei case, for the party needed to minimize as much as possible the damage the case would do to its relations with the intellectuals. This helps to explain the relative lightness of Yang's sentence and the government's strenuous efforts to deny the procedural irregularities in the case.

In an article written on the eve of the Communist victory in mainland China, Mao Zedong answered those who charged the CCP with being dictatorial by replying, "My dear sirs, you are right, that is just what we are. All the experience the Chinese people have accumulated through several decades teaches us to enforce the people's democratic dictatorship, that is, to deprive the reactionaries of the right to speak and let the people alone have that right." Although incidents like the Yang Wei case still occur, one need only imagine how Mao Zedong would have replied to Tom Brokaw's question to appreciate the difference between Mao's China and Zhao's.

The reaction of the Chinese students in the U.S. to the purge of Hu Yaobang has turned out to be a reliable omen of worsening relations between the regime and the intellectuals at home, with consequences that are described in parts III and V below. Today overseas student attitudes continue to be a more reliable indicator of the regime's acceptability to the educated class than the staged expressions of support that appear in the controlled media. To judge by this measure, the regime has failed to persuade its people that it faced a rebellion rather than a peaceful protest in 1989 and that it put it down with minimal force.

Part of the propaganda effort has been a stream of accusations against China Spring for manipulating the Democracy Movement to overthrow the government. During the repression the Shanghai authorities re-arrested Yang Wei, and literary theorist Liu Xiaobo, who had ties to China Spring and participated in the last stage of the Tiananmen hunger strike, was labeled a "black hand" of the movement. The Chinese government labeled CAD not merely reactionary, as it did in 1987, but counterrevolutionary.

The true role of the CAD in the events of spring 1989 was minor. Most of its members remained in the U.S. and sent little more than moral support to China. The organization's strength had been sapped by a financial crisis and a split between Hu Ping and the former chairman, Wang Bingzhang, that culminated in a lawsuit against Wang for alleged private use of some of the organization's funds.

After the June 1989 repression, Chinese students and scholars in this country organized themselves for the first time on a broad basis to lobby and demonstrate. They may become the kind of lobby that has previously been lacking in American politics to draw attention to Chinese human rights issues. It remains to be seen whether China Spring will be submerged in this movement or strengthened by it.

PART III
The Crisis of Reform

SIX

Reform at the Crossroad: Chinese Politics in 1988

The politics of 1988 were dominated by the relationship between Deng Xiaoping, at age 84 still China's top decision-maker despite his semi-retirement, and Zhao Ziyang, the 69–year-old party general secretary, Deng's heir apparent. The year opened with Zhao's influence at a high point. He demonstrated his position as Deng's chief reform strategist by sponsoring a bold initiative to establish an export-oriented economy along China's coast. At year's end, when price reform suffered a setback, it seemed that Zhao's political career might also suffer, but he emerged from the crisis with his power intact—although his grip on the succession remained uncertain.

The broad commitment to economic reform was no longer at issue among the Party leaders, but controversy attended efforts to work out the details of reform and efforts to manage the social and ideological consequences of "opening up" the economy and social life. Deng's remained the only voice that could authoritatively settle such controversies among the leaders. Although both Zhao Ziyang and 60–year-old Prime Minister Li Peng, Zhao's chief rival for power among the younger leaders, relied increasingly on experts and specialists to frame policy options, China's policy-making process still remained personalistic: Deng's nod determined major policy decisions and power relationships. And Deng continued to rely on his intuitive style of "crossing the river by feeling the way from rock to rock."

Deng's impulsive mid-year decision to implement a still-embryonic proposal for price-system reform illustrated both his unquestioned personal authority and the limits that this authority placed on the influence of the rising technocracy. The episode also demonstrated the risks of such a decision-making style, as Deng's instincts proved flawed. Accelerating inflation generated a strong popular reaction that forced the government quickly to reverse the price-reform policy, which had been announced with much fanfare. In addition, since price reform was apparently a prerequisite for further reform of industrial enterprises, its failure was seen by many as a signal that reform as a whole had reached a dead end. For many, the Third Plenum of the Thirteenth Central Committee, which reversed the price reform, was the symbolic end of the decade of reform that had begun at the epochal Third Plenum of the Eleventh Central Committee in December 1978.

The year 1988 ushered in a season of discontent that is perhaps unique in China's post-revolutionary history. The failure of price reform in the fall accelerated the radical decline in the regime's authority that had begun earlier in the year. For the first time one could hear anti-Deng sentiments openly expressed among a broad spectrum of Chinese. The rising sense of anomie was as much a consequence of reform's successes—increased freedom of speech, rising expectations, social and geographic mobility—as of its failures—inflation and corruption.[1] The mood among intellectuals, in particular, reflected a profound questioning not only of China's political leaders and political system, but even of its national culture and national character. Some viewed the increasing social disorder and intellectual alienation as signs of a dangerous breakdown of the social contract; others saw these as normal signs of a freer "civil society" emerging as a result of rising prosperity and liberalization.

If the events of 1988 demonstrated Deng Xiaoping's continuing dominance of Chinese politics, they also showed that his decision-making style was becoming less suitable to China's increasingly complex political economy and turbulent society. Although Deng reiterated his desire to retire from the front line of government frequently during the year, he was unable to consummate a succession of power. The shape of the post-Deng leadership remained murky, and the chances remained high that the leadership would be politically insecure.

Zhao's Role and the Coastal Development Strategy

The year opened with a bold reform initiative that demonstrated Zhao's pre-eminence as Deng's chief strategist for reform. The policy-making process leading to this new program, called the "coastal development strategy," also illustrated Zhao's openness to proposals from young, liberal reformers, his willingness to champion practical new ideas regardless of how far they might diverge from those of some of the older party leaders, and the political risks attending the adoption of proposals that had not been thoroughly discussed within the Party leadership and the bureaucracy.

The new program, also referred to as "joining the great international circle," departs in several ways from the "open policy" put into effect in 1979. Under the open policy Beijing had successively designated four Special Economic Zones, fourteen coastal cities, three delta areas, and Hainan Province as places with preferential conditions for foreign investment and bases for the development of exports.

First, instead of concentrating foreign investment and trade in certain areas, the new policy opens up to foreign investment the entire coastal region from Liaoning to Guangdong—an area estimated to have a population of 100 to 200 million.

Second, under the new policy both capital and management are expected to come mainly from overseas investors rather than through joint ventures.

Third, both capital and raw materials may be freely imported, referred to as "putting both ends of the production process on the world market" (*liangtou zaiwai*). The old policy of discouraging imports of parts and raw materials has been dropped for two reasons: because of the difficulty experienced by foreign-owned firms in dealing with Chinese suppliers; and in order to reduce inflationary pressures on the Chinese economy that are generated when export-oriented firms compete with domestic-oriented firms for raw materials.

Fourth, the new strategy—under which China contributes only labor to the exported product, not capital or raw materials—is a strategy of exporting China's cheap excess labor power. Where the old open policy emphasized that foreign investors should supply China with advanced modern technology, the new policy stresses labor-intensive industries like clothing, handicrafts, and light industrial products.

In short, the new policy is one of "export-led growth" or "export-oriented industrialization." It is explicitly modeled on the experiences of Taiwan and the other Asian "small dragons." Zhao's plan is to develop a fifth "dragon" along China's coast—one much larger than all the rest.

The genesis of the coastal development strategy illustrated both Zhao's links to a circle of young, pragmatic technocrats and his continued dependence on Deng Xiaoping for the political authority to implement radical economic reforms. The strategy originated with a handful of economists, most prominently Wang Jian, a 33–year-old assistant research fellow at the State Planning Commission. Wang and others argued to Zhao in late 1987 that an export-oriented strategy would enable China to solve the two main problems created by the success of the earlier stages of reform: a shortage of raw materials and a surplus of rural labor. They also argued that an export-oriented strategy could help China surmount the two main obstacles that would face economic reform in the near future: enterprise reform and price reform. Exposing Chinese enterprises to the discipline of international market competition would force them to become efficient, they argued. Creating a large number of enterprises oriented to the world economy would provide a bridge for the adjustment of domestic prices to world market levels.[2]

After making two tours of the coastal regions, in January 1988 Zhao reported these ideas to Deng Xiaoping. In addition to the factors already mentioned, Zhao also emphasized that the low value of the U.S. dollar had raised the price of Japanese, Taiwanese, and Korean exports to the United States and that this offered an excellent opportunity for China to enter the market with its cheaper labor. Deng approved the proposal, stating that the policy "must be pursued with great boldness and with speed; on no account can we lose this opportunity." Based on Deng's support, the Politburo gave its endorsement at its Fourth Plenum on February 6.

Merely announcing the policy, however, did not guarantee its success. Zhao had not taken the time to create a consensus for the policy among other senior leaders or among the provincial officials whose cooperation would be required for the policy to succeed. The plan faced broad political and bureaucratic skepticism, one sign of which was that in his Government Work Report to the Seventh National People's Congress, Prime Minister Li Peng placed Zhao's plan only fourth among the tasks facing the government. The three tasks that took priority were promoting the development of agriculture and industry; improving science, technology, and education; and continuing enterprise reform. Those items Li listed after the coastal development strategy included political reform, cultural and social policy, and defense modernization. In discussing coastal development, Li—unlike Zhao—emphasized careful preparatory work rather than speed and called for attention to the development of inland as well as coastal areas.[3]

The plan also confronted innumerable practical obstacles. In order to succeed, the new strategy will eventually require a further devaluation of the *renminbi;* Chinese enterprises can now earn more *renminbi* by selling products at home than by exporting them. But fears that such devaluation would aggravate inflationary pressures prevented any moves in this direction in 1988, and near the end of the year the government announced that there would be no devaluation in 1989.

Even if domestic obstacles like devaluation can be overcome, the export-oriented coastal development policy will face resistance abroad. Unless the quality of Chinese workmanship improves, China's products will not be able to compete in the world market. And even if the products do meet international standards, the export drive is likely to run into protectionist barriers in the United States, Japan, and Europe.

Nonetheless, by the end of 1988, considerable achievements were claimed for the coastal development policy. For the first eight months of the year exports from six of the coastal provinces were reported to have increased 21 percent over the same period of 1987, to a sum of US$11.77 billion, representing 44 percent of China's total exports.[4] It was too early to evaluate whether such figures represented merely the natural momentum of a dynamic sector of the economy, or whether the policy changes in Beijing really had initiated a fundamental economic reorientation in the coastal regions.

The Role of the Technocrats. Events at the Seventh National People's Congress, meeting from March 25 to April 13, were evidence of the rise of technocracy, which had been a striking feature of Chinese politics in 1987.[5] Seventy-one percent of the delegates were newly elected, and they were younger and better-educated than members of previous congresses.[6] The congress streamlined the central state organs by reducing the number of ministries and commissions to 41 from 45, restructuring a number of the organs, and appointing younger and better-educated ministers to many of the posts.

The congress elected Acting Prime Minister Li Peng, a prototypical "red technocrat," to a full term as prime minister, the top post in the state hierarchy. Son of a communist martyr and adopted son of Zhou Enlai, Li was educated in the Soviet Union as an electrical power engineer and served for many years in the Chinese energy bureaucracy.[7] In a press conference after his accession to the premiership, Li denied the view widely held abroad that he is a spokesman for a conservative wing of the leadership, describing himself instead as an implementer of Party policies. The fact that no important policy initiatives were associated with his name during 1988 lent plausibility to this characterization.

In his Government Work Report to the Congress, Li emphasized the need for a cautious and orderly pursuit of the established policies for economic reform, a steady pace of growth, the improvement of science and technology, more efficiency in government, and the maintenance of social order. To facilitate the movement toward a market-regulated economy, the Congress adopted constitutional amendments permitting the transfer of land-use rights and the existence and development of privately owned enterprises. It adopted laws which gave the managers of state-owned enterprises the authority to make business decisions without seeking permission from higher government organs.

Before and after the Seventh Congress, debate continued within the technocracy over the future path of reform. Movement toward a market-regulated economy had been a goal of the reformers for several years. In 1988 this reform faced two interlocking obstacles — government control of the prices of some major goods and government interference in the management of enterprises. At this policy crossroad, the leaders turned to their advisers in governmental and semi-governmental research institutes and the universities. They gave these specialists free rein to frame proposals, provide studies of foreign models, and conduct surveys in order to predict popular responses to alternative measures.

One group of economists, headed by Wu Jinglian of the Chinese Academy of Social Sciences and the State Council Research Center for Economic, Social, and Technological Development, argued for carrying out price-system reform first. These economists argued that a shift from controlled to market-determined prices was necessary to enable enterprises to operate efficiently. Acknowledging that price reform would entail some worsening of inflation, Wu pointed to the overnight liberalization of prices by Adenauer in postwar Germany as an example of how such inflation would be self-limiting as the domestic market was established.

Price reform seemed to its proponents not only economically necessary in 1988 but also politically opportune. According to the State Statistical Bureau, in the preceding ten years the inflation-adjusted incomes of urban residents had increased by 85.7 percent, thus providing a cushion of well-being that would enable urban residents to absorb the impact of a temporary inflation. The vast bulk of the Chinese population, the peasants, would be much less severely affected by inflation than urban dwellers because the main component of inflation so far had been the rise in food prices and peasants grow rather than buy most of their food. In some respects, peasants would even benefit from inflation, which would raise the prices of the grain and other agricultural products they sell, as well as of the products of their village industries, which are not controlled. Although in some countries—Poland, Burma, and Iran, for example—inflation has been accompanied by economic stagnation, in China inflation has been accompanied by economic growth. In principle, this provided the government with enough resources to be able to plan wage increases for many of the urban residents. By reforming the wage system and the price system concurrently, the leaders could assure that price reform would bring no decline in the people's average living standards.

Moreover, proponents of price reform saw in it a built-in tradeoff for the inevitable loss of popularity the regime would face as a result of worsening inflation—a substantial reduction in bureaucratic corruption, a problem which has generated enormous popular discontent. Price-reform advocates pointed out that corruption is fostered by the two-track price system, under which there is a gap between official and market prices and those who have the discretion to supply a good at an official price are tempted to demand part or all of the difference between that price and the market price as a finder's fee. Therefore, narrowing the price gap would reduce the size of bribes, and removing it eventually would remove the main cause of corruption.

Other economic specialists, however, warned that the worsening inflation induced by price reform might be more serious and longer-lasting than Wu Jinglian and his allies predict. In 1988, inflation had already reached the highest levels since prices were stabilized in the early 1950s. By the end of the year, the official inflation rate had reached 18.5 percent, with the actual rate substantially higher. Official statistics showed that 21 percent of urban workers had suffered a decline in living standards in 1987. In addition, survey research by the Economic System Reform Institute indicated that public anxiety about prices was so keen that price reform might well trigger a psychological inflationary spiral. The Institute warned that the political danger of inflation lay less in people's fears about the current price of goods than in their worries about inflation devaluing their savings and undermining the worth of their future pensions, which are calculated as a percentage of base salary and do not reflect the bonuses and other perquisites that make up an increasingly high proportion of most workers' incomes.[8]

An alternative reform proposal, put forward by Li Yining of Beijing University, called for placing emphasis on strengthening the managerial autonomy of enterprises. It was known as the "3–5–8" plan because it had three-year, five-year, and eight-year targets. Li's proposal was based on the idea, accepted by virtually all Chinese economists, that a major cause of inefficiency in state-run enterprises is government interference in their operations. According to this view, each ostensibly state-owned enterprise in China is in practice the property of—that is, controlled by—a specific governmental bureau, usually at the provincial, municipal, or county level. The bureau enjoys the benefits of its "property"—such as control over taxes remitted, access to manufactured goods which can be traded with other bureaus, and the ability to make job appointments. In exchange, the bureau gives the enterprise free land and money for investment, protects it from competition, helps it acquire low-cost raw materials, and allows it to set profitably high prices for its manufactures.[9]

Many reform economists have long held that while this situation persists, price reform will fail. The market will be unable to discipline enterprises because they will continue to be protected by their bureaucratic owners and will take advantage of price reform to raise prices and increase their monopoly profits. Li Yining's special contribution to the debate was to argue that enterprise reforms enacted or tested to date have been unable to free enterprises from bureau control. These have included allowing enterprises to retain profits, substituting taxes for profit remittance, signing performance contracts with managers, and expanding the limits of managerial autonomy by law.

Li proposed "stockification"—turning enterprise assets into

stocks, and giving or selling a portion of these stocks to the enterprises' employees, to other individuals, or even to other companies, while also keeping a portion for the state. Once transferred to new owners, Li argued, the enterprise would be able to resist official interference, thus becoming free to respond to market signals in pursuit of profit and efficiency. Joint-stock companies would still be socialist, Li argued, because each company's stock would be owned by a broad range of people in society, especially the enterprise's staff and workers, and because a sizable portion of the stock would remain in the hands of the state.

The way in which the choice of price reform over enterprise reform was made indicated the limits of technocracy in China today. Deng Xiaoping suddenly announced the decision to go ahead with price reform, although the debate among the experts had not yet reached its conclusion.

The Rise and Fall of Price Reform.

On June 22, during a meeting with Ethiopian President Mengistu Haile Mariam, Deng Xiaoping remarked that conditions were ripe to reform prices and wages. "We are in the process of storming this pass right now," Deng told Mengistu. "We expect it will take us five or six years."[10]

Deng's pronouncement, apparently unexpected, became policy, and Zhao Ziyang called upon Wu Jinglian, Li Yining, and other economists to work up concrete proposals to implement the policy. These proposals were debated at the Politburo meeting held in the seaside resort of Beidaihe in July and August. In August, the New China News Agency announced that the Five-Year Plan for price reform had been adopted by the Politburo and would be submitted to the Central Committee in September for its (pro forma) approval.

What emerged from Beidaihe was apparently a watered-down version of Wu Jinglian's proposal. The plan, which was never publicly released, evidently called for a step-by-step raising of the prices of major industrial raw materials, transport rates, electric power, and grain. Over the course of five years, the price increases were expected gradually to narrow the gap between state-set prices and free-market prices, with the state-set prices nearing or equaling market prices at the end of the transition period. In short, the

105

goal was to abolish both the "double-track price system," and the concomitant direct state role in allocating goods, and to create a situation in which the state could control the economy through macroeconomic levers like credit, money supply, and investment ("the state adjusts the market and the market guides enterprises"). In order to assure that most people's incomes would keep pace with the inflation induced by the reform and that living standards would not fall, the Politburo also intended to reform the urban wage system at the same time.

Before the details could be announced, however, the psychological inflation predicted by some experts began to occur. People ran to the banks to withdraw their funds and to the stores to buy whatever goods were available. Perhaps more serious than the popular panic was uncontrolled price-raising by industrial enterprises, which took advantage of the new atmosphere to seek larger profits. Zhao Ziyang was soon forced to present the consensus advice of the other leaders to Deng Xiaoping: in order to stem the tide of price rises and of popular discontent, price reform must be abandoned and central economic control must be tightened to bring inflation under control.

The policy was reversed less than two weeks after the Politburo made its decision to proceed with price reform. The State Council passed a six-point decision announcing that no major steps would be taken in price reform during the next year and promising that inflation would be lower in 1989 than in 1988. Subsequently, the Third Plenum of the Thirteenth Central Committee, which met from September 26 to 30, adopted a decision to "place the emphasis of reform and construction for the next two years upon bringing order to the economic environment and rectifying the economic order." In his speech to the Plenum, Zhao Ziyang announced, "Price reform should not and cannot be further carried out without reform in other areas."[11]

With the abandonment of price reform, attention turned to Li Yining's alternative enterprise reform proposal. In his speech to the Third Plenum, Zhao stated, "Next year, the pace of price reform should be slowed down while enterprise reform must be emphasized."

But the spectacular reversal on price reform left few observers optimistic about the prospects for thoroughgoing enterprise reform. The political obstacles to enterprise reform are even more daunting than those which forced the abrupt reversal on price

106

reform. For Li Yining's proposal to succeed, as he himself has acknowledged, several accompanying reforms would also have to be achieved. First, official ideology would have to be thoroughly overhauled to find a way to justify what is essentially an abandonment of socialism in favor of private ownership. Second, extensive political reform would be necessary to narrow the powers of government bureaus and force them to respect the newfound independence of enterprises. Third, the owners of stock in Chinese enterprises would have to be able to buy and sell their shares in a stock market, with prices allowed to rise and fall according to the efficiency of companies' operations; for such a market to function speculation in stocks would have to be allowed. Fourth, hitherto nonexistent markets would have to be created in land, capital, labor, and technology, in order to enable the new companies to realize their economic potential. Finally, establishing a market environment that would discipline the enterprises to operate efficiently would require implementation of the already-stalled price reform.

By the end of the year, no concrete measures had been taken to implement Li Yining's far-reaching vision. Many Chinese feared that reform had reached a dead end. According to some, all the feasible reform measures had been accomplished, and the ones remaining were too difficult and too intertwined to implement. China's economy was doomed to enter a long period of stagnation.

A less pessimistic view held that the next step of reform could be taken not in Beijing but in the provinces, and not in the state-owned economy but in the private economy. According to official statistics, private enterprises produce only about 1 percent of China's total industrial output value. But the real figure is doubtless much larger, perhaps as much as a quarter or a third of industrial output value in some provinces, especially if one counts those among the vast number of ostensibly collective "township enterprises" that are actually privately owned. Such enterprises are especially active in Guangdong, Fujian, and Zhejiang. If local enterprises continue to grow at the current rapid rate, the next stage of China's reform may not be reform from above of state enterprises, but rather reform from below led by the small and medium-sized privately run enterprises, which might create their own market mechanisms in dealings with one another. Early signs indicate that local levels of government and most state and private enterprises were paying little attention to emergency retrenchment policies man-

107

dated from above in the fall of 1988 to try to regain control over the economy and slow inflation.

The Worsening Social Mood.

Among many Chinese, concern about the prospects for a second decade of reform intersected with a crisis of confidence in their leaders and even in themselves as a nation. This social and intellectual crisis is a major political irony of the reforms. Although reforms had been undertaken in 1978 in a bid to redeem the Party's legitimacy by radically improving the economy, by 1988, the inflation and devolution of power brought by the successes of reform had contributed to a decline in the regime's authority and to a wave of profound questioning about China's national character.

The roots of discontent lay in the achievements of reform. Rapid economic growth caused inflation, and the transition toward a market-regulated economy created a two-track price system which engendered corruption. The failure of government salaries to keep up with inflation led bureaucrats and functionaries to demand bribes to perform their duties. By 1988, bribes had begun to be routinely required in big cities to install phones or to start electric service, and even to get mail delivered or to receive medical attention. Such bribes had become institutionalized and semi-legitimate, increasingly collected openly by offices or groups of office-mates. Throughout society, the Party's encouragement of a new ethic of entrepreneurship had led to a general blurring of boundaries between legitimate and illegitimate economic and social behavior and to an increasing sense of normlessness.

Although the incomes of most peasants, factory workers, office workers, and private entrepreneurs had increased, the growth of incomes lagged behind rising expectations. Each social group seemed less impressed by its own gains than by the seemingly more rapid advance of others—perhaps with the exception of peasants in the more prosperous suburban areas, who were the group that benefited most from the first decade of reform.

Years of intermittent political decentralization and liberalization had finally created an atmosphere in which social groups could give open vent to their sense of frustration. The year saw a striking rise in reports of protests, strikes, and demonstrations by workers, students, and occasionally peasants. The crime rate increased by 45.1 percent over the 1987 rate,[12] and there were frequent reports of serious crimes, including train robberies and other acts of violence. During a July conference on public security, both Prime Minister Li Peng and Minister of Public Security Wang Fang blamed the economic situation for what they described as a severe increase in economic crimes, corruption, theft, economically motivated crimes of violence, and incidents of mass unrest and counterrevolutionary activities.[13] There were reports that special mobile police units and antiterrorist units had been established to deal with unrest. It was rumored that police officials had visited both Poland and Chile to study anti-riot methods. The death penalty was frequently imposed—and widely publicized—not only for violent crimes but also for economic crimes, including bribery, embezzlement, fraud, smuggling, and corruption, where relatively large sums of money were involved or other exacerbating circumstances were found. Although no aggregate statistics were released, such executions numbered at least in the hundreds, more probably in the thousands.[14]

Given the postponement of price reform, which had been expected to help cure corruption, the leadership stepped up efforts to stem official corruption by administrative means. Both serving and retired Party officials were ordered to cut their ties with businesses. Deng Xiaoping was said personally to have ordered that the Kanghua conglomerate be broken up and that it sever its relations with the semi-official China Foundation for the Handicapped, which is headed by his son, Deng Pufang. A system of hotlines was set up to encourage citizens to report Party corruption, although citizens' trust in the system seemed to be low.

The mood among the intellectuals reached a point somewhere between pessimism and despair. Intellectuals were the only major segment of society whose living conditions had declined on the average during reform. The government, which runs virtually all the institutions employing intellectuals, allowed their salaries to lag far behind inflation due to worsening budget deficits and the relatively low priority given to education. It became common to remark, in rhyme, that, "To wield a surgeon's knife is not as good as wielding a barber's razor," and "Researching the atomic bomb doesn't pay as much as peddling tea-eggs."

A wave of complaints over the low salaries and poor living

conditions of intellectuals found its way into the halls of the Seventh National People's Congress, where many delegates raised the issue, including Beijing University President Ding Shisun. Prime Minister Li Peng acknowledged in a news conference that

> educational expenditures are insufficient, the intellectuals' salaries are too low, and incomes are inequitable. There are phenomena of bureaucratism and corruption in the government, and the popular masses and college students are dissatisfied with this and have raised some criticisms and suggestions. I consider this to be normal.[15]

Pressed by its own budget deficits, the government could only suggest that universities offer consulting and educational services to society or set up sideline enterprises to increase income. Students at Beida (Beijing University) sarcastically threatened to set up a shoeshine stand outside the Great Hall of the People during the People's Congress in order to implement this suggestion.

The discontent of intellectuals and students went beyond dismay over intellectuals' standards of living. As in previous years, students and intellectuals protested for continued reform and against government restrictions on foreign study and government repression of political activities. Beida students carried out a series of demonstrations in June, ostensibly in protest against the beating death of a graduate student at the hands of some hoodlums near the campus, but actually raising the by-now standard issues of freedom of speech, human rights, and democracy. The official New China News Agency blamed the protest on incitement by Voice of America.

Chinese students abroad also continued to act as a critical lobby, writing an open letter in April 1988 to protest what they said was a tightening of the policy on sending students abroad. While denying that there had been any significant change in policy, the State Educational Commission acknowledged that from now on China would require most of its students going to the United States to accept the status of "state-sponsored student," under a J-1 visa, which is much harder to convert to permanent residency in the United States than normal student visas. The commission also acknowledged that the mix of specialties and countries approved for foreign study would be altered.

Leading intellectuals spoke increasingly freely at home and

abroad. The more independent their words, the more popular such thinkers seemed to become among intellectuals. Fang Lizhi, the astrophysicist known as "China's Sakharov," and Liu Binyan, the investigative reporter, who were both purged from the Chinese Communist Party (CCP) in 1987, were allowed to go abroad in 1988, Fang to Australia and Liu to the United States. Fang made a series of statements abroad and at home to the effect that Marxism is obsolete and that China needs a multi-party system. He reportedly outraged the top leaders by reiterating the widespread belief that relatives of some Party leaders are putting money away in foreign bank accounts. Liu Binyan spoke widely in the United States and Europe, among other things praising the Democracy Wall activists of 1978–79, calling for the establishment of independent periodicals in China, and predicting that fundamental changes in the Chinese political system were germinating within the shell of the old system.

The Democracy Wall activists had committed the mistake of voicing similar ideas ten years too early. Most of the best known among them, such as Wei Jingsheng, Wang Xizhe, Xu Wenli, Chen Erjin, and Liu Qing, remained in prison. But one of the earliest casualties of that episode, Ren Wanding, resurfaced in 1988, five years after his release from prison, with an essay challenging the Communist Party to "let the people decide their future through the ballot box" and warning that "for the next few decades at least, China is likely to be a confused and unstable place."[16]

In June, the Party's venerable ideological journal *Hongqi* (Red Flag) was replaced by a new one called *Qiushi* (Seeking Truth), which was intended to be more lively. At the Fifth National Congress of Literature and Art Circles held in Beijing in November, Politburo Standing Committee member Hu Qili promised minimal Party intervention in literature and art but also tried to reassert the doctrine that it is the social responsibility of the writer to serve the Party and socialism.[17]

Despite such efforts, the Party no longer seemed to have either the ideological authority or the political will to induce intellectual conformity or to repress expressions of discontent. The intellectuals as a whole seemed to have gone beyond seeking more freedom of thought and flexibility within Marxism—their apparent goal as recently as a year or two earlier—to rejecting Marxism as wholly irrelevant to their concerns. Except for a handful of professional philosophers, few bothered to pretend to an interest in Marxism; many openly treated it as a cynical joke. In published works, Marxism was usually referred to perfunctorily, if at all.

The depth of alienation of the intellectuals was sharply revealed by the popular six-part television series *River Elegy* (*Heshang*), written with the participation of some of the leading intellectuals of the younger generation, including journalist Su Xiaokang and historian Jin Guantao. The series was an exploration of the nearly century-old theme of the roots of China's backwardness and combined inquiries into China's geography and prehistoric civilization with analyses of more recent problems with modernization. Its boldly Toynbeean argument, applied to the vast sweep of Chinese history and to Chinese civilization as a whole, was that China's anciently rooted, inward-looking, peasant-based civilization was moribund. The only way forward for the nation was a merger with world civilization—i.e., complete Westernization.[18] The TV series received widespread praise, except among some Party elders who attacked it angrily and were able to delay a second airing.

With *River Elegy*, a decade of increasingly searching critiques of the Cultural Revolution had finally grown into an inquest into Chinese civilization itself. The conclusions drawn from the inquest were nightmarishly reminiscent of the themes that had tormented Chinese intellectuals about their civilization since the late nineteenth century—the fear that the Chinese race is falling behind other races, that some vital cultural essence has been exhausted, and that China's peasant-based culture is inherently and fatally deficient in the modern values of democracy and science. The series conveyed the sense of a nation caught in a historical trap with no way out. As a judgment on China's achievements and prospects, the film's evaluation of Chinese civilization might seem to outsiders to be too harsh, but it was extraordinarily revealing of the intellectuals' state of mind.

The consensus seemed to be that Western democracy and even the Taiwan system represented proper models for Chinese political reform. The press increasingly and more forcefully advocated ideas that had not been promoted publicly since the crackdown in January 1987, such as a free press, truly competitive elections, separation of powers, and allowing the NPC to function as a real legislative body.

Yet many intellectuals were pessimistic that any such developments would actually take place in the near future. Deng continued to hew to the conservative political line defined by his "four basic principles" (dictatorship of the proletariat, socialism, Marxist-Leninist-Maoist thought, and party leadership). In addition, reform theorists around Zhao Ziyang propounded a theory labeled the "new authoritarianism," which argued that in the current period reform required strong authority, not democracy. According to the new authoritarians, the urgency of reform and the enormity of the obstacles to it brooked no delay for consensus formation or compromise. They argued that the most dangerous threat to reform came not from conservatives in the leadership but from social groups adversely affected by inflation, unemployment, and other transitional problems. Citing the works of Samuel P. Huntington and the experiences of South Korea, Singapore, and Taiwan, the new authoritarians called for nondemocratic rule by a reformist elite who would push the reform program through against all resistance. They argued that such a program differed from China's old authoritarianism in that it would be used not to deprive people of their freedoms but to break through the obstacles that still limited people's freedoms.[19] Early in 1989, Zhao himself reaffirmed that "China cannot implement a Western style multi-party system. . . . Political reform is definitely not going to abolish the leading role of our party."[20]

With Mao's death, the Party's source of legitimacy had shifted from serving as a revolutionary vanguard to serving as a technocratic elite forging the way to modernization. But Deng's dismal performance in the second half of 1988 struck a blow at this legitimation. Perhaps the most striking sign of society's mood was a widespread willingness to criticize the hitherto sacrosanct Deng for his stewardship of the reforms. Personal attacks on Deng and his children were reportedly included in wall posters at Beijing University. Many writers renewed sharp criticism of the overcentralization and personalization of power in the Chinese system. The fact that the mood among the intellectuals did not lead to an open political challenge to the regime in 1988 was due to several factors: the intellectuals' fear of political disorder and their distaste for taking physical risks, the absence of a political alternative, the openness of the Party leadership to input from leading intellectuals (and the shared family and personal networks among the two groups), and, most important, the fact that other major social groups, especially the peasants, were not equally disgruntled.

Leadership Succession and the Prospects for Reform.

Far from clinging to power, Deng continued his efforts, which have extended over several years, to create a stable arrangement for his own succession. Toward the end of the year he claimed that Zhao Ziyang and Li Peng were now in control and that he was enjoying a leisurely semi-retirement, although the events of the year belied such statements. Deng continued to be indispensable, in fact, to any major policy decisions, which bodes ill for the fate of reform once he passes from the scene.

None of the five top leaders beneath Deng in the hierarchy seems likely to be able to replace him as the authoritative decision-maker who can unify an increasingly fractious nation for further risky steps of reform.

Zhao Ziyang remained the strongest candidate. During the debate over price reform and after its reversal, rumors flew that Deng was dissatisfied with Zhao, threatened not to support him during the summer Politburo debates, and was angered by complaints lodged against him by party elders Wang Zhen and Bo Yibo during the price reform fiasco. Whatever the truth of these rumors, Zhao seemed to emerge from the episode with his authority unscathed.[21] To be sure, there were several self-critical sentences in his report to the Third Plenum. For example, he stated that "If we had paid closer attention to solving this problem [of unbudgeted capital construction] early this year, the current situation would have been better. It seems we noticed this problem too slowly and tackled it too late." But the self-criticism was collective rather than individual, addressing a failure of the entire leadership and not only of Zhao himself. But Zhao remains without a power base in the army, he is too liberal to win the kind of unquestioning acceptance from all sections of the Party that Deng has enjoyed, and to date his authority remains dangerously dependent on Deng's backing.

Among other candidates for the succession, Li Peng has an even narrower base of support than Zhao. Li, like his adoptive father Zhou Enlai, appears to have the personality of a policy implementor rather than that of a political leader. Yao Yilin has always served under the shadow of his mentor, Chen Yun, and lacks the broad experience and prestige of members of the senior generation of leaders. Hu Qili seems too young, too liberal, and too politically cautious to come out on top in a power struggle.

The least-well-known member of the Politburo Standing Committee cannot be excluded as a come-from-behind candidate for the succession. He is Qiao Shi. Almost nothing is known about his political base, his personality, or his beliefs that would indicate how well he could establish power or what policies he would favor if he did win. But because he controls the security apparatus, he has to be taken seriously as a possible winner in a succession crisis.

An institutional dark horse in the succession is the army. The Party's ability to control the army has remained a crucial political question. For years the army has expressed its dissatisfaction with the ideological and social disorder that has accompanied liberalization. The overhaul of the officer corps in recent years appears to have reduced the split between army and Party leaders. Yet Deng has as yet been unable to realize his often-stated goal of retiring as chairman of the Central Military Commission; he was re-appointed to the post at the Seventh National People's Congress. Although Deng told foreign visitors that it was Zhao Ziyang who actually ran the military commission, Zhao's status on the commission continued to be that of first vice-chairman. The long-time vice-chairman of the military commission, Yang Shangkun, aged 81, continued to hold that post even as he was elected President of the People's Republic. Yang's brother, Yang Baibing, remained director of the General Political Department.

The generals have played key roles in power transitions in the past, for example in the arrest of the "Gang of Four" after the death of Mao. Deng's departure may disturb the delicate balance between military and Party elites and force a weak or unstable successor to turn to the military for support. In such an event, the façade of Party rule would probably be maintained, with the generals exercising their influence largely behind the scenes.

Whatever its inner structure, the post-Deng regime will most likely take the form of collective leadership. The question will be whether any post-Deng leadership will be able to create enough consensus and concentrate enough power to overcome the strongly entrenched bureaucracies and deep conflicts of interest among regions, agencies, and social classes that stymied the forward movement of reform in the latter half of 1988—and whether, while trying to do so, the leadership will be able to win at least tolerance, if not support, from an increasingly restive populace. Without Deng, both these tasks will be harder than ever.

SEVEN

Paradoxes of Reform and Pressures for Change

On April 27, 1989, 150,000 Chinese calling for democracy and human rights marched through Tiananmen Square, breaking through cordons of tolerant police, surrounding truckloads of unarmed troops, and receiving the cheers of Beijing residents.

It was a historically significant event in two ways. Seventy years after the May Fourth Incident of 1919, the April 27 Incident showed that the Chinese people are still yearning for the "science and democracy" that they started searching for then. And thirteen years after the April 5th Incident of 1976, when students demonstrated in Tiananmen Square against the "feudal fascist dictatorship" of Mao Zedong, the April 27 demonstrations revealed that the Deng regime is facing a legitimacy crisis of its own. The new legitimacy crisis is equally severe but different in nature from the one that faced the late Mao regime. After Mao's death Deng won a new kind of mandate from the people by offering the promise of competent management and economic reform in place of Mao's revolutionary utopianism. Today, when the economy is in trouble and reform appears to blocked, the Chinese people no longer seem to accept Deng's authoritarian-technocratic mandate to rule.

The signs of the legitimacy crisis can be seen not only in the student demonstrations but also in peasant grumbling, worker strikes, official corruption, urban crime, and a wave of criticism on the part of the intellectuals, who are slipping out of the role of behind-the-scenes advisers into that of a public opposition. The Chinese people are far from being dissatisfied enough to risk revolution, and the government is too strong to be overthrown. But the pressures that are building call for some sort of change.

Is it possible that China might change in the direction of democracy as we understand it—not the "socialist democracy" of one-party authoritarianism that China has had until now, but democracy that puts a Chinese framework around the essential attributes of political freedom and electoral competition? As recently as the early 1980s, the most I felt able to argue was that democratic ideals could not be counted out as a long-term force in China.[1] During the Democracy Wall events of 1978–79 and the local-level elections in 1980–81, there were only a handful of students and younger workers who called for freedom of the press and multi-party democracy. In 1979, when Deng Xiaoping articulated "four basic principles" that every Chinese should accept—proletarian dictatorship, socialism, Marxism-Leninism-Mao Zedong Thought, and the leadership of the party—hardly anybody challenged the principles openly.

I recall puzzling long and hard over the writings of a senior party theorist, Wang Ruoshui. In the early 1980s Wang wrote some theoretical articles about Marx's theory of alienation. In this theory Marx argued that powerful forces like religion, capitalism, and the state, which deprive mankind of its freedom, are created by and live off the projected energies of mankind itself and thus can be brought under control by mankind. Wang argued that alienation exists not only under capitalism but also under socialism, and he said that it takes both economic and political forms. Wang's argument seemed to imply that the Chinese Communist Party was an alienated force oppressing the people, and that it could be tamed by democratic popular control. But it seemed incredible to me that the deputy editor of the central party newspaper *People's Daily* could be saying such things, even indirectly. When I described Wang's theory in writing, I hedged my bets by describing the logical implications of his argument as I saw them, but by pointing out that he might not necessarily intend them.[2]

In April 1989 I had the opportunity to attend a conference with Wang Ruoshui in California. One morning I gathered my courage to sit down with Mr. Wang at breakfast and ask him whether he had intended all along to argue for multi-party democracy in China. "Oh certainly," he told me. "I intended that implication. But under the political conditions of the time I could not say so openly."

I don't think that any Western China specialist—and probably very few Chinese—imagined that fewer than ten years later, such ideas would be widely accepted not only among students and intellectuals, but also within the party itself. It is true that Wang Ruoshui, along with Liu Binyan, Fang Lizhi, Wang Ruowang, and several other intellectuals, were expelled from the party in 1987 for their liberal ideas. Yet their expulsion seems only to have made them more popular.

How strong are the democratic trends in China? Students and intellectuals, after all, are only a tiny minority in this vast peasant country. Most of the people care little about politics and are absorbed in scratching out a living. China has a long tradition of authoritarianism and faces enormous economic problems. The leaders at the top are obsessed with keeping order in a tumultuously changing society. They command strong military and police forces. With forty years' experience of one-party dictatorship behind them, how likely is it that the leaders will voluntarily throw some of their power into the unpredictable hands of the people, especially in the midst of an economic crisis?

One can approach these questions by drawing up a balance sheet on China's achievements and problems as they appear to both outsiders and Chinese intellectuals. I will do so in two realms, economic performance and intellectual freedom. The exercise will provide an understanding of the contradictions at play in China today and of the prospects for a transition to a more democratic system.

Let us start with economic performance. Today, life expectancy at birth in China is 69 years, up from an estimated 40 years in 1953 and ranking with the more developed countries in the world, and infant mortality is only 35 per thousand.[3] China has achieved these and some other relatively good "quality of life" indicators, even though it is still one of the world's poorest countries on a GNP-per-capita basis, because of a combination of distributional social policies and aggregate economic growth. On the social side, the communist government has invested major efforts in medical care, education, food production, and, more recently, in consumer goods, and has maintained a relatively even distribution of wealth. On the aggregate side, China's growth record in the past forty years has actually been among the world's fastest. Under Mao, China achieved an average annual growth rate of about 6 percent.[4] It has also established a virtually complete industrial system which can produce everything from trains and planes and fighter jets to computers and medical instruments. Under Deng, the rate of economic growth has accelerated, with more attention paid to consumer goods and to the development of foreign trade.

This is the plus side. However, China has paid enormous political, social, and ecological costs for its economic growth. A conspic-

118

uous example was the vast, mainly man-made, famine of 1959–61, which claimed twenty to thirty million lives, the largest famine in world history. Second, aggregate statistics hide the fact that China's fast population growth has canceled out much of the increased economic output when food or other output figures are calculated on a per-capita basis. The Chinese people remain extremely poor. The educational and transport systems are overburdened nearly to the breakdown point. Economic growth is constrained by an energy shortage. Urban Chinese enjoy a per person average of less than ten square meters of housing.[5] Beginning as early as the eighteenth century and continuing through the Mao years and down to today, the growing numbers of Chinese have inflicted mounting, permanent damage to their air, water, and land on a scale unknown even in more industrialized nations.[6]

These problems worry us as outsiders. What especially worries the Chinese today is the perception that economic reform has reached a dead end. Deng's reforms have achieved enormous results in three areas. First, in agriculture, Deng disbanded the communes and leased the land back to the peasant households for private management. This resulted in a threefold increase in the value of agricultural output as well as the release of tens of millions of excess laborers for small-scale local industry. Second, in commerce and industry, Deng allowed the growth of small individual and ostensibly collective (usually actually private) factories, stores, and service trades. This private and semi-private sector has grown rapidly, employs a large portion of the labor force, and produces at least a fifth of China's industrial product.[7] Third, Deng opened up the Chinese economy to foreign trade and investment. So far, over $79 billion of foreign investment has flowed into China and foreign trade now constitutes 28 percent of GNP.[8]

Since 1982, the Party leaders have seen the next item on the reform agenda as establishing market discipline for the state-owned enterprises, in order to raise their effiency which is now abysmally low. This is important because the roughly 80,000 state-owned enterprises—especially the five-thousand-odd bigger ones—are the dominating force in industry, raw materials production, energy, transport, and other key sectors.[9]

Chinese economists believe that two reforms are necessary to rectify this situation. First, enterprises must be freed from their bureaucratic owners and turned into independent economic entities which have decision-making power over their own operations.

119

Second, it is necessary to de-control the prices of major industrial raw materials (like steel and coal), transport, electric power, industrial crops, and grain. In 1988 Deng Xiaoping became impatient with the debate among his economic advisers over how to carry out this two-pronged reform and announced that price reform would be the first step. As a result an inflationary panic set in. The government had to reverse course and announce that price reform would be postponed indefinitely, and that economic policy would concentrate on getting control over inflation.

To many Chinese, these developments spelled the end of reform. If price reform is impossible, they believe enterprise reform will be even more impossible—since it not only faces numerous obstacles of its own but depends for its ultimate effect on the simultaneous implementation of price reform as well. They feel reform has reached a dead end.

But this may be too pessimistic. As Dwight Perkins has argued in *China: Asia's Next Economic Giant?*,[10] China's human and natural resource endowments are so favorable that the long-term prospects for development are excellent, so long as the leaders maintain political stability and keep in place policies that do not crush the incentives for economic performance. Only a little more than a year ago, the U.S. President's Commission on Integrated Long-Term Strategy even ventured to predict that the Chinese economy might overtake the Soviet Union and Japan to become the world's second largest economy by the year 2010.[11]

At this moment no one knows how China will find its way from point A—the stalemate of reform—to point B—the realization of its economic potential. One possible path would be via the continued rapid growth of the small-scale private and collective enterprises which are especially vigorous in the coastal region. In the coming years such enterprises are likely to ignore the orders coming from far-away Beijing for an economic slowdown and to continue their rapid growth. If the days of reform from above are finished, the days of reform from below may be just beginning.

Let us leave the economy on this ambiguous note and turn to an evaluation of intellectual freedom in China today. To borrow a metaphor from Liu Binyan, the relationship between China's political structure and its civil society is like an eggshell with a chick growing inside it. Outwardly, the apparatus of totalistic political control still exists, but inwardly an independent society is developing.

120

Let me give the example of a magazine I know about. Unlike the Soviet Union, where a separate censorship bureaucracy exists, China has always exercised the censorship function through the network of party committees which control the publishing houses. The party committee of each publishing house takes reponsibility for censoring the books and magazines that it publishes. A friend of mine wanted to publish a magazine without its being censored. He worked through his personal network and found an friend fairly high up, someone he had tilled the land with during the time of the cultural revolution when both were exiled to the same May Seventh Cadre School. The friend agreed to publish the magazine without reviewing it, trusting my friend not to push too far beyond the bounds of the permissible.

This merely transferred the task of censorship from the publisher to my friend, turning censorship into self-censorship. In this sense the system still works, because there is still no legal definition of, or protection for, freedom of speech and publication. But it is also correct to say that the system is breaking down, because many editors and publishers are now less interested in discharging their obligations of party discipline than in testing the boundaries of what they can get away with.

And they are getting away with more and more. In late April 1989, the Shanghai Municipal Party Committee fired Qin Benli, the redoubtable editor of the Shanghai *World Economic Herald*, for publishing statements supporting the student demonstrations. This incident illustrates that party control, while still an ultimate reality, is increasingly costly and ineffective. To exercise their control, senior party leaders have to wait until something so outrageous is published that someone brings it to the higher party councils for resolution. And then the leaders must endure a political firestorm to punish the writers who have been too free with their pens. The expulsions from the CCP in 1987 of Liu Binyan, Wang Ruoshui, and others caused an worldwide counter-reaction and to some extent helped provide the impetus for 1989's student demonstrations. So too the firing of Qin Benli caused an uproar in Chinese press circles, with some reporters even planning to sue the Shanghai Municipal Party Committee for abusing its powers.

We have to understand that people like Liu Binyan and Qin Benli have been through much worse before. They were labeled "rightists" in 1957 and some of them spent up to twenty years in jails and labor camps. This has provided them with a powerful sense of anti-authoritarianism and the toughness to stand up to the kinds of relatively minor punishments the party watchdogs are able to dish out today. Considering that about half a million intellectuals were punished in the 1957 campaign and millions more in the cultural revolution, one can imagine the obstacles the party leaders face in enforcing ideological conformity.

The embryonic growth of an independent civil society in China is obscured from view by the Chinese practice of *gua*—to hang or to hook in. Every publication, every research institute, every enterprise in China is protectively "hooked" into the party's control network—sponsored by or registered with some party-recognized organization. So far as I know, no totally independent organizations exist. Yet the people who operate the control network no longer have faith in the ideology. As a consequence, publications and institutes are increasingly operating as independent social forces, including not only those set up outside the party and subsequently hooked into it, but also those set up by the party itself, such as the research institutes of the Academy of Social Sciences and the theory department of *People's Daily*.

A good example of the chicken-and-eggshell phenomenon, where civil society grows up within the framework of party control, is the recent controversial television program *River Elegy* (*Heshang*). This highly critical and pessimistic six-part series was produced and broadcast by the government's central television station. It is an example of increased liberty, but after the series became controversial, some top party leaders were able to delay its being broadcast for a second time, which shows that liberty remains limited by arbitrary power.

This discussion of freedom has focused on the relations between the intellectuals and the regime. It is neither a full discussion of changing state-society relations nor a rounded evaluation of China's human rights record—a record that includes the continued jailing of political prisoners like Wei Jingsheng, repression in Tibet, persecution of Catholics loyal to Rome and of Protestants who do not accept the leadership of the officially recognized religious authorities, inequitable trial procedures, physical abuse of prisoners, the excessive use of the death penalty, and coerced abortion and sterilization.

Nonetheless, the discussion provides a basis for addressing the prospects for fundamental change in China's political system. I would like to approach that topic by saying something more about

River Elegy. The television series evokes the extraordinary mood of dissatisfaction which is sweeping the Chinese intellectual world today. But I will argue that this self-critical mood is a good sign for the prospects for democracy.[12]

River Elegy was written with the participation of some of the leading younger and middle-aged intellectuals. The head writer was a well-known investigative reporter, Su Xiaokang. The chief academic advisor was the historian Jin Guantao. Among those interviewed in the series are the Beijing University economist Li Yining, the advocate of the policy of issuing stock in government enterprises, and Wang Juntao, who was one of the candidates for election in the Haidian district people's congress election in 1980 and is now vice-director of the private Beijing Social and Economic Sciences Research Institute. We can take the series as representing the thinking of many Chinese intellectuals today.

I have seen the TV series on videotape, borrowed from one of my Chinese students in New York, where it was being handed from student to student and being discussed enthusiasically. It consists of six one-hour documentaries. In visual terms the series is nothing special by Western or Taiwan or Hong Kong standards. It is mainly a patchwork of Chinese and foreign footage taken from the files of the Central Television Station, plus some "talking head" interviews.

The importance of *River Elegy* lies in its theme. The series asks why China is still so backward, and what it has to do to join the modern world. The fact that Chinese should be raising this question in the next to last decade of the twentieth century is significant in itself, because it is a question first raised more than a hundred years ago. It is painful for the Chinese still to have to be discussing it after so many decades of modernization efforts pursued at such great cost. The authors clearly feel that socialism has failed, and say so almost in so many words.

But the argument of *River Elegy* cuts deeper than this, and more painfully. The authors probe beyond China's difficult century-long history of modernization efforts into its geography, prehistoric civilization, and peasant culture. They argue that Chinese culture grew out of an ancient peasant civilization, based on intensive agriculture and dense population, which was profoundly conservative and isolationist. This civilization cannot adapt to the modern world. It is moribund (*shuailuo*).

River Elegy thus revives questions of national identity and na-

123

tional survival which go back to the Westernization Movement and the 1898 Reforms of the late 19th century. It raises issues which I thought the Chinese intellectuals had long ago settled. What does it mean to be Chinese? Can the Chinese people (or race, *minzu*) survive in the modern world in competition with other peoples? Is there anything in Chinese civilization worth saving or keeping, or must the entire cultural heritage be rejected in order to adapt? Is China's culture so inherently deficient in the necessary modern values of democracy and science that the Chinese people must totally re-make themselves, paying the price of giving up their cultural identity in order to survive as a people in the modern world?

The series takes the Yellow River as a symbol for China, its people, and its civilization. As the title suggests, the authors believe that the old China symbolized by the river is dead. They mourn its passing, but they urge their countrymen to accept the fact that it is gone forever. The only way for China to regain its vitality and to modernize, they say, is for China to reject its old civilization and to merge completely with the West. Although the authors do not say so, in effect they are calling for the same "complete Westernization" that "China's Sakharov," Fang Lizhi, was expelled from the party for advocating.

As I heard the voice on the videotape discuss these problems, I kept thinking back to the writings of Liang Qichao, the most famous reform thinker of the 1890s and early 1900s. Liang's ideas were partly formed by his trip to the U.S.—in 1903. Although there are some differences between Liang's views and those of *River Elegy*, the television show largely echoes Liang's diatribes against the weak, passive culture of the Chinese people, his predictions that the Chinese race will die out in a Darwinian racial competition for survival, and his calls for the creation of a Chinese "new citizen." It is as if the Chinese intellectuals have at long last awakened from a dream full of hope that they started at the time of the May Fourth Movement, to find that nothing has changed, that they are still caught in a trap that is a hundred years old, and that they must start searching again for a way out.

This nightmarish sense of China's historic immobility is not idiosyncratic to the authors of *River Elegy*. For the last ten years, writers in all literary, humanistic, and social science fields have engaged in a vast national process of reflection into the experience of the Mao years. Among the works which, from one aspect or another, explored the issue were the "wound literature" of the late 1970s, Liu Binyan's reportage, Wang Ruoshui's alienation theory, works on the history of the cultural revolution, debates among party historians about the path taken by Chinese socialism in the 1950s, and analyses of "feudal" influences in Chinese culture.[13] With *River Elegy*, a decade of explorations into the roots of Maoism evolved to its logical conclusion, an inquest into the nature of Chinese civilization itself. The consensus has been that the cultural revolution was made possible by the peasant mentality of utopianism, egalitarianism, and authoritarianism shared by both Mao and the Chinese people.

That the Chinese intellectuals have reached such a deeply pessimistic view of their country's situation must seem paradoxical against the background of the relatively optimistic way in which I have portrayed recent developments in China. Despite serious problems, as I argued earlier the nation has scored some important achievements in modernization and economic growth. If the country has indeed achieved less than it should have and paid an exorbitant price, the fault does not lie with Chinese civilization but with the political structure of Chinese socialism and the policy mistakes of the leaders.

The main fallacy of *River Elegy* is its assumption that Chinese civilization today is still traditional Chinese civilization. This ignores the very facts that make *River Elegy* and other works like it possible—the historic experience of Maoism, the ability of the Chinese to draw lessons from that experience, and the force of the new attitudes that *River Elegy* and works like it embody. The national effort of historical introspection, painful though it is, is actually one of the most hopeful indicators that we have for the prospects of democratic political reform in China. As many Chinese tell me, if it were not for the cultural revolution, China's chances for democracy would not be as good today as they are. In a sense, it is precisely because the Chinese intellectuals are so pessimistic about China that I am relatively optimistic.

The conditions may be favorable, but the problem is what political scientists call "democratic transition." Democratization entails political uncertainty, because it diffuses control over the evolution of events from the elite outward to other elements of the population. Transition theory teaches us that where the state is strong, democratization will not occur unless it serves the immediate political interests of an important sector of the elite to take the

125

risk.[14] This is where the April 27 incident in China comes back into the picture. From the standpoint of the analysis of democratic transition, what is significant about the April 27 events is not so much the student demonstrations themselves—although the moderateness of the students' behavior is important—but the official reaction to them as represented by several sympathetic statements of Zhao Ziyang.

For the first time the Chinese communist leadership responded to spontaneous pressure from below not by repressing it as reactionary or bourgeois, but by acknowledging the legitimacy of autonomous political participation by people outside the ruling party. In immediate terms, this signaled that Deng's power was waning and that the exercise of authority by Zhao has already begun. For the time being, adopting a democratic posture has helped Zhao both to weather the student crisis and to firm up his grip on the succession. The longer-term question is whether Zhao and his younger generation of communist leaders will see democratizing reform as the best chance that they have to solve the regime's legitimacy problem. If they do, the events of April and May 1989 will mark a breakthrough in Chinese history.

Being a student of Chinese affairs is an exhilarating but humbling profession. China is a paradoxical place. Ten years of reform have brought unprecedented achievements in economic growth and political liberalization. Yet dissatisfaction is at an all time high. The regime is in a legitimacy crisis, yet hardly anyone wants it to fall. China's greatest asset is its civilization, yet its inheritors, the Chinese intellectuals, despair of it as the root of China's problems.

In some ways, the Chinese seem trapped by their own history. They have not resolved the problems of modernization and democratization that have been on the top of their national agenda for nearly a hundred years. After forty years of socialism, China faces economic problems to which no one has a solution; and lying behind these are even more monstrous human and ecological problems that the government has no funds or time to pay attention to because of the immediate problems of reform. There is a despairing sense of having entered a historical dead end where reform is bankrupt, the regime is incompetent, and the culture is moribund. Despite all this, China not only endures but actually seems to be in the midst of vigorous growth and open-ended change.

PART IV
Political Change in Taiwan

EIGHT

Democratizing Transition in Taiwan
(with Yangsun Chou)

A t 6:05 on the evening of September 28, 1986, Taiwan oppo-
sition leader Fei Hsi-p'ing stood up in a meeting room of
Taipei's Grand Hotel and announced, "The Democratic Progressive
Party is established!"

Capping a series of remarkable moves by both the ruling Kuomintang and the nonparty opposition (*tang-wai*, hereafter TW), this
announcement and its aftermath marked a potentially epochal step
in Taiwan's political evolution. It also broke precedent in the
worldwide evolution of Leninist-style political systems, none of
which has ever before tolerated the formation of a significant opposition party. The bold changes in Taiwan drew attention on the
other side of the Taiwan Straits, where political reform was also a
focus of attention, and raised questions for U.S. foreign policy.
Taiwan's party system reform warrants a careful examination of
the participants' motives, the reform process, the potential impact
within Taiwan and outside, and the reforms' theoretical significance.

1950–1986: Liberalization of a Leninist Party-State

The Kuomintang was shaped by its founder, Sun Yat-sen, under
Comintern tutelage in the 1920s as a Leninist-style party. The basic
party structure established then endures today: selective membership recruitment, a revolutionary and nationalist ideology, a centralized decision-making structure under a Central Committee, a
policy-making Central Standing Committee and a policy-
implementing secretariat with organization, intelligence, and propaganda departments, control of the army through a political cadre
system, maintenance of a youth league, leadership over the policies
and personnel of the state apparatus, and—until recently—

129

intolerance for the existence of any opposition party. (Like the CCP with the "democratic parties," the KMT has long coexisted with two other small parties which do not constitute a serious opposition.)

From the beginning, the Leninist structure stood in tension with non-Leninist strains in the party's tradition—a fact which made the KMT different from other Leninist parties. Under its ideology, Sun Yat-sen's Three Principles of the People, the KMT did not define its role in terms of the struggle between progressive and reactionary classes. Instead, it justified itself as a moral and technocratic vanguard capable of guiding national construction and gradually introducing full constitutional democracy. (In this way, the KMT ideology of "revolutionary democracy" resembled the ideologies of other Leninist party-states in their post-mobilization phases, such as the Soviet "state of the whole people" and "Chinese-style socialism.") After its break with the CCP in 1927 the KMT adopted an ideology of anti-communism, with pro-capitalist domestic policies and a pro-West foreign policy, and all of this further opened it to the influence of non-Leninist ideas. Upon establishing its rule on Taiwan the party justified its restriction of political and other rights—including the right to organize new political parties —not as necessities of the revolutionary state but as temporary measures arising from the condition of civil war between the KMT and CCP regimes. These restrictions were thus not embodied in the basic constitutional order but in "Temporary Provisions Effective During the Period of Communist Rebellion" and, under the authority of these provisions, in a limited regime of martial law (*chieh-yen*).[1]

Even before 1949, in keeping with Sun's ideas of tutelary democracy, the KMT tried to make nominal progress away from party dictatorship toward constitutional democracy, for example by promulgating a new constitution in 1947 (the same constitution in effect in Taiwan today, although it is modified by the Temporary Provisions just mentioned). Starting in 1950 in Taiwan, gradual steps were taken to implement local self-rule at the provincial and lower levels, while maintaining the national government structure brought over from the mainland. In that year the Taiwan Provincial Assembly was established, its members indirectly elected by municipal- and county-level legislators for two-year terms. In 1954 for the first time the provincial assemblymen were directly elected, now for three-year terms, which were eventually changed

130

TABLE 8.1. Membership of Elected Central Government Organs

	National Assembly	Legislative Yuan	Control Yuan
Number of members under constitution	3,136	882	257
Number elected on the mainland	2,841	760	180
Number who came to Taiwan	1,576	470	104
Of those, still serving	899	222	35
Supplementary seats elected in Taiwan	91	74	24
Overseas Chinese members selected by the President	0	27	10
Total number of delegates now serving	990	323	69
Average age of those now serving	74	71	70
Percent aged 69 or below	23.6%	31.4%	38.5%
Percent aged 70–79	47.1%	34.7%	27.1%
Percent aged 80 or above	29%	33.8%	34.2%
Average deaths per year, 1981–86	43.6	14.1	1

Source: *Shih-pao chou-k'an*, No. 85 (October 11–17, 1986), p. 31.

to four-year terms. In 1969 elections were held for Taiwan delegates to the central government's Legislative Yuan and National Assembly, and indirectly for the Control Yuan. As is well known, however, the majority of seats in these organs continued to be held by mainland delegates who had been elected in 1947 (see table 8.1).

Local elections brought a number of non-KMT politicians into the political arena, but it was not until the rise of the TW in the late 1970s that the KMT faced a strong, quasi-organized opposition. The one possible exception to this statement was the abortive formation of a "China Democratic Party" (Chung-kuo min-chu tang) by Lei Chen and several other politicians in 1960. But the regime's rapid and severe response to this attempt showed that its Leninist instincts remained strong, and the CDP dissolved with Lei Chen's arrest.

By the 1970s economic growth had brought major changes to Taiwan society. Average annual per capita income had increased from $50 in 1941 to $3175 in 1985.[2] The average annual rate of economic growth was 11 percent from 1964 to 1973 and 7.7 percent from 1974 to 1984.[3] Despite increasingly severe export competition from mainland China (in terms of labor costs) and South Korea (in terms of high-technology goods), Taiwan's 1985 exports totalled almost $34 billion, with the United States taking 48 percent of the total and Japan 11 percent.[4] The egalitarian policies pursued under the principle of "People's Livelihood" had prevented extreme polarization of wealth: the total income of the richest fifth of the population was only 4.4 times that of the poorest fifth.[5] The middle class now constitutes an estimated 30–50 percent of the total population. Over 46 percent of the population has attended at least junior middle school.[6]

While economic and social change created a more sophisticated public, the diplomatic and foreign-trade situations provided salient political issues. Taiwan's diplomatic isolation has steadly increased since its expulsion from the UN in 1971, de-recognition by Japan in 1972, and the breaking of formal diplomatic relations by the U.S. in 1979. Except for the city-states of Singapore and Hong Kong, Taiwan's economy is the most trade-dependent in the world. In a recent *China Times* poll of leaders in twelve industries, the respondents said that the weakest points of the Taiwan economy were the overconcentration of export markets, the lack of diplomatic relations with most countries in the world, and excessive import dependency on a few suppliers.[7] In other opinion polls the public gives the government highest marks for its economic policies and lowest marks for its diplomatic performance, which many view as too inflexible.[8] These issues have played an increasingly prominent role in electoral campaigns and legislative debates.

The emergence of the TW can be dated from the 1977 election, when non-party politicians won 22 seats in the provincial assembly and four posts as mayor or county magistrate. In the following year the term *"tang-wai"* itself came into common use when Huang Hsin-chieh, Shih Ming-teh, and others organized a *"Tang-wai* campaign assistance corps"* (Tang-wai chu-hsuan t'uan) to coordinate the campaigns of non-KMT candidates throughout the island. In subsequent elections held in 1980, 1981, 1983, and 1985, the KMT was generally able to get about 70 percent of the vote and TW and independent politicians about 30 percent.

Until 1986, the TW was not a party but a loosely knit movement consisting primarily of small personality-based factions absorbed in large part in local issues. What drew these factions together was dissatisfaction with the ruling party's position on the interlocked issues of Taiwan's future in the international arena and the role of the KMT in the Taiwan political system. Both the candidates and the electoral supporters of the TW consist predominantly (although not exclusively) of Taiwanese, not surprisingly since 85 percent of the island's population are conventionally counted as Taiwanese, and since under Taiwan's electoral system by far the majority of the offices open for electoral competition are at the provincial level and below. Although both the KMT and the state apparatus have been heavily Taiwanized, the KMT remains mainlander-dominated at its highest levels, and it defines Taiwan's status as part of China as being settled beyond discussion.

The character of the TW as a predominantly Taiwanese political force in a mainlander-ruled polity has naturally made the issue of Taiwan's relationship to the mainland central to TW politics. On this issue the TW politicians are ranged along a radical-moderate continuum. Few Taiwanese favor reunification with the mainland. But the moderates are willing to forego for the time being any open challenge to the KMT's rule and to its one-China ideology, while the radicals—although they cannot say so openly under censorship —appear to favor some form of Taiwan independence, without KMT rule and, in some cases, under socialism (but not under the PRC). Some among both radical and moderate TW politicians have called for transport, commercial, postal, and other contacts with mainland China. They do so, however, not in order to promote reunification but because they believe that the KMT response to the mainland's diplomacy has been too rigid, and that such contacts are necessary in order to begin the search for a new relationship with the mainland and a less isolated position in the world. Other TW issues include opposition to the exclusive use of Mandarin on Taiwan television and to the promulgation of KMT ideology through the schools.

The radicals emerged as a strong force in the 1977 "Chung-li Incident" (a violent demonstration about alleged election tampering in Chung-li city). They showed still greater strength in 1979, when they mobilized a series of demonstrations which culminated on December 10 in a violent clash between demonstrators and police that became known as the "Kaohsiung Incident." In response, the government arrested Shih Ming-teh, Huang Hsin-chieh, and over 60 others, tried and jailed eight, and closed the offices of *Mei-li-tao* (Formosa) magazine, which was the organization behind the demonstrations.

Beginning in 1984, TW politicians produced a series of magazines which directed strong attacks at government policies and leaders on a wide range of policy and personal issues. The government banned and closed many magazines, but the TW evaded control by reopening the magazines under new names and by publishing magazines in the disguised form of monthly or weekly book series. In 1985, two apparently government-backed libel suits were filed against TW magazines. Although the plaintiffs were successful in both cases, from the government's point of view the broader results were less satisfactory. The verdicts were controversial; the defendants argued that their freedom of speech and, in one case, legislative immunity, had been abridged; the defendants' supporters staged demonstrations, including a series of sendoffs for defendant Lin Cheng-chieh as he prepared to serve his year-and-a-half prison term.[9] It became apparent that conviction in a libel case could be turned into political capital.

Moderates continue to dominate among opposition politicians on the island (the radicals' main base is overseas), but the exigencies of Taiwanese politics have imparted an increasingly militant flavor to the moderates' tactics. Despite the successes of KMT rule and the amelioration of mainlander-Taiwanese social relations, Taiwanese voters still have deep-seated feelings of having been colonized, and they respond emotionally to the martyr symbolism around such jailed leaders as the Kaohsiung Eight. In this political culture, mass rallies, emotional rhetoric, and confrontational demonstrations are tools of electoral survival for policy moderates. Even while adopting such tactics to some degree, moderates like K'ang Ning-hsiang suffer constant criticism for being too soft on the KMT. The fractious Taiwanese political style alarms many mainlanders, outside as well as inside the ruling party, who are used to a more courtly, controlled manner of maneuvering. It seems especially to alarm those in the security bureaucracy. Ample room existed in the mid-1980s for a tragic misunderstanding between the two political cultures, which might have led to a vicious circle of confrontation and repression.

From Liberalization to Democratizing Reform

In contrast to South Korea under the generals and Marcos' Philippines, however, where challenges to the regime were met fairly consistently with repression leading to further polarization, the response of the KMT to the growth and increasing militance of the opposition until late 1985 was a mix of selective repression with institutional liberalization. The regime tried to repress the radical wing of the TW while stepping up recruitment of Taiwanese into the party, army, and government, including some in high posts, and gradually liberalizing electoral institutions and the media—what Edwin A. Winckler calls a movement toward "soft authoritarianism." [10] Despite opposition from the security bureaucracy and many mainlanders, President Chiang Ching-kuo had been trying to accommodate with the TW as it developed. As early as 1978, he directed KMT officials to meet with TW figures under the auspices of a prominent newspaper publisher, Wu San-lien.[11] But such contacts stopped after the TW's relatively poor performance in the 1983 elections.

The reform undertaken in 1986 represents a fundamental change of course, to what we would call democratizing reform. The formation of an opposition political party does not by itself make Taiwan a pluralist democracy, but it is the most important single step that could have been taken in that direction. If the reform goes no further than to legalize the new party (and others which may be formed), it will have a large impact on Taiwan politics and, through enhanced electoral competition, will make the ruling party more accountable to the electorate. We discuss other possible future developments in a section below.

The explanation for the change of course lies in large part with President and party Chairman Chiang Ching-kuo, who occupies a position of supreme influence in the Taiwan political system similar to Deng Xiaoping's in the mainland. Both the initiative for the reform and the power to implement it over substantial intra-party opposition lay with him. The inner story of his decision is not known, but the public record provides enough information to reveal the general concerns that motivated him.

The long-term impetus for both liberalization and democratization came from three factors described earlier: the KMT's ideological commitment to constitutional democracy, the economic, social, and political maturation of the population, and the increasing electoral appeal of the TW. But to understand Chiang's decision to shift from one type of reform to the other, we need to look at the more immediate problems facing the regime in 1986.

The first of these was the succession problem. Chiang is 76 years old and suffers from diabetes. Although he has a formal successor as president in Vice President Lee Teng-hui, much of his power is personal rather than institutional, and there is no one currently in the senior ranks of government who is likely to be able to replace him as the lynchpin of cooperation between party conservatives and liberals and among party, state, army, and security officials. In December 1985, on the 38th anniversary of the implementation of the ROC constitution, Chiang addressed one element of this problem by stating that he would not allow himself to be succeeded as president by any member of his family nor by a military regime. To show the firmness of his opposition to a dynastic succession, he posted his second son and potential successor, Chiang Hsiao-wu, to Singapore as deputy commercial counsellor in the Taiwan mission. In June 1986, he appointed civilian official Wang Tao-yuan as Minister of Defense, signalling his intent to diminish the role of military men in the cabinet. He also assigned his younger brother, Chiang Wei-kuo, to be secretary of the National Security Council, a move seen as providing a further guarantee for a peaceful and legal succession.[12] The President may have felt that difficult and controversial, but necessary, reforms should be undertaken before he passed from the scene rather than be left for his less well-equipped successors to handle. Moreover, reform could contribute to a smoother transition by increasing the legitimacy of the regime, reducing the motivation for the population to become involved in political disorders, and setting in place improved mechanisms for long-term recruitment of new leaders at all levels.

Additional concerns motivating the reform were a series of internal and foreign shocks in 1985 and 1986. The first was the revelation that the 1984 assassination of U.S. businessman and writer

Henry Liu (Liu Yi-liang, also known as Chiang Nan) had been carried out at the behest of the head of the Defense Ministry Intelligence Bureau. The second was the bankruptcy of Taipei's Tenth Credit Cooperative due to mismanagement by officials with ties to KMT politicians, an incident which led to the resignations of two cabinet ministers.[13] A third was a defeat suffered by the government in its policy of resistance to the PRC's "unification diplomacy." In May 1986, officials of the state-owned airline were forced into face-to-face negotiations with PRC airline representatives in order to arrange the return of a hijacked cargo plane and crew from Guangzhou. Although the government denied that the negotiations signaled any change in its "three-no" policy (no negotiations, no compromise, and no contacts), the events weakened the confidence in this policy among both foreigners and the domestic Taiwanese public.

Such incidents suggested the need to revitalize the ruling party and government. On the international scene, in addition, political reform offered the possibility of enhancing the image of a regime that is especially vulnerable to foreign opinion because of its trade dependence and diplomatic isolation. Especially in the United States, where human rights issues exert a substantial influence on foreign policy, the maintenance of martial law has long been a public-relations embarrassment for Taiwan's supporters—a fact often brought to the President's attention by sympathetic high-level American visitors.

Finally, the initiation of bold reform steps in 1986 offered the possibility of strengthening the KMT's appeal in the elections scheduled for December 6 to fill seats in the Legislative Yuan and the National Assembly. Chiang must have known that by initiating reform in the months leading up to a major election he ran the risk of entangling the reform process with the pre-election maneuvering by both sides. His decision to do so suggests that he thought the advantages outweighed the dangers.

Managing Political Reform

"The way of the reformer is hard," Samuel P. Huntington has observed.[14] The reformer must maintain a concentrated hold on power in order to be able to disperse it, and must implement reform measures quickly enough to prevent the consolidation of conservative opposition, but not so quickly as to allow the pace of events to get out of control. These problems indeed faced Chiang Ching-kuo in 1986.

The first challenge was to turn a personal decision for reform into a party program. Chiang sought the understanding of the strong group of senior and middle-level party conservatives, concentrated in the ideological, military, and security sectors, who feared that any relaxation of martial law or the party ban would create an opening for communist subversion, Taiwan independence activity, or an alliance of the two. At the Third Plenum of the KMT's 12th Central Committee in March 1986, Chiang reminded the delegates of the party's long-standing goal of implementing constitutional democracy, and said that the time had come to make further progress toward this goal.[15] After the session, on April 9, he appointed a twelve-man task force of Standing Committee members to suggest reform measures. This powerful temporary organ became a virtual politbureau above the Standing Committee, entrusted with the power to establish the party's reform strategy in line with Chiang's wishes. It was headed by former President Yen Chia-kan, a technocrat, and former Vice President Hsieh Tung-min, a Taiwanese politician associated with the KMT moderate wing, and composed of the most powerful figures in the party, both liberal and conservative.

In June, the task force reported a bold, but vague, six-point reform proposal:

1. To conduct a large-scale supplementary election to the central representative organs (the Legislative and Control Yuans and the National Assembly) in order to address the problem of superannuation and deaths of members.

2. To put local self-government on a legal basis. (The progress made so far in instituting local self-government in Taiwan has been carried out under an administrative order rather than a law. The pertinent legislation has been tabled in the Legislative Yuan since 1952. The main problem has been that the law would provide for direct popular election of the Taiwan provincial governor and the mayors of Taipei and Kaohsiung. These officials are currently appointed by the central government, and the KMT has feared that their direct election would create strong popularly based rivals to its own politicians.)

3. To simplify the national security laws. (Under martial law, the government has established a complex set of security orders,

some overlapping with the provisions of the regular legal system, and many provisions of which have not been used.)

4. To provide a legal basis for formation of new civic associations. (Formation of new civic associations is banned under martial law. The current law on civic associations does not provide for the registration of new parties, and the election and recall law does not provide for their participation in elections.)

5. To strengthen public order.

6. To strengthen party work.[16]

After receiving its report, President Chiang ordered the committee to work out more detailed proposals for the third and fourth items first.

Meanwhile, Chiang reopened the "channel" (*kou-t'ung*) to the TW, hoping to co-opt TW leaders into sharing a stake in an orderly reform process. In May, he directed KMT party officials to hold talks with representatives of the TW through the good offices of four mediators. The mediators were senior presidential adviser T'ao Bai-ch'uan, aged 83, a long-time KMT liberal and former member of the Control Yuan, and three National Taiwan University professors, Hu Fo, Yang Kuo-shu, and Li Hung-hsi—men who had already been involved in behind-the-scenes negotiations in 1984 between the government and the TW that averted a confrontation over the illegal formation of the *"Tang-wai* Research Association on Public Policy" (TRAPP), a quasi-political party.[17] The KMT was represented by the three deputy secretaries general of the party Central Policy Commission, Liang Su-jung, Hsiao T'ien-tsan and Huang Kuang-p'ing. Eight delegates were selected to represent the TW, including K'ang Ning-hsiang and You Ch'ing; one of them, the brother of imprisoned TW leader Huang Hsin-chieh, declined to participate.

According to informed observers, the President's intention was to allow TRAPP to register legally and to organize local branches that could nominate candidates, carry out election campaigning, and serve as a political party in all but name. In return, he hoped to delay the formation of a full-scale opposition party until after the election. At the first "channel" meeting, held on May 10 at a Taipei restaurant, the two sides accepted three common principles: respect for the constitution, cooperative efforts to maintain political harmony, and agreement in principle by the KMT to allow the TW to register TRAPP under the provisions of the civic associations law.[18] But this agreement displeased some TW politicians, who argued that it put the TW in an inferior position to the KMT, which was itself unregistered under that law. The second scheduled channel meeting on May 24 broke down over this issue.

The approach of the election had made it difficult for the TW to compromise. The KMT's excellent performance in the 1983 elections convinced many TW leaders that they would need the best possible campaign organization to hold their own in the coming contest, which would be the last electoral opportunity until 1989. In addition, the fall of Marcos in the Philippines and the increasing militance of the opposition party in South Korea encouraged impatience with a slow pace of change. Overseas, as we will detail below, exiled politician Hsu Hsin-liang and others had already started to form a "Taiwan Democratic Party." Given the militant style of Taiwanese politics, many TW politicians felt that the voters would not view them as a serious opposition if they did not insist on their right to organize within the island.[19]

While continuing to insist that TRAPP and its branches were illegal, the government did not move against it. But Minister of Justice Shih Ch'i-yang warned in late September, just a few days before the DPP was founded, that the premature formation of a full-scale political party would be illegal and would be treated as such.[20]

Despite this warning, the TW politicians meeting at the Grand Hotel on September 28 decided to take the next step. The meeting had originally been called to finalize the TW list of candidates. (The room had been reserved ostensibly for a meeting of the Rotary Club.) That morning, however, Fei Hsi-p'ing, K'ang Ning-hsiang and other moderates recommended altering the agenda to consider establishing a preparatory committee for a new party. More militant delegates argued for establishment of the new party on the spot. This might be the last gathering of a large number of TW figures for a long time; moreover, the government was less likely to arrest the participants while they were official election candidates than at any other time. Once a new party was established, they argued, there would be time enough to appoint committees to draft its program and charter. The name of the new party was suggested by senior TW figure and Taipei representative to the Legislative Yuan Hsieh Ch'ang-t'ing, who argued that it should include neither "Taiwan" nor "China" in order to avoid taking a position on the issue of Taiwan's future relations with the mainland. After discussion, 132 of those present signed their names to the declaration of founding of the DPP.[21]

Some participants left the Grand Hotel after the historic meeting of September 28 convinced that they would be arrested as soon as they came outside. DPP leaders hastened to assure President Chiang through private channels that the new party respected the ROC constitution and opposed communism and Taiwan independence,[22] but its leaders were unwilling to take such a conciliatory stance publicly.

Indeed, there was strong opinion among KMT conservatives to respond to the formation of the DPP by arresting the participants. President Chiang's preference, however, was to declare the new party illegal and refuse to recognize it, without taking police steps, meanwhile speeding the pace of drafting the new civic organizations law that would legalize it retrospectively. He directed the twelve-man task force to hold urgent meetings to draft specific recommendations for reform of the martial law system and political parties ban. He held a series of meetings in late September with top party, military, and intelligence officials to seek support for his views.[23]

On October 15, Chiang was able to push resolutions through the KMT Central Standing Committee adopting the two key reform proposals. The first called for the abolition of martial law and its replacement with a national security law. Under this proposal the national security law (expected to be submitted to the Legislative Yuan in early 1987) would generally ban the same crimes as were banned under martial law, but would define them more carefully, decrease the penalties, and put the cases of civilian defendants before civilian courts. The national security law would also replace martial law provisions for entry and exit control, seacoast and mountain-area defense, and so on. The second resolution called for the revision of the law on civil organizations so as to reverse the ban on formation of new political parties. According to press leaks in late 1986, the revised law, which would be submitted to the Legislative Yuan somewhat later than the new national security law, would allow the registration of new political parties which adopt party constitutions and platforms; compete legally for power through the electoral system; and support anti-communism, the constitution, and national unity (i.e., not Taiwan independence).[24] These three conditions are likely to become a focus of contention between the DPP and the government in early 1987. DPP leaders contend that the government has no right to insert KMT party policies (anti-communism and anti-Taiwan independence) into the registration requirements imposed on other parties. Observers generally assume these differences can somehow be resolved, perhaps through further use of the KMT-opposition "channel."

Meanwhile, the KMT demanded that the DPP refrain from moving beyond the preparatory phase of party formation. The KMT also challenged the DPP to make clear its political stand. President Chiang announced that the new party would not be tolerated if it did not accept the three basic principles just described.[25] On October 11, the DPP gave its first, somewhat ambiguous, public response, stating that it stood for respect for the constitution and that it would not cooperate with any political force advocating violence.[26]

Reform Tested: November-December 1986

The period immediately preceding the December 6 election posed a major test for the firmness of Chiang Ching-kuo's reform decision and his managerial skill, and a test as well for the statesmanship of the DPP. The key question was how the long-repressed, potentially explosive issue of Taiwan's status would be introduced into the political dialogue. If this question had not been raised, the reform would have been illusory; if it had been pressed too far or too fast, the reform might have been aborted.

The stance of the DPP came into clearer focus on November 10, when—despite the government's warning that such an action would be illegal—it held its first National Representative Congress and adopted a party charter, a 34-article "Basic Program" and a 139-article "Action Program."[27] The congress elected Chiang P'eng-chien (David P.C. Chiang) as chairman. Chiang, a member of the Legislative Yuan, was a defense lawyer at the trial of the Kao-hsiung Incident defendants, and is considered a representative of the younger and more radical wing of the DPP. His chief rival for the post was Fei Hsi-p'ing, a mainlander member of the Legislative Yuan supported by DPP moderates. On the key question of Taiwan's future, the basic program advocated "self-determination" by ballot of "all residents of Taiwan." The DPP also called for rejoining the UN, leaving unstated whether the application should be in the name of China or of Taiwan. As its party flag, the DPP adopted a white cross against a green background, with a silhouette of the island of Taiwan in the middle of the cross, symbols which bear no visible relationship to those of the KMT or the Republic of China. Although the term "independence" was thus avoided, the party's position appeared to contradict the KMT's insistence that the status of Taiwan as a part of China is already settled.

Both the government and the DPP faced their next challenge with the attempted return from abroad of radical TW politician Hsu Hsin-liang. A Taiwanese and former KMT member, Hsu had broken with the party and was elected as a TW candidate to the post of T'ao-yuan county magistrate in 1977, at the time of the Chung-li Incident. In 1979 he was deprived of this position by the Control Yuan for his participation in the demonstrations preceding the Kaohsiung Incident. Hsu went into exile in the United States, where he joined the Taiwan independence movement. In late 1984, he was elected first deputy general secretary of the newly formed "Taiwan Revolutionary Party" based on the American east coast. In various of his writings or in declarations which he has signed, he has called for "the complete disappearance of [the KMT regime] from the face of the earth" and the waging in Taiwan of an urban guerrilla war of socialist revolution.[28] In 1981 the Taiwan government issued a warrant for Hsu's arrest on charges of rebellion.

Like Kim Dae-jung and Benigno Aquino, Hsu was drawn by the prospect of an election to try to re-enter the political arena at home. In May 1986, he announced his departure from the Taiwan Revolutionary Party and the establishment in Los Angeles of a preparatory committee for a Taiwan Democratic Party (T'ai-wan min-chu tang). In October, after the formation of the DPP, Hsu transformed his new party into an overseas organization of the DPP. He announced his intention to return to Taiwan to campaign for the DPP, and, following Kim Dae-jung's precedent, invited a number of Taiwanese and Americans—including Ramsey Clark and Linda Gail Arrigo (an American graduate student and the wife of the jailed Shih Ming-teh)—to accompany him on the flight home.

Because of Hsu's popularity with the Taiwanese electorate, his actions created a dilemma for both the KMT and the DPP. Although the government had issued a warrant, it did not wish to arrest him on the eve of the election. Most DPP politicians also preferred not to be encumbered at this sensitive juncture with the problem of his arrest, but neither could they square their party platform with asking him to stay away.

Hsu was eventually kept out of the country, but not without three violent incidents, one of them Taiwan's largest since the Kaohsiung incident. The first occurred on November 14 when a Hsu ally, Lin Shui-ch'üan, and five colleagues attempted to precede him back to Taiwan. Lin was denied entry at the airport because he did not have a visa. Several hundred TW supporters who had come to the airport to welcome Lin clashed with airport police, and two persons were injured. The second and major incident occurred on November 31, when in expectation of Hsu's arrival an estimated ten thousand supporters gathered at Taiwan's Chiang Kai-shek International Airport. Hsu, meanwhile, was held up at Narita Airport in Japan, where the airlines honored a Taiwan government request to deny him permission to embark for Taiwan. After a standoff of nine hours at the airport, police used water cannons and tear gas on the crowd. Twenty-six police vehicles, as well as vehicles of the China Broadcasting Company and the China Television Service, were overturned and damaged, and over a score of policemen injured. In the third incident, on December 2, Hsu managed to arrive at the Taiwan airport on a Philippine Airlines plane under an assumed name. He was denied entry, but several thousand demonstrators, some reportedly armed with staves, clashed again with police, leading to a number of arrests and injuries.[29]

For the KMT reformers, the strength of popular support for Hsu after six years' absence came as a shock, especially in view of his advocacy of violent anti-KMT revolution. The events also surprised some leaders of the DPP. Although the party had never recognized Hsu's overseas branch, it felt obliged to participate in the welcoming activities because of Hsu's popularity and because of the DPP's friendly links with Taiwanese organizations in the U.S. The DPP stance was that it welcomed Hsu's return because of humanitarian considerations and out of respect for human rights. But after the second violent incident, while denouncing the use of water cannons and tear gas by police, the DPP also criticized the violence of the demonstrators, called on the government to identify and prosecute the perpetrators, and stated that any DPP member involved would be punished under party discipline. The party further announced that it was cancelling a series of planned rallies in order to avoid any possible further outbreak of violence.[30]

The December 6 elections were held only four days after Hsu Hsin-liang's third attempt to return. The results contained several messages for the leaders of both parties.[31] First, to the relief of both, they went off peacefully. Second, although the election confirmed the dominance of the KMT, the DPP showing was also strong. The results must be interpreted in light of the structure of the Taiwan political system, which places limits on campaign publicity, expenditures, and access to the mass media, and in which there is normally considerable vote buying and other irregularities.[32] Despite these disadvantages, the DPP won 18.90 percent of the vote in the National Assembly election, electing 11 of its 25 candidates, and 22.17 percent in the Legislative Yuan election, electing twelve of its nineteen candidates. Counting independent and minor-party votes, the total non-KMT poll was a bit above 30 percent of the vote.[33]

The strength of militant sentiment in the electorate was shown by the overwhelming victories won by some of the most more radical DPP candidates. The largest number of votes of any candidate island-wide was won by Hsu Jung-shu, wife of Chang Chün-hung, in prison because of his participation in the Kaohsiung Incident. The second heaviest vote-getter was Hung Ch'i-ch'ang, a former member of the radical "Editors' and Writers' Association." The fourth largest number of votes went to Hsu Hsin-liang's brother, Hsu Kuo-t'ai. Hsu had been at the head of the airport demonstrators both times that his brother attempted to return.

However, some moderate DPP leaders also fared well. Senior TW politician K'ang Ning-hsiang, who had suffered a surprise defeat in his run for the Legislative Yuan in the 1983 election, was resoundingly re-elected from Taipei city. Other important moderate victors were Huang Huang-hsiung, Ch'iu Lien-hui, and You Ch'ing.

A further indication of the strength of the opposition came in the surprising victories of three DPP condidates in occupational constituencies, which the KMT normally closely controls. (Not all seats in the two directly elected bodies are elected by geographic constituencies; a number are reserved for occupational groups.) In the trade-union constituency, DPP candidates defeated the heads of both the provincial and the national-level trade union organizations for one seat each in the Legislative Yuan and National Assembly. Another DPP candidate won election to the National Assembly from the commerce sector.

On the other hand, the strength of the KMT showing paid tribute to that party's deep organizational base and to the preference of many among Taiwan's affluent population for continuity and stability. Among KMT candidates, strong showings were made by candidates with fresh images, reform leanings, or athletic, show-business, or academic credentials. The outstanding example was the victory of reformist Chao Shao-k'ang, the top vote-getter in Taipei city. On the other hand, in an unprecedented defeat for retired military men, Taipei voters rejected a former air force vice-commander.

Prospects

For the DPP, the biggest question is whether it can stay together, given its essential nature as a coalition of independent factions. The party's factionalism is reflected in the rules it adopted at its November 10 congress. The DPP made itself an elite party, with new members admitted only on the nomination of at least three members. (By early November, total membership was reportedly about 1400.[34]) The purpose of this rule is apparently to prevent both competition among factions for control of the organization through recruitment of new members and infiltration by the KMT. Despite its small size, the party has a 31-person Central Executive Committee, an eleven-person Central Standing Executive Committee, an eleven-person Central Consultative Committee, and a five-person Central Standing Consultative Committee, thus offering representation in policy-making organs to every faction. In order further to protect each faction's prerogatives, the national congress is to meet yearly (as against every five or six years for the KMT) and the party chairman is limited to one nonrenewable one-year term. There is reason to wonder whether a party constructed so carefully to prevent concentration of power can survive as a party.

The question is all the more pressing given the ideological split among moderate and radical members. The DPP will be under intense pressure from the KMT and the electorate to define the meaning it gives to "self-determination" and to define the policy and organizational relationship between itself and the Taiwan independence movement. There is a demand from Taiwanese organizations overseas, such as the influential, tacitly pro-independence Formosan Association for Public Affairs (FAPA), that the DPP establish overseas branches. This possibility is tempting because of the political support such overseas branches could provide in Washington.[35] Yet overseas branches are likely to serve as points of influence for independence forces. The DPP may split over issues like this, or the government may repress the new party if it evolves a clear pro-independence position.

This prospect clearly worries the PRC government as well. Given the PRC's announced policy that Taiwan may keep its own political system even after reunification, the PRC is in no position to object to any political reform the Taiwan authorities want to carry out. In keeping with its United Front policy, Beijing has welcomed the formation of the new party.[36] According to Hong Kong sources, the Chinese authorities see no likelihood of the DPP taking power in Taiwan in the near future.[37] However, a PRC foreign ministry spokesman has reiterated Beijing's opposition to Taiwan independence, pointedly adding "or self-determination."[38] The PRC even seems to be using the existence of the new party as the basis for a fresh appeal to the KMT for early reunification. "The future of the Kuomintang," stated Peng Zhen in his speech commemorating the 120th birthday of Sun Yat-sen's death, "hinges on its cooperation with the Communist Party."[39] For the U.S. as well, the prospect of a vocal pro-independence force in the island is also unwelcome, chiefly because of the disturbance it would cause in American-PRC relations.[40]

DPP politicians interviewed early in 1987 in Taipei state that these concerns are misplaced. Self-determination, they say, means simply that the residents of the island should be consulted in any decision concerning its future, rather than having their fate determined by the KMT, PRC, and U.S. without their participation. They argue that it is only common sense to say that the island's residents face a long-term choice among three alternatives: maintaining the status quo, re-uniting with the mainland, or becoming independent. By calling for self-determination the DPP is not advocating any of these, but only the right of the residents to decide. It remains to be seen whether the KMT will accept this position as falling within the bounds of acceptable political discussion, and whether the DPP itself can remain united on the position.

Whether or not the DPP survives in its present form, the lifting of the ban on party organizations may well introduce still other competitors into the political arena. By late 1986, three potential parties were already beginning to take shape under the following

tentative names:[41] the Democratic Unity Party (Min-chu t'ung-i
tang), under former KMT Legislative Yuan member Lei Yü-ch'i,
which would represent predominantly middle class non-Taiwanese
and would stand for peaceful reunification with the mainland; the
People's Livelihood Cooperation Party (Min-sheng hsieh-li tang),
under Kaohsiung politician Su Yü-chu, a local party which would
have a chiefly poor working-class constituency and the support of
some retired soldiers; and the China Patriotic Party (Chung-kuo ai-
kuo tang), under right-wing KMT journalist Chung Shu-nan, who
has spoken of forming this new party to oppose the DPP, but is
unlikely to do so since he would then have to leave the KMT.

At least five additional political groups or social forces can be
identified which are not closely tied to the KMT and have not yet
been included in the DPP. These include a group of pro-unification
nationalists around *Hsia-ch'ao* magazine; a group of activists concerned mainly with ecological issues; Christian groups, including
the Presbyterians, who are politically active, and the fundamental-
ist New Testament Church; a number of local independent politicians; and liberal academics and professionals. Under the new civil
associations law such forces might organize parties or interest
groups, or they may align with the DPP or remain unorganized.

Conspicuous by its absence from these lists is a potential labor
or welfare-state party. Taiwan has never had a strong, independent
labor movement; instead, the KMT has always been careful to
assure its own political dominance of labor. The success of the DPP
in this election in winning two seats in the labor constituency will
probably motivate the KMT to redouble its organizing efforts in
the unions to shore up its control.

The future evolution of Taiwan's political system will, of course,
depend even more upon the post-reform adaptation of the KMT
than on the shape taken by the opposition. Those who lightly compare Taiwan's situation to those of South Korea or the Philippines
forget that the KMT, for all its problems, is a vigorous organization. Its strengths include a nationalistic ideology with considerable appeal, much fresh blood among its membership, including
many Taiwanese (constituting an estimated 70 percent of the party
membership) and a cadre of skilled technocrats, strong local political machines, control over the media and, through the political
commissar system, control over the military. The KMT would
probably perform well in elections even without the special advantages it enjoys under the current electoral system, and it is unlikely

to give up all of these advantages in the course of reform. Hence it is unlikely that the Taiwan political system will quickly evolve into a true two-party system.

Rather, assuming the democratic reforms are carried forward, Taiwan is more likely to remain for the foreseeable future a hegemonic party system like that of Mexico, or possibly to evolve from such a system into a Japanese-style dominant-party system in which the KMT controls over half the votes while a variety of smaller parties share the remainder. Also possible, if the DPP stays together, is the development of a "one-and-a-half-party system" with a dominant KMT and a permanent minority opposition party.

To the extent that a hegemonic, dominant-party, or party-and-a-half system allows freedom of political organization and advocacy, it provides mechanisms that strengthen political competition and hence, government accountability to the people. However, KMT rule is so intimately intertwined with all aspects of the Taiwan system that there would have to be other far-reaching reforms before democratization could be said to have gone very far. Among the obstacles to fuller democratization are, first, anti-democratic biases built into the constitutional structure. As long as the majority of seats in the Legislative Yuan and National Assembly are reserved for mainland constituencies, there can be no realistic possibility of shaking KMT control of these organs. This problem has already been targetted for reform; it was the first point of the six presented by the 12-man working group in June. In addition, as long as the President is indirectly elected by the National Assembly and the Taiwan governor and Taipei and Kaohsiung mayors appointed by the central government, the Taiwan electorate cannot control the selection of the country's top officials.

Other barriers are government and party control of the press, and banning and censorship of the opposition press; advantages to the ruling party, described earlier, provided by the rules of the electoral system; the practice of imprisonment for political crimes (according to Amnesty International, as of August 1986 there were approximately 110 political prisoners in Taiwan[42]); interpenetration of party and government structures along classic Leninist lines, for example, the relationship between the Government Information Office and the party's Cultural Work Commission, or between the government's Overseas Chinese Commission and the party's Overseas Work Commission (similarly, party-contolled military intelligence organs perform functions which in non-Leninist

149

states are the purview of state organs); the political commissar system in the army, which gives the KMT control over the military; and, finally, the existence of state and party-managed enterprises.

Although some of these problems are on the current reform agenda, most of them are not; completion of the current reform, however, may create momentum for further democratization. On the other hand, the possibility always exists that a coalition of party conservatives, military and security personnel, and economic technocrats could call a halt to the reform process under various scenarios: if the call for Taiwan independence grew too strong, if there was violence, or if a succession crisis led to instability at the top.

Theoretical Implications

Taiwan's reforms are being closely watched in China, which is also involved in political reform. Although we have no hard evidence of the unofficial reaction, news of Taiwan's progress has probably been among the factors spurring public impatience with the slow pace of political reform on the mainland—impatience recently expressed in the form of student and worker demonstrations in several cities.

Whether the Taiwan reforms can serve the mainland in any way as a model is a more difficult question. So far, during the current wave of discussions of reform in the PRC, the question of allowing the formation of opposition parties has not been publicly raised (except, reportedly, in wall posters). But some democrats both outside and inside the CCP advocated a multi-party system during the 1978–81 Democracy Movement, so it is likely that such ideas still have supporters today.[43] To PRC pluralists, the changes in Taiwan can only encourage the belief that China's cultural background and Leninist patterns of organization do not preclude reform of the party system.

Even so, prospects for multi-partyism on the mainland have to be counted as slight. As we noted at the outset, the KMT has been an anomaly among Leninist parties because it lacks a Marxist ideology and has been, through most of its history, pro-Western and pro-capitalist. The applicability of its experience to other Leninist parties is thus limited. Moreover, the mainland Chinese population is far less prosperous and educated than Taiwan's, and in this sense the social conditions for pluralism are less promising. Also in contrast to Taiwan, the mainland's succession problem seems, at least outwardly, to be well under control, and the PRC's international standing is high. And unlike Taiwan, the PRC is not dependent on the U.S. economically and militarily, and hence has less concern with American and other foreign public opinion. In short, the PRC leaders lack the various stimuli for party system reform that motivated Chiang Ching-kuo. While reform in the role of the single ruling party is a major part of the mainland reform agenda, there is no sign so far that the leaders are considering reform of the party system itself, or even that they intend to allow the question to be publicly discussed.

If the Taiwan case carries no easy lessons for the mainland, it does seem relevant to other cases of democratizing reform and to the growing theoretical study of the democratization of authoritarian regimes. In a 1984 article, "Will More Countries Become Democratic?", Samuel P. Huntington suggested that the particular conjunctions of circumstances that had created the world's democracies were not likely to be repeated.[44] But the large number of democratic transitions in recent years—Spain, Portugal, Argentina, Peru, and others—have required political scientists to develop new perspectives on the problem.

One line of thought has been that there are circumstances in which relatively democratic institutions are more functional for elites than authoritarian ones.[45] Given permissive economic, social, and international conditions, a turn toward democracy may be an attractive option for an elite facing succession problems, an economic crisis, mass unrest, international pressure, or other problems. In such conditions relatively democratic institutions offer the possibility of improving a regime's abilities to legitimate itself, to regulate social conflict, to recruit successors, to gain access to and make use of information for policy making, and so on.

Our analysis of Chiang Ching-kuo's motives for the reform suggest he is in fact seeking these benefits. Indeed, for Taiwan, democratization may be profitable in the even more concrete sense of helping to stimulate the confidence of foreign investors and trade partners. In contrast to the disincentive effects of the instability and apparent lack of political consensus in a society like South Korea, one of Taiwan's main competitors for investment funds, the perceived progress in Taiwan and the perception that this progress adds to political stability should help to bring in investment.

151

Since democratization in Taiwan is just beginning and still faces many problems, it is too early to say how fully the Taiwan case will confirm this functional theory of democratic transitions. But the theory seems to provide a useful perspective for understanding the reform decisions made by the end of 1986. So far, the Taiwan experience has confirmed the proposition that democratizing reform can strengthen a regime. In addition, Chiang Ching-kuo's handling of the reform process provides useful lessons for reformers elsewhere in the skills of consensus-building and conflict management.

NINE

The Effect of Taiwan's Political Reform on Taiwan-Mainland Relations

Taiwan has exerted an increasing influence on mainland China in recent years. Beijing's new "coastal development policy," announced in January 1988, is explicitly modeled on Taiwan's experience. The new move in Chinese economic reform toward turning state-owned enterprises into joint-stock companies draws some of its inspiration from the success of the Taiwan model. In the political sphere, Chinese democrats have pointed to the reforms in Taiwan to argue that neither a Leninist party structure nor a Chinese cultural heritage is a bar to democratization, and that similar reforms in mainland China are overdue if China is to stop falling behind its smaller rival in the race to modernize.

Less noted and more complex are the effects which Taiwan's political liberalization, growing international self-confidence, and economic prosperity have had on Taiwan-mainland relations. These effects are the subject of this chapter. My argument is that political reform in Taiwan has changed the fundamental assumption on which China's Taiwan policy has hitherto been based—that the Kuomintang has the power unilaterally to negotiate the future of the island with the CCP. Democratization has so complicated the internal politics of Taiwan that it is now impossible for any deal to be struck with the mainland that does not command wide popular support on the island. Given the enormous risks that unification would pose for the people of Taiwan, this new political reality bodes ill for reunification on anything like the terms that have hitherto been offered by Beijing.

Beijing is beginning to readjust its strategy to take account of the new situation, but it may no longer have any realistic options that will enable it to achieve its goal. The other actors in the drama —the KMT, the Taiwan electorate, and proponents of Taiwan independence—are also adjusting their strategies to take account of the changed situation on the island and to respond to the new strategies of Beijing. All the actors see the United States as an important potential help or hindrance, but they often misunderstand the American position.

Mao Zedong used to say that it did not matter if Taiwan took a hundred years to rejoin the motherland.[1] But in a 1980 speeech Deng Xiaoping expressed an increased sense of urgency about the Taiwan issue, listing reunification as one of the three great tasks of the decade.[2] Deng may have felt that Taiwan's importance for China's economic and security interests was greater than ever, given Taiwan's economic dynamism and China's growing aspirations as a regional power. And he may have felt that the completion of China's territorial unification was a historical mission of his generation of CCP leaders, which he was duty-bound to complete in his lifetime. Perhaps he realized that the passage of time would only make reunification harder to achieve.

Whatever his reasons, Deng has pursued reunification aggressively and imaginatively, building up pressure on the KMT to enter negotiations. His strategy has had two prongs. On the one hand, he has offered a series of radical concessions. In 1979 the National People's Congress Standing Committee issued a "Letter to Our Taiwan Compatriots" seeking people-to-people contacts and peaceful reunification. In 1981 NPC Standing Commitee Chairman Ye Jianying articulated Nine Points, offering Taiwan "a high degree of autonomy" in a reunified China. In 1983, in an an interview with Professor Winston Yang, Deng Xiaoping guaranteed Taiwan the right to maintain not only its own social and economic system but even its own military. And in 1984 Deng suggested the application to Taiwan of the notion of "one China, two systems," originally created for use in Hong Kong.

These concessions have not been merely tactical. They have in an important way altered, or at least rendered ambiguous, the substantive goals of the CCP's reunification policy. Deng's central goal remains that which the CCP has always pursued, to find some way of putting into practice the idea of "one China" which both the Taipei and the Beijing governments officially recognize in principle; or, to restate the same thing, to implement Chinese sovereignty over Taiwan. In doing this, a second goal is also unchanged: to assert the higher, or national, status of the Beijing government and to establish the lower, or local, status of the Taipei government. But a third and more concrete goal has become ambiguous, i.e., the establishment of actual physical control over the island. The idea of "one country, two systems" seems to suggest that such physical control is not an immediate aim of Chinese policy. (In this regard, Chinese authorities stress that Taiwan differs from Hong Kong.)

Yet, by extinguishing Taiwan's international persona, the first two elements of Deng's policy would lay the groundwork for the subsequent imposition of physical control at a time of the mainland's chosing. Its ability to do this would also be enhanced by the substantial economic integration that would be achieved between the island and the mainland under the one country two systems policy. People on Taiwan are understandably cautious about handing over their bargaining chips to the people on the other side in exchange for a promise of respect for local autonomy.

Lending color to these concerns, Deng has unwaveringly maintained the second prong of his strategy, which is the threat of military force if Taiwan declares independence, obtains nuclear weapons, suffers from domestic insurrection, is subjected to foreign military intervention, or delays reunification beyond Beijing's ability to be patient. The CCP leaders have been challenged over and over again, by the U.S., by overseas Chinese journalists, and by the leaders of Taiwan to abandon this threat, and they have always refused.

A crucial element of the CCP's Taiwan policy has always been the insistence that its only interlocutor is the KMT, a rival political party which has emerged during the still unfinished Chinese civil war in control of some pieces of territory which include Taiwan as well as—the CCP has found it convenient from time to time to stress—some other pieces of territory that do not happen to be administratively part of the province of Taiwan.[3] For the CCP, almost any arrangement is conceivable between the two political parties so long as it does not entail a change in the status of Taiwan as a subordinate political unit under Chinese sovereignty. This status Beijing regards as "already settled" and not open to negotiation (a position the KMT shares). Thus, Beijing has always refused to consider dealing with Taiwan as a state or government, or with the people residing on Taiwan as a distinct people or nationality. To allow negotiations on any of these bases would risk abandoning the principle that the negotiations are intended to implement—

Beijing's sovereignty over Taiwan. Therefore, what the CCP seeks is negotiations not between the two "sides" but between the two (political) "parties."

CCP strategy has assumed that the ruling party in Taiwan is controlled by mainlanders committed to reunification, and that it has the power to resolve the fate of Taiwan. It is this set of assumptions which political reform has rendered untenable. Control of the party and of the island is tipping from mainlander to Taiwanese hands, and from the elite to the electorate. This tipping is manifested in four ways.

First, the "Taiwanization" of the political system—initiated in the mid-1970s with the recruitment of increased numbers of Taiwanese into the upper ranks of the ruling party—has now reached the highest levels of party and government. For the first time in Taiwan's history the President is a Taiwanese, and the new party Central Standing Committee and the new Cabinet, both formed in July 1988, are each more than one-half Taiwanese in composition. The Legislative Yuan will come under the control of Taiwan-elected members by about 1992, due to deaths and voluntary retirements among the superannuated mainland members combined with the election of increased numbers of local "supplementary" members. Although mainlanders retain the highest positions in the party apparatus and the military, Taiwanese are moving higher and higher in both.

The new party and state elite still professes loyalty to the traditional party platform of one China in order to avoid a rupture with older mainlander party members and to avoid giving the PRC a *casus belli*. Yet they appear to be much less emotionally committed to unification than previous leaders and more committed to the interests of the Taiwan populace.

Second, party, electoral, representative, and public opinion institutions have developed to the point where the electorate is able to enforce considerable accountability and responsiveness upon the government. The major opposition party, the Democratic Progressive Party, although still formally illegal, has proven itself politically viable and enjoys substantial popularity. Elections are fiercely competitive despite structural constraints which load the dice in favor of KMT candidates. An aggressive print media keeps the government under a constant barrage of opinion columns, leaks, speculation, and second-guessing.

The Taiwan electorate seems to understand that a formal declaration of independence would be a costly, risky venture with few payoffs. The voters prefer to promote continued political reform at home that will increase their power in the political system, and innovative diplomacy abroad that will increase their government's international political profile and influence and hence their own convenience in traveling around the world and doing business. The electorate would probably not be averse in principle to some sort of formal reunification with mainland China provided that their rights and freedoms were credibly guaranteed and their access to international markets protected or enhanced. But the Taiwan electorate does not want to take even the slightest risk of coming under the actual physical control of the mainland authorities. This attitude is likely to continue even if the mainland regime substantially changes its political complexion. The islanders are unlikely ever to want to put their fate in the hands of outsiders, except in the unlikely event that the outsiders are much richer than they are.

Third, all kinds of alternative futures for Taiwan are being publicly debated. Although it remains illegal to discuss "Taiwan independence," or even to advocate discussing it, it is nonetheless widely debated both as such, and in the form of discussions over the meaning of the Democratic Progressive Party's platform of "self-determination."[4] Numerous other proposals have beeen debated, such as such as "two countries, two systems," "the cultural approach," "one country under separate administrations,"[5] and a "unification-pluralistic politics model."[6] Most of these proposals call in one way or another for legitimizing the status of the Taipei authorities within the larger Chinese national entity, and are therefore incompatible with the CCP's insistence on the Taipei government's illegitimacy. Beijing views all such proposals as going down the road of Taiwan independence either intentionally or unintentionally.

Perhaps the most influential of these proposals has been Wei Yung's "multi-system state" model (tuo-t'i-chih kuo-chia), also known as the German model and multiple recognition, under which, pending eventual unification, the two sides would co-exist on an equal footing in the international arena, with neither reduced to the status of a local government. Both sides would continue to assert the notion of one China but would accept diplomatic recognition from countries that also recognized the other. Dr. Wei is a KMT member and government official and his proposal has been widely favored by influential politicians and academics in Taiwan.

From time to time it has been rumored that his proposal was on the verge of official acceptance. The CCP leaders view the proposal as a thinly disguised device to cement the *de facto* independence of Taiwan.

Fourth, beginning in late 1988, the Taipei government has adopted a loosely-defined strategy of "flexible diplomacy" under which it has tried to increase its official presence in international organizations and foreign capitals by abandoning the all-or-nothing insistence on being the only Chinese government and on being labeled the Republic of China. (The strategy is influenced by, although not identical with, the multi-system state notion of Wei Yung.) On this basis Taipei was able to upgrade relations with several countries, including Canada, Britain, and France, who are attracted by Taiwan's growing financial clout. President Lee Teng-hui paid a state visit to Singapore in early 1989 in the capacity of "President Lee from Taiwan." Taiwan sent a high-ranking delegation to the Asian Development Bank meetings in Beijing in May 1989, even though the delegation could not carry the label Republic of China there. Eventually, flexible diplomacy is likely to confront Beijing with the unpalatable choice—most likely in a poor country attracted by Taiwan's offers of generous economic aid—between co-existing in the same capital with an embassy labeled Republic of China or withdrawing its own legation in protest. Beijing will probably chose the latter option, but at some cost to its diplomatic prestige.

Flexible diplomacy is connected with political reform. It is made possible by the Taipei government's new-found self-confidence in its democratic legitimacy within the island, since it tacitly dispenses with the legitimizing fiction that the Taipei government represents all of China. And it is a sign of the government's increased responsiveness to the demands of the local electorate, who are anxious to gain better access to and security within the international system. The CCP leaders see the new strategy as dangerous, because it aims to establish a viable international personality for Taiwan that will enable it to survive indefinitely outside the motherland's control.[7]

Taken together, the four developments just sketched mean that it is too late for any decision on the future of Taiwan to be taken over the heads of the people of Taiwan. The Taiwan electorate has entered the reunification game as a third player, indeed as the one which holds the most valuable cards and has veto power over any agreement. This development is far more threatening to CCP strategy than the obstacles it confronted in the past: the activities of the Taiwan independence movement, which the CCP correctly regards as having limited influence; the anti-communism of the mainlanders on Taiwan, which the CCP has always regarded as negotiable; and the economic and security interests of the U.S. in Taiwan, which the CCP believes it can preserve in a unified China. It means that the CCP's Taiwan strategy has failed.

While bold and imaginative, the concessionary prong of CCP strategy failed to assure the Taiwan elites that their interests would be adequately protected in a future unified country with two systems. The military prong of the strategy was never very credible and has become even less so over time, not only for directly military reasons but because China's domestic reform strategy and new-look foreign policy have given it ever rising stakes in a peaceful Asian environment. The combination was insufficient to induce the KMT into negotiations during the time when there were still only two players in the game, while in several ways the strategy gave added impetus to the emergence of the Taiwan electorate as the third player.

By continuing to place pressure on the KMT to solve the Taiwan problem in the near future, yet failing to provide a sufficiently attractive modality for doing so, the CCP provided a major incentive for the KMT to firm up its domestic legitimacy and stability by undertaking the political reform that has led to the emergence of the third player. The very imaginativeness and constant refining of Deng's proposals to the KMT helped unleash the flurry of alternative blueprints from scholars and politicians on the Taiwan side. The continuing threat of CCP use of military force has helped the KMT reformers maintain stability through the risky reform process, because it has discouraged the opposition from appealing to Taiwan independence sentiment. On both ends, the threat of PRC military intervention has helped to compress the Taiwan political spectrum toward the vital center.

As recently as a few years ago, the CCP leaders seemed to believe that only the KMT, with U.S. support, was keeping the people of Taiwan out of the motherland's embrace. The CCP has now formed a more accurate impression of the Taiwanese state of mind based on several years of face-to-face contact among people from Taiwan and the mainland. Much of this has occurred on American campuses. In addition, starting in 1987, many people from Taiwan visited the mainland, including in 1988 a Mainland China Affairs

Observation Team that included representatives from the Democratic Progressive Party. The Chinese leaders have also had access to the reams of reportage published in Taiwan by journalists and other visitors to the mainland, reflecting the overwhelming impression that the mainland is far too backward for reunification to be desirable now.

Signs have emerged since 1988 that the CCP leaders have begun to recognize the failure of their Taiwan policy and are exploring new ways of dealing with Taiwan. One was the "James Hsiung Incident," which in the summer of 1988 afforded interesting insight into the leaders' state of mind. Hsiung, a prominent Chinese-American professor of political science at New York University, had met several times in recent years with Deng Xiaoping and Yang Shangkun, the senior leaders directly in charge of Taiwan policy. He reported to a seminar at the Asia and World Institute in Taipei that the CCP leaders had become concerned about the Taiwanization of the KMT and the potential overhaul of the Legislative Yuan. They worried less about T'ai-tu (the Taiwan independence movement) than about tu-T'ai (Taiwan gradually consolidating its *de facto* independence under KMT rule). They had taken note of the widespread discussion in Taiwan of the ideas of the multistate system and multiple recognition and felt that such ideas would lead toward *de facto* independence. They were anxious to consummate China's reunification once and for all, without any political preconditions. If the KMT would enter into negotiations, Hsiung reported, the CCP would be willing to consider such concessons as abandoning the right to use military force against Taiwan, establishing a coalition government of the two political parties, writing a new constitution that would not include the "four basic principles" (socialism, dictatorship of the proletariat, Marxism-Leninism-Mao Zedong Thought, and CCP leadership), and even changing the national name and flag.[8]

The picture which Professor Hsiung painted of the top leaders' worried state of mind and willingness to make new concessions is consistent with more public evidence. When Zhao Ziyang met with George Shultz on July 15, 1988, he stated that "both sides support the policy of one China. . . . Both sides hope for mutual cooperation. . . . Both sides want to carry on the fine tradition of China's national culture."[9] This statement was compatible, although not identical, with some of the ideas reportedly offered by Professor Hsiung's high-ranking leaders, such as reunifying China on the basis of shared Chinese identity rather than the "four upholds." In August 1988, when CCP United Front Work Department Chairman Yan Mingfu met with a group of Taiwanese, he stated that the CCP's refusal to rule out the use of military force in Taiwan was directed not against the Taiwan residents but only against potential foreign interference, and that the CCP would be willing to negotiate an agreement with the KMT that both sides would not use force against the other.[10] The official PRC journal *Outlook* elaborated that "the CCP will never use force against the patriots and those in favor of reunification of the motherland. If China must resort to force it will only be against aggressors and traitors."[11] This is only a change of emphasis in the long-standing CCP position, but it may be a significant one.

The Hsiung incident made clear that the rumors one occasionally hears about secret negotiations over the status of Taiwan between representatives of the KMT and the CCP were false at that time, because it is unthinkable that the CCP leaders would have been discussing their potential concessions with Hsiung if they had had a channel for presenting them directly to the KMT. This reasoning leads to the conclusion that the public negotiations through the international press were the only ones going on. But these public negotiations were real. For many years Taipei had refused to respond in any way to CCP offers, which encouraged the CCP to increase its concessions step by step. Taipei started to reply in 1988, challenging the CCP to up its ante. President Lee Teng-hui several times repeated three conditions for improving relations with the mainland—that Beijing must abandon its military threat against Taiwan, its four basic principles, and its blocking of Taiwan's activities in the international arena.[12] The CCP leaders' comments to Professor Hsiung showed awareness of and serious interest in these conditions.

Political reform in Taiwan has strengthened the hand of the KMT in these public negotiations, by strengthening the KMT's legitimacy and popularity in Taiwan and demonstrating to the CCP that the Taiwan apple will not simply fall from the tree. But on the other hand, for the KMT as for the CCP, political reform has reduced its freedom to maneuver. Reform has placed new limits on the KMT's ability unilaterally to conclude a settlement with the Beijing authorities if a mutually agreeable one could be negotiated. The third player confronts not only the CCP, but also the KMT.

But the impact of the Taiwan electorate on the KMT-CCP relationship has not been merely that of a potential veto power. The electorate's rising power in Taiwan has given it the ability to force the KMT into acts of diplomatic flexibility that it views as risky. The KMT has faced enormous political pressure from the opposition parties, intra-party critics, members of the Legislative Yuan, and the press to find a way for Taiwan to "re-enter the international community." The electorate has used the CCP's apparent flexibility as a goad to press the KMT to try for some new solutions to Taiwan's international isolation (so long as these do not involve a sell-out of the Taiwan residents' interests). The KMT response has fallen into two parts. In relations with the mainland, starting in late 1987 the KMT took a series of bold new initiatives, including permission for mainlanders to visit Taiwan to comfort ill relatives or attend funerals, legalization of indirect trade (which according to PRC statistics amounted to US \$2.4 billion in 1988[13]), permission for Taiwan academic and sports figures to visit the mainland, permission for most mainland publications, films, and other media to be imported into Taiwan, and permission for some mainland students and scholars studying in the U.S. to visit Taiwan. In relations with the rest of the world, the KMT has adopted the strategy of "flexible diplomacy" described earlier.

For the KMT, these steps are risky. Externally, they risk playing into the PRC strategy of "Hong-Kongizing" Taiwan. According to this scenario, Taiwan's economic ties with the mainland might create a powerful pro-unification constituency among Taiwan entrepreneurs, a constituency subject to manipulation from the mainland because of its economic interests held hostage there. At the same time, increased people-to-people and quasi-governmental contacts across the Strait could erode the international credibility of Taiwan's insistence on its legal personality as the sole legitimate government of China, leading to an erosion of foreign support.[14]

Internally, the major risk lies in the possibility that relaxation of tensions with the mainland will impair the KMT's claim to a privileged position within the Taiwan electoral system. That system is currently structured in such a way that the opposition cannot win control of the government no matter how many votes it gets. The reforms so far proposed by the KMT, significant though they are, fall short of changing this fundamental bias. In a way that is legally intricate but politically simple, this structure derives its ultimate rationale from the fact of the civil war and the threat from the mainland. If this threat is seen to recede and the civil war to

162

enter a twilight phase of informal peace, the question of why the KMT should not compete equally with the other parties, which has already been insistently raised, will become unanswerable.

On the other hand, the net effect of the reforms has been to weaken the appeal of Taiwan independence as a political option. Although almost all the leaders of the opposition Democratic Progressive Party personally favor Taiwan independence, the mainstream of the leadership has decided that for the time being it is politically unwise to push for independence, mainly because of the anticipated strong reaction from the CCP. They have chosen to concentrate their efforts instead on pressing the KMT for more rapid democratization, in the expectation that this will eventually bring them closer to winning power while in the meantime strengthening the electorate's ability to block any unacceptable reunification settlement. So far, most of the electorate seems to have accepted the democratization-first strategy. The openly pro-independence New Tide movement remains a small minority within the Democratic Progressive Party and appears to have a relatively small base of support among the voters.

These developments have confronted the organized Taiwan independence movement, most of whose members are overseas, with a set of unappetizing political dilemmas. On the one hand, the Taiwan independence forces fear that political reform will legitimize and strengthen KMT rule; yet if they continue to hold themselves aloof from participation in the political system, they risk becoming ever more irrelevant in the eyes of the electorate. Increasing Taiwan-mainland contacts carry the risk of movement toward a negotiated settlement with the mainland that would make the success of the independence cause even more remote than it already is, but to oppose these contacts puts the independence movement at odds with the desire of most of the electorate for a more activist diplomacy. The independence movement fears a weak KMT that fails to deal resourcefully with the CCP's smiling diplomacy and hence allows Taiwan to fall into a unification trap, but it also fears a strong KMT that wins political victories in the international arena and so deprives the independence movement of much of its reason for being. In short, Taiwan's political reform presents the independence movement with a choice between using it as a window to step up pressure for independence, or rejoining established political institutions to work within the electorally oriented opposition. The Formosan Association for Public Affairs, the main

Taiwanese political organization in the U.S., is split into a faction that wishes to concentrate on working for independence and one that wishes to work mainly on promoting democratization. At the moment of writing, the latter group is dominant.

There has been much misunderstanding among Chinese on both sides of the Taiwan Strait about U.S. policy toward reunification and the potential U.S. role in shaping future Taiwan-mainland relations. The declared American policy remains that which was stated in the 1972 Shanghai Communiqué—that the U.S. "does not challenge" the position that "there is but one China and that Taiwan is a part of China," and that the U.S.'s only national interest in the issue is "in a peaceful settlement of the Taiwan question by the Chinese themselves."

But this position is freighted with ambiguity. It can be read as saying that the U.S. agrees with the Chinese position that Taiwan is a part of China, or as saying that the U.S. does not necessarily agree, but does not want to argue about the issue for the time being. While no one involved in Taiwan is under the illusion that the U.S. now actively supports Taiwan independence, the ambiguity in the American position allows some to believe—with hope in the case of Taiwan independence leaders, with fear in the case of the PRC leaders—that the U.S. might swing its support to Taiwan independence in some future eventuality. Chinese on both sides of the issue are aware that influential Congressional leaders such as Senator Claiborne Pell (D., R.I., Chairman of the Senate Foreign Relations Committee), Senator Ted Kennedy (D., Mass.), Representative Stephen Solarz (D., N.Y.), and Representative Jim Leach (R., Iowa), are sympathetic to the goals of the Formosan Association for Public Affairs.

Among some pro-Taiwan-independence politicians, the opinion is prevalent that, as one such person told me, "If Taiwan declares independence, I believe the U.S. will support us. Taiwan's strategic value as an 'unsinkable aircraft carrier' is too great for America ever to abandon it. America will welcome an independent Taiwan that is friendly to its interests." In parallel fashion, as the prospect of reunification recedes, Beijing tends to blame U.S. arms sales for emboldening the KMT, to see the U.S. hand behind KMT reforms, and to perceive a hidden American agenda of protecting economic and strategic interests in Taiwan. A November 1988 article in the official weekly *Outlook* was revealing of this belief—perhaps too much so, for it was quickly withdrawn. It charged the U.S. with "increasing its interference in Taiwan's affairs, strengthening its political, military, and economic infiltration and control with a view to consolidating the situation in the Taiwan Strait of no peace no war, no unification no independence, no economic rapprochement or estrangement."[15]

While these particular charges are exagerrated, the U.S. has contributed importantly to the frustration of PRC goals by asserting a national interest in peaceful resolution of the Taiwan issue and by selling arms to Taipei to assure its capability for self-defense. While deploring American involvement, the PRC has called upon the U.S. to take active steps to achieve the peaceful resolution of the issue that it says it wants by pressing the KMT into negotiations, or even by serving as a mediator. The Chinese placed great hopes in a reformulation of the American position which was offered by Secretary of State Shultz in Shanghai in April 1987. The Secretary stated that "our steadfast policy seeks to foster an environment in which such developments [toward a relaxation of tensions] can continue to take place."[16] The reformulation was confirmed by the Assistant Secretary of State for East Asian and Pacific Affairs, Gaston Sigur, who stated at about the same time that American policy seeks to "facilitate an environment in which an evolutionary process toward a peaceful solution, worked out by the parties themselves, can occur."[17] The PRC has interpreted the Shultz statement as a new American moral commitment to take active steps to encourage peaceful resolution of the unification issue, although American officials have insisted it is nothing more than a restatement of existing policy, politely rephrased to take note of Beijing's sensitivities.

Since George Bush is regarded as an "old friend" by the leaders in Beijing because of his service there as U.S. Ambassador, Beijing is likely to place even more pressure on him than it did on Ronald Reagan to help bring the Kuomintang to the negotiating table. PRC hopes may also have been raised by the appointment of Richard Solomon to the post of Assistant Secretary of State for East Asia. Solomon, who was Henry Kissinger's National Security Council China aide when U.S.-China rapprochement began in the 1970s, is widely thought to have been the person who drafted Shultz's April 1987 Shanghai toast.

But on my reading, the hopes and apprehensions on both sides of the Taiwan Strait about an American secret agenda or a change of policy are misguided. Despite intended ambiguities, policy countercurrents, confusion engendered by the separation of powers, and occasional reformulations in wording, American policy remains what the government says it is: the U.S. does not care whether Taiwan is eventually reunified with China or becomes independent, just so long as the issue is resolved peacefully. If this analysis is correct, then America is unlikely to play an active role in future reunification politics except in the improbable eventuality of rising military tensions in the Taiwan Straits.

The future prospects for Taiwan-mainland relations can be sketched in terms of three scenarios, in increasing order of probability.

The first is for increasing tension in the Taiwan Strait. This scenario could come about at the initiative of either the Taiwan or the mainland side. On the Taiwan side, it could be engendered if Taiwan acquired nuclear weapons, if there were a military coup or widespread social disorder in Taiwan, or if the Taiwan independence forces gained much strength. On the mainland side, this scenario would be triggered if the Beijing authorities decided for some reason to step up efforts to isolate Taiwan diplomatically and to increase the level of military threat. But for reasons implicit in the foregoing analysis, all these events are highly unlikely.

The second scenario is for an eleventh-hour negotiated agreement. The KMT and the CCP might agree to recognize the *de facto* independence of the island under the thin disguise of an affirmation of China's unity.[18] Such an agreement might contain the following essential points. Both sides would agree that there is only one China, and Taiwan is part of that China; that fellow Chinese on both sides of the Taiwan Strait will not use military force against each other; and that fellow Chinese on both sides of the Taiwan Strait will not interfere with one another's participation in international organizations or diplomatic activities with foreign countries. The two political parties would agree to settle once and for all on paper the question of Taiwan's status, thus seeking to strengthen existing legal and political barriers to Taiwan independence. The agreement would help to assure the mainland authorities that Taiwan would not fall under the influence of a hostile power, and would make it easier for the PRC to gain access to Taiwan's capital and technology. But the CCP would make major concessions in agreeing not to use force against Taiwan and to allow Taiwan to conduct its activities in the international arena. The question of the form of Taiwan's association with the mainland would be left to the future to resolve, and Taipei would be under less pressure than before to resolve it on Beijing's terms. Thus, such an agreement would serve the KMT's interests more than those of the CCP. For this reason, such an agreement cannot be accounted a strong likelihood.

In any case, an agreement of this sort could be effective only if it won the support of the Taiwan electorate. Under the present disposition of public opinion in Taiwan, such support is certainly not guaranteed, but it is possible. Although a major motivation for the two political parties to reach such an agreement would be to block the Taiwan independence option, the residents of Taiwan would not necessarily see the agreement as working against their interests. It would remove the threat of PRC military action against Taiwan and would increase the ease with which Taiwan residents could conduct their international political and economic activities. In these ways it would increase the ability of Taiwan to survive and prosper. In the long run it would make it even more difficult for the mainland authorities to impose their control on the people of Taiwan against the will of the residents.

The third scenario is for the continuation of the current situation. The *de facto* independence which is growing increasingly viable economically and diplomatically, despite continuing political tensions over it, has to be accounted most likely to continue, since at the time of this writing the CCP authorities continue to argue adamantly against Taiwan's flexible diplomacy and against the idea of dual recognition, refuse to abandon the threat of the use of military force, and continue to work energetically against Taiwan's attempts to re-enter international society under any rubric but that of a local level of Chinese goverment.[19]

According to the analysis presented in this paper, this last scenario offers no realistic chance of achieving reunification, unless there are momentous changes in the international environment or the situation within Taiwan. Yet so far the PRC leaders prefer it. This policy at least keeps the Taiwan problem open, and with it the possibility that the strategy may somehow still encounter the improbable historical circumstances that will allow it to succeed. Moreover, keeping the Taiwan strategy of the 1980s in place postpones the domestic political costs of acknowledging its failure. Perhaps not until Deng Xiaoping's passing can the Chinese leadership afford to come to terms with the fact that winning back Taiwan, if it can be done at all, may turn out be a more time-consuming process than even Mao Zedong foresaw.

PART V

Prospects for Chinese Democracy

TEN

Chinese Democracy in 1989

In the late 1960s millions of Red Guards, who had earlier taken to the streets full of faith in Mao, found themselves discarded in the countryside where they discovered that the peasants were still living in primitive conditions after two decades of socialist development. In 1971, Mao Zedong's "closest comrade-in-arms" and trusted successor Lin Biao perished in the course of his alleged military coup attempt against the Great Helmsman. These events prompted significant numbers of Chinese to ask themselves what was wrong with their country's political system.

All over the country, thousands formed small dissident groups to discuss how such things could have happened. Some wrote letters of protest or advice to Chairman Mao; a few may have plotted violent action against the regime. These groups were rooted out by the police in campaigns called "cleansing of class ranks" (1968–69) and "one-strike, three-anti" (1970–71). Hundreds of their members were executed.[1] Although the regime surmounted this particular crisis of political control, its ideological control continued to weaken.

Only one group of dissidents of the early 1970s became known in the West, after its members hung a wall poster in Canton in 1974 under the pseudonym Li Yizhe. The poster attacked Maoist autocracy in the thin disguise of what it called the "Lin Biao system." As a solution to the flaws of dictatorship, the Li Yizhe group called on the National People's Congress (NPC) to exercise its powers.[2] The Li Yizhe group thus introduced what was to become a consistent strategy of Chinese democrats, namely, attempting to ameliorate or circumvent one-party dictatorship by taking seriously the provision, found in every constitution of the People's Republic of China (PRC), that the National People's Congress is the supreme organ of government. This strategy was prominently reflected in many articles written during the debate over political reform in 1986–87. It surfaced again during the May 1989 crisis when Cao Siyuan, a self-styled lobbyist affiliated with the Stone Group Corporation (a privately-owned computer company in Beijing), and Hu Jiwei, a reformist member of the NPC Standing Committee, attempted to convene a meeting of the Standing Committee to overturn Premier Li Peng's May 20 declaration of martial law. After the crackdown on June 4, Cao was arrested and Hu subjected to political denunciation.

By 1989, what had started as congeries of small, isolated, clandestine groups which did not know of each other's existence, had grown step by step—through the Tiananmen Square Incident of 1976, the Democracy Wall movement of 1978–79, and the student demonstrations of 1985 and 1986–87—into a national force that apparently had the participation or sympathy of almost all urban residents in China. In the process, the movement for Chinese democracy became more complicated in its social composition and in its mix of political goals and tactics.

Although the movement crossed a major watershed in 1989, when many intellectuals gave up hope that the regime of Deng Xiaoping was capable of reforming itself politically from within, both before and after June 4, the democratic movement of 1989 retained strong continuities in personnel, goals, and tactics with its predecessors. The mainstream democratic movement has always maintained hope that the authorities would initiate the changes for which it was calling. Indeed, the movement's moderation is striking. Chinese democrats have consistently positioned themselves as remonstrators rather than opponents, pressing the party to reform in its own interests and in keeping with its own ideals.[3] This position did not change in 1989. The movement's main organizations—comprised before June 4 of the Capital Federation of Autonomous College Student Organizations (*Gaozilian*), the Capital Federation of Intellectual Circles (*Beizhilian*), and the Beijing Workers' Autonomous Federation (*Gongzilian*), and, after June 4, of the Chinese Democratic Alliance (*Minzhu Zhongguo zhenxian*), the Association of Chinese Students and Scholars in the United States, and the Chinese Alliance for Democracy (also known as China Spring)—have all said that they do not seek the overthrow of the Chinese Communist Party (CCP). Even after the regime's use of force on June 4, the main elements of the democracy movement have not changed their commitment to nonviolent methods in bringing about political change.

172

Several factors account for the moderation of the democracy movement. The Chinese democrats have long believed that the regime was capable of reform from within, and the democrats themselves continued to believe in socialism, albeit of a democratic variety. But a moderate approach was also prudent, for the regime retained command over the police and the military, and it previously showed itself willing to use these instruments of coercion to suppress the opposition. Finally, the democracy movement was made up almost entirely of students and intellectuals, a small minority within Chinese society. These people lacked the numbers and the willingness to confront the regime head-on. These factors combined to incline Chinese democrats to press for a "self-limiting revolution" in the People's Republic of China.

Reform from Within

Perhaps the most important factor of those mentioned above is that the regime's ideology claims to be democratic and leaders of the opposition have thus had reason to hope for reform from within. All four constitutions of the PRC affirmed popular sovereignty, contained provisions for citizens to vote and run for office, and guaranteed the rights of free speech, assembly, petition, and demonstration. Even if largely rhetorical, such provisions pay tribute to the strength of democratic yearnings in China and set standards that the regime has to pretend to meet in some fashion.

Mao resolved the contradiction between rhetoric and reality with the concept of "democratic dictatorship," which held that the system was democratic because the totalitarian vanguard party was serving the highest interests of the people—whether they liked it or not. Those subjected to repression were not the people but their enemies. However cynical the argument, many Chinese believed in it and in Mao's benevolence and wisdom. Many blamed the problems that they encountered in their own lives on individual cadres rather than on the system and the assumption was widespread that Mao did not intend the abuses that were carried out in his name. Paradoxically, the practice of writing letters of remonstrance and appeal to Mao was common in the darkest days of his regime, perhaps more common than in his relatively lenient periods.

Such beliefs had faded by the time of the Tiananmen Square

Incident of April 5, 1976, especially among the sophisticated factory and office workers and Communist Youth League members of the capital who formed the main force of the demonstrators. But the demonstrators still directed the brunt of their criticism at those around Mao and not at Mao himself. This made it possible for Deng's regime, which never contemplated full de-Maoization, to reverse the verdict on the incident only two years after Mao's death.

Hopes for democratization from the top down revived after Mao's passing. Under Hu Yaobang's leadership of the CCP Organization Department, millions of individuals were exonerated from unjust criminal and political verdicts and rehabilitated, some posthumously. Property was returned, jobs restored, reputations cleared. Hu sponsored the "debate over practice as the sole criterion of truth," which opened the way for the expression of fresh ideas that party theorists had been nurturing in "cowpens" and May 7 cadre schools during the years when they were condemned to internal exile.

Most participants in the Democracy Wall movement in 1978–79 were convinced that Deng wanted democratization and welcomed their suggestions. Only a few like Wei Jingsheng argued that Deng was a "new dictator," that temporary tolerance for unsolicited advice was not equivalent to a restructuring of power, and that a democratic climate without democratic institutions could easily dissipate whenever a change of course was initiated at the top. In the eyes of most intellectuals, the arguments of Wei and those who thought like him were premature. The intellectuals believed that reform is invariably a lengthy process; moreover, although Deng could not afford to move too fast because of conservative resistance in the party, he nevertheless was proceeding with deliberate speed in a democratic direction and had to be given plenty of time. Most democratic activists saw Deng's arrest of Wei and his fellow-thinkers as regrettable but inevitable. At the time it was felt by many that what Wei had said was true enough, but it was not the time to say it.

In 1980, Deng himself called for political reform, reviving the hope that he would pilot China toward democracy. In a major speech delivered in August, he set modest goals and stressed that political reform was meant to strengthen, not weaken, party leadership.[4] Some people around Deng, such as Liao Gailong, took the speech as license to argue for more far-reaching reforms, including the vitalization of the people's congress system.[5] For some of the democrats, reform of the people's congress election system opened the vista of a parliamentary road to influence. They competed vigorously in the county-level elections held in 1979–81.[6] Until 1989, Deng continued to entertain the notion of political reform and allowed it to be discussed sporadically. An especially vigorous public discussion took place during 1986–87, after Deng had stated that political restructuring must be part of the reform agenda.

It is clear in retrospect that Deng meant what he said when he warned that reform must not infringe on the four cardinal principles, namely, keeping to the socialist road, upholding the people's democratic dictatorship, leadership by the CCP, and Marxism-Leninism and Mao Zedong Thought, but this warning was not so clearly understood at the time he issued it. His words and actions were ambiguous. His speeches contained little abstract political discussion, making it hard to determine the intellectual logic of his position. Some thought the ambiguity was tactical, as he maneuvered to maintain a fragile coalition of reformers and conservatives. Others viewed Deng as intellectually confused, unaware that he could not reform the economy without reforming politics. My guess is that Deng shared the assumption of many Chinese political thinkers, including Mao, that democracy is an instrument of mobilization whose function is to strengthen the links of citizens to the state, rather than a set of procedures for limiting state power to protect individual rights.[7] Thus, Deng did not see a contradiction between his vision of democracy and a benevolent dictatorship exercised by him and his party.

Although one may argue that Chinese democrats misread Deng, they were probably not entirely wrong in thinking that Deng's closest aides and designated successors, Hu Yaobang and Zhao Ziyang, were willing to consider relatively far-reaching measures of political reform. Hu, head of the CCP Organization Department in 1977–78 and CCP General Secretary from 1982 to 1987, sponsored a two-part "Conference for the Discussion of Guidelines for Theoretical Work" (*Lilun gongzuo wuxu hui*) in January-April 1979, at which liberal party thinkers he had rehabilitated or promoted began the overhaul of Chinese Marxism-Leninism needed to provide an ideological basis for reform.[8] Under a pseudonym, at least one of the works produced at this conference found its way into a publication at Democracy Wall.[9]

According to people who worked with Hu, his driving motive

was to guarantee that another Cultural Revolution could never occur. Thus, he advocated subjecting the ruling party to outside challenges and criticism. Although his vision of political pluralism did not envisage a rotation in power between the CCP and other political parties, Hu was willing to consider a number of other suggestions, such as expanding the role of the NPC and dividing it into two or three chambers. Hu also believed that the women's organizations, the Communist Youth League, trade unions, and professional associations should have greater independence from the CCP, saying, "If we control them so tightly, why bother to have separate organizations?"[10]

Hu was popular among intellectuals for his openness to their ideas, and was criticized by the army newspaper in 1982 for laxness in maintaining ideological discipline. He was purged from his party secretaryship in January 1987, after student demonstrations persuaded the party elders that he was allowing "bourgeois liberalization" to get out hand. It was his death on April 15, 1989, that triggered the student demonstrations.

Zhao Ziyang's record was more ambiguous. His chief commitment was to economic growth, and for him the main question seemed to be what sort of political structures would best meet the needs of economic development. It seemed inevitable that the marketization he favored would lead indirectly to the eventual breakup of dictatorship. But beyond this some advisors found him receptive to the argument that development in the modern age would eventually require lifting constraints on information and tolerating social pluralism and its more open political conflict. Zhao was associated with the theory of the "primary stage of socialism," which legitimated a diversity of social interests. His aide Bao Tong articulated the concept of "the new order of the socialist commodity economy," which rationalized wider use of elections and more political openness.[11] In 1986, Bao Tong authorized the establishment in Beijing of the Fund for the Reform and Opening of China, financed by the American businessman George Soros, and operating, at least officially, independently of Chinese government control. According to one report, Zhao commissioned the preparation of a political reform proposal that included ideas for multi-party competition and an independent press.[12] These actions indicated that Zhao was interested in a substantial opening and pluralization of the political system, at least over the long term.

On the other hand, Zhao presented a notably cautious program in the section on political reform of his report to the 13th Party Congress in October 1987. In the months before his fall from power, people around him promoted a theory called the "new authoritarianism," which argued that in the present, relatively early state of development China needs an enlightened autocrat to direct economic development while keeping order and protecting people's rights. We will probably never know to what extent this argument reflected Zhao's technocratic convictions, and to what extent it was propounded as a means to induce Deng Xiaoping to hand over power to Zhao quickly and without dividing it among several successors.

In any case, during the May-June crisis Zhao's tactics shifted. According to the subsequent official charges against him, he supported Deng Xiaoping's hard line on the demonstrations while he was on a state visit to North Korea in late April. But upon his return he changed his position, calling for the withdrawal of the controversial *People's Daily* editorial that branded the demonstrations a "turmoil" and advocating other concessions.[13] His conciliatory words and actions in public indicated that calls for the resignation of Li Peng and Deng Xiaoping did not displease him. On the eve of the declaration of martial law, officials and intellectuals associated with Zhao issued a six-point statement blaming the crisis on Deng and calling for special NPC and CCP meetings to examine errors of the past and, by implication, to summon Zhao (who had already been unofficially purged) back to power. In the aftermath of the June 4 crackdown, many members of Zhao's liberal brain trust fled the country. They now appear to maintain links with the exile democratic movement headed by Yan Jiaqi, a political scientist and former advisor to Zhao. Because they represent a faction within the CCP that may some day return to power, their alliance with the democracy movement allows Chinese democrats to continue even now to hope for reform of the communist regime from within.

That Zhao's interest in democracy during the crisis may have been tactical does not render it insignificant. Transitions from authoritarianism to democracy normally come about when authoritarian rulers see tactical advantages for such shifts. If Zhao's effort to play the democracy card had succeeded, he might have reverted soon to a more authoritarian position in order to consolidate his power and address China's economic problems. But meanwhile, Zhao's behavior demonstrated that those who hoped for change of the Chinese communist system from within had some grounds for their hopes.

Whatever the personal views of various party leaders, by the end of 1988, the actual achievements of officially-sponsored political reform were meager. They included regularization and expansion of the role of people's congresses, direct elections of county-level people's congress deputies, limitations on terms of office for some party and state officials, establishment of employee councils in state-owned enterprises, and the enactment of several hundred laws conducive to procedural regularity. The reform program also endorsed collective leadership in the party, orderly succession, the rule of law, and independence of the judiciary, but these desiderata remained weakly institutionalized.[14]

There were signs that some in the leadership favored further steps toward political reform in 1989, including passing a law making the press more free and independent but still subject ultimately to party guidance; enacting a law on demonstrations permitting peaceful gatherings while still enabling the government to restrict their scope;[15] reducing the role of party officials in student organizations, trade unions, enterprises, and schools, while preserving the party organs in these units as watchdogs; and further strengthening the role of the National People's Congress as a legislative and oversight organ under overall party guidance. In the crisis of spring 1989, even such half-way steps might have sufficed to satisfy many of the demonstrators. In the long run, they were unlikely to satisfy Chinese democrats, any more than similar solutions seem to have satisfied Polish or Hungarian democrats. The push for real freedom of the press and of association, as well as for truly competitive elections would have resumed, probably sooner rather than later. But in the meantime, the liberal images of Deng, Hu, and Zhao, whether they were justified or not, helped to keep Chinese democrats looking for change from above.

The Democracy Movement's Ideals

The second reason for the Chinese democrats' long-standing posture of loyalty to the regime is the nature of their own ideals. With few exceptions, the opposition's vision of Chinese democracy has been compatible with a socialist order. At Democracy Wall in 1978–79, most of the proposals were made from the perspective of party

178

members or nonparty loyalists. They called for very modest measures of political openness and competition, more in the spirit of Mao's idea of a party with an "open door" to society than in the spirit of a Western multi-party system. In 1986–87, the high point of the intra-party and academic debate over political reform that had been initiated by Deng, major proposals included establishing a civil service system; strengthening the National People's Congress by reducing its size and enlarging its system of committees; separating the party from the government; giving a clear legal definition to vertical and horizontal jurisdictions in the bureaucracy; publishing more financial data to assure greater governmental "transparency"; providing firmer guarantees of an independent judiciary; consulting more systematically with experts and technocrats in policy-making; and paying more consistent attention to procedures in governmental decision-making.[16] The emphases were on openness and procedural regularity.

None of the 1986–87 proposals that I have seen was anti-socialist or calculated to lead to the overthrow of the party. To be sure, the idea of socialism had become so diluted that it would have been hard to identify an anti-socialist proposal unless its author labeled it as such. Most of the democrats' proposals dealt with economic structures indirectly if at all and, among the economic reformers, even proposals for privatization and marketization of the economy were cast as versions of socialism. (For example, a proposal for issuing stock in state enterprises was presented as promoting "ownership by the whole people.") After the purge of Zhao Ziyang, a *People's Daily* editorial charged that in a 1987 intra-party meeting even Zhao advocated abandoning the insistence on upholding socialism on the grounds that nobody knew any more what socialism was.[17] Similarly, proposals for competitive electoral politics would not have been cast as open challenges to the principle of party leadership even if they were intended as such. Indeed, the moderate guise of most proposals may signify little except that Chinese are adept at waving the red flag to oppose the red flag.

My own reading of the political reform debates and personal encounters with some of the participants, however, lead me to believe that in most cases the reformers wanted to keep China socialist as they understood the term. For example, Yan Jiaqi, Li Honglin, Su Shaozhi, and Cao Siyuan, who were named in Beijing Mayor Chen Xitong's post-crackdown report as progenitors of the "turmoil" and "counter-revolutionary rebellion" in Beijing,[18] were among the leading participants in the 1986–87 discussions of political reform. All were party members; all seemed to espouse some version of socialism.

With some individual variation, the vision of the reformist party intellectuals centered on a system in which the communist party continued to be dominant but was checked by competitive elections and a free press in order to keep it honest and close to the people. This dominant party would run its own affairs and those of the government with openness and in accordance with laws and established procedures. For most of these intellectuals, the idea of party pluralism owed little to admiration for the American political and social system, which they criticized for its disorderliness, polarization of rich and poor, and political apathy. Although all believed that China could emulate some aspects of the American political structure, few could conceive of, or really wanted, an American-style system for China. Rather, their expectation was that party competition would develop out of China's existing system of "democratic consultation" with the nine minor political parties.[19]

Cao Siyuan used the term "socialist parliamentary democracy" to describe his vision. Yan Jiaqi emphasized "proceduralism." The vision of these party intellectuals was not fully articulated in print, probably because its realization depended upon a step-by-step approach that could pass muster with the supreme autocrat. But it was probably not far from the vision held by Hu Yaobang and some of Zhao Ziyang's supporters, if not by Zhao himself. Marxists such as Su Shaozhi, Li Honglin, and Wang Ruoshui argued vigorously that democracy is not only a part of the Marxist tradition but its fundamental aim. In short, what the party democrats had in mind was not the overthrow of socialism but democratic socialism.

That the democracy movement's mainstream was not anticommunist does not, however, gainsay the fact that a fundamental conflict existed between the democrats and the regime over the nature of socialist democracy, as well as over the pace of progress toward it. This conflict sharpened markedly beginning in 1987. In retrospect, the purge of Hu Yaobang in January 1987 was a major turning point. His demotion was accompanied by suppression of student demonstrations occurring at that time, and was followed by the expulsion from the CCP of three ranking intellectuals (Fang Lizhi, Wang Ruowang, and Liu Binyan), soon followed by others, and by the initiation of a campaign to oppose "bourgeois liberalization."

The events of early 1987 radicalized a portion of the intellectuals, because the man in whom they rested many of their hopes for the party fell, and the influence of Wang Zhen, Deng Liqun, and others whom the intellectuals regarded as hostile increased. In 1989, the key initial demands of the student demonstrators in Beijing were to reverse the verdict on Hu and to denounce the campaign against bourgeois liberalization. An immediate sign of the serious impact of Hu's ouster was the unprecedented signing of an open letter to the party Central Committee by more than 1000 Chinese students in America, about 700 of whom used their real names. This open letter became the first of several such letters and established the network that was used in 1989 to mobilize the students against the Li Peng regime. Meanwhile, the anti-bourgeois liberalization campaign was conducted so fecklessly that it created an atmosphere in which, as Fang Lizhi said, "no one is afraid of anyone any more" *(Shei ye bupa shei).*

More fires broke out than the party's ideological watchdogs could control. The Shanghai *World Economic Herald* published daring articles on the failures of reform and the need for more radical economic and political solutions. A magazine called *New Enlightenment* made its debut in October 1988, having evaded the party's control system for periodicals by registering itself as a book series. The four issues that were published before the spring crackdown contained essays by eminent theorists, many of them party members, who were at odds with the regime's ideological authorities. Contributors to these four issues, who were soon to play prominent roles in Tiananmen or who were arrested in the subsequent crackdown, included Liu Xiaobo, Bao Zunxin, Jin Guantao, Li Honglin, Yu Haocheng, and Wang Ruoshui. *The Chinese Intellectual*, long published overseas, produced its first domestic issue in January 1989, also as a book series.

Other constituents of a nascent civil society that was gradually working itself loose from effective CCP control were the Stone Group Corporation and its Institute of Social Development, the Beijing Social and Economic Research Institute (SERI), the Capital Steel Research Institute, and the Happiness Bookstore. These institutions had somewhat ambiguous relationships to the CCP. Most of them were nominally "hung" *(gua)* from some part of the CCP organizational network, but they operated independently. The same was true of some institutions that the party itself had established, such as the Economic System Reform Institute, the Rural Development Research Institute, some institutes of the Chinese Academy of Social Sciences, and some sections of the China International Trust and Investment Corporation. Politically-oriented intellectuals used these institutions as bases from which to test the bounds of tolerance more and more adventurously.

The regime was confronting the beginnings of a "desertion of the intellectuals," against a backdrop of rising inflation and corruption, the abortion of price reform, and the ever more intense, long-standing succession conflict.[20] Deng Xiaoping and Beijing Mayor Chen Xitong were not entirely wrong in attributing the origins of the "turmoil and rebellion" to the sharp challenge to the ethos of the regime presented by intellectuals using increasingly sophisticated tactics. But their analysis of events turned into a self-fulfilling prophecy. By proclaiming the intellectuals' democratic socialism to be nonsocialist, Deng set up a head-on conflict with the intellectuals who would have preferred to work within the system.

On January 6, 1989, Fang Lizhi wrote an open letter to Deng calling for the release of political prisoners, including Wei Jingsheng, to mark the upcoming 40th anniversary of the PRC. Thirty-three noted intellectuals followed with a letter of support on February 16. Also in February, 42 leading Beijing scientists joined the call for the release of "youth imprisoned or sent to labor reform for ideological problems." And in March, 43 writers and theorists called on the NPC to grant amnesty to Wei Jingsheng and others.[21] A young democratic activist named Chen Jun, who had links with China Spring, was planning to use the scheduled April 1989 meeting of the National People's Congress to submit "A Report on Amnesty '89," amidst much publicity, which he was skilled in generating. Petition campaigns in Hong Kong, France, and the United States were launched in support of the amnesty request. A shift of many of China's most prestigious intellectuals to a pro-Wei position ten years after his arrest signalled how far the conflict between the regime and the intellectuals had developed.

The intellectuals' impertinence annoyed Deng. He was confronted with a coalescing group of influential nonparty and party intellectuals, informally linked to the hated China Spring, who were conducting a sophisticated international publicity campaign around an issue that was divisive within the regime and embar-

182

rassing to him personally. To hold firm would look churlish; to yield would legitimize an independent opposition. The regime felt trapped and its responses revealed as much. The regime declared the call for an amnesty illegal, clumsily blocked Fang Lizhi from attending the banquet to which President George Bush had invited him, confiscated an international petition to the NPC delivered from Hong Kong in support of the amnesty drive on the grounds that it was propaganda, and used a weak pretext to expel Chen Jun from the country. Not only were these responses ineffective, they tarnished the regime's international image.

The student movement thus emerged against the background of a general crisis in the regime and a specific crisis in relations between the regime and the intellectuals. But in rhetoric, tactics, and demands, the students at first avoided pressing their advantage too aggressively. They positioned themselves within the established tradition of moderate democratic remonstrance. They cast themselves not as dissidents but as loyal followers, appealing to the authorities to live up to the values they themselves had articulated. The purpose of the hunger strike, which was symbolically undertaken in front of the Mao Mausoleum, in the shadow of the monument to the martyrs of the communist revolution, was to force the leaders to recognize the movement as being patriotic. The message was that the students valued the welfare of the state above their own lives. It was thoroughly in the tradition of Qu Yuan, who had lived in the fourth century B. C., and who committed suicide to show his loyalty to the ruler who failed to heed his advice. Indeed, Qu probably represented a more influential precedent for the opposition's tactics of nonviolence than the examples of Mahatma Gandhi, Martin Luther King, or Corazon Aquino, so often mentioned in the Western media.

The students' demands followed the logic of two decades of Chinese democratic activism. Absolute power corrupts, and a good socialist government must allow itself to be supervised by the people. The demonstrators asked that the Chinese government recognize popular sovereignty and political rights that are guaranteed by the PRC constitution. They carried signs that read "We firmly support the correct leadership of the Chinese Communist Party" and "The people love the people's police."[22] They demanded that the government end corruption, overcome bureaucratism, promote reform, and improve education. In effect they paraphrased the words of the regime's spokesmen.

The two key demands were for a free press and for dialogue—
the latter implying recognition by the authorities of the students'
autonomous organizations. By a free press, the demonstrators did
not mean entrepreneurial, commercial, unregulated mass media
that compete for readers and live off advertising, but simply a press
that reports the truth. Except for such experiments as the *World
Economic Herald*, in the spring of 1989 most Chinese media remained under the effective direct or indirect control of the CCP's
Propaganda Department or its local bureaus. What was published
or broadcast remained determined by the policy needs of the party,
although Chinese journalists have long argued that both the people
and the regime would be better served if journalists had the authority to publish what they knew to be true. Because corruption
and special privilege are among the features of the communist
system that most alienate the people, the students and the professional journalists who later joined them argued that a truthful
press would be the best mechanism for cleaning up, and hence
saving, the regime.

A draft press law defining the professional rights and responsibilities of Chinese journalists has been undergoing revision for
years. According to some reports, the law was finally scheduled for
enactment in late 1989.[23] The provisions of this law had been sharply
debated, but even a relatively conservative version would have
gone a long way toward meeting the demands of the demonstrators. The government needed only to have made some final revi-
sions and handed the draft to the NPC to enact. But this possibility
was overtaken by events.

The second key demand—for dialogue—was also ostensibly
compatible with the regime's own logic. As part of its political
reform, the government had promoted the development of the nine
minority democratic parties and increased its practice of "democratic consultation" through the Chinese People's Political Consultative Conference and informal forums with "democratic personages." It was a CCP tradition for leaders to go to work units and
solicit the people's opinions. In the course of Deng's reforms the
party had re-established a system of offices for "letters and visits
work" to which individuals could come with complaints. On April
4, 1989, the National People's Congress passed an Administrative
Proceedings Law, which enabled citizens to take government organs to court to protect their rights.[24] Accordingly, the students'

demand for dialogue received widespread support, including from school administrators and political hacks, and from the official trade union federation.[25]

The regime attempted to respond on its own terms to the demand for dialogue. Cabinet spokesman Yuan Mu received a student delegation for a nationally televised discussion on April 29. Li Peng held talks with student leaders on May 18. United Front Work Department director Yan Mingfu and other party leaders went to Tiananmen Square to speak with hunger-strikers. And finally, in his May 19 speech announcing the imposition of martial law, Li Peng emphasized that "dialogue between the party and government on the one hand, and the broad [masses of] students and personages of various circles on the other, including dialogue with students who have participated in parades, demonstrations, classroom strikes, and hunger strikes, will still be actively continued at many levels, through many channels, and in many forms, in order fully to hear opinions from various quarters."[26]

However, the dialogue that the authorities had already engaged in as well as the type of dialogue they promised in the future was not what the students demanded. The government attempted to treat its encounters with the students as opportunities to feel the public pulse without decentralizing power. Yuan Mu and Li Peng acted as hosts and as authority figures, avuncularly urging the students to return to classes, defending the government's position, and delivering threats. The students in turn stated that such encounters were unsatisfactory and acted out their dissatisfaction by behaving impolitely at the meetings. They demanded that the two parties be placed on an equal footing, that the government's representatives in the dialogue be of high rank, that observers and reporters be present, and that the government give prompt responses to the students' questions. The students also demanded that their representatives be elected by autonomous student groups distinct from the puppet student unions established under party sponsorship.[27]

Here was the Trojan horse that the regime could not accept. Had this demand been granted, the students would have achieved the legalization of the first completely independent political organization in PRC history, and the effective negation of Deng Xiaoping's four basic principles, as Deng understood them. This demand explains why Deng had early on "determined [the student movement's] nature" (*dingxing*) to be "a planned plot, a turmoil, whose essence is to negate fundamentally CCP leadership and the socialist system."[28]

The Chinese leaders have been obsessed since 1956 with what they see as the deterioration of the Leninist system in Poland and Hungary. In this connection, the formation of a "Capital Autonomous Workers' Association" during the demonstrations was a particularly alarming development. Although it was a tiny group, its existence evoked the specter of a Chinese "Solidarity." Leaders of this group were arrested even before the general crackdown of June 4.[29] As Li Peng told the other leaders shortly after declaring martial law: "There was no way out. You give a step, they advance a step; you retreat two steps, they advance two steps. It had gotten to the point where there was nowhere else to retreat. If we were going to retreat any further, we might as well have handed China over to those people."[30] The leaders preferred military repression to seeing China become another Poland.

Chen Xitong, in the regime's most thorough indictment of the democrats to date, contends that the democratic movement wanted to achieve the violent overthrow of the government.[31] The regime needed to portray the spontaneous, uncoordinated acts of defensive violence by people throughout the city of Beijing on the night of June 3, when the troops moved in, as part of a coordinated plan in order to justify calling the democrats' activities a "counter-revolutionary rebellion." Chen quoted some unsigned leaflets as calling for the use of violence to overthrow the CCP, but he was unable to name the organizations or individuals responsible for them. Nor could he find direct quotes from any specific democratic activist calling for the overthrow of the party or the use of violence. Chen could only find personal attacks on Deng and Li Peng, criticisms of the Chinese socialist system, and appeals for thorough-going reform.

The only exception, one worth pausing over, is Chen's charge against literary theorist Liu Xiaobo, who was arrested after June 4 and is believed to be in danger of receiving a heavy sentence for his activities.[32] Liu was one of four intellectuals who began a 48–72 hour hunger strike on June 2. Chen accused Liu of membership in China Spring and quoted him as having stated in a published interview: "We must organize an armed force among the people to effect Zhao Ziyang's comeback." But an investigation by a Chinese-language news magazine in New York has established that these words were a mistranslation. The interview was conducted by telephone in Chinese, but the transcript was prepared in English in New York by the activist Chen Jun, for publication in the West. Chen provided a copy of the transcript to the *Independence Evening News* of Taiwan, which translated a statement by Liu to the effect that all social forces must be mobilized back into Chinese as "armed forces in society must be organized." The text was reprinted in Hong Kong and from there picked up by Chinese intelligence and quoted by Mayor Chen.[33] These facts are important not only because they may affect Liu Xiaobo's fate, but also because they confirm the nonviolent character of the democratic movement even after the declaration of martial law.

After the June 4 killings and the subsequent wave of arrests, many intellectuals broke completely with what they call the Deng-Li Peng-Yang Shangkun regime. Liu Binyan, who was often criticized by younger intellectuals after he was purged from the CCP because he continued to express hope in the communist party, has denounced the regime and predicts its fall within two years.[34] This attitude is widespread. But the loss of hope in the Deng regime has not brought with it a break in the moderate, remonstrative tradition of Chinese democracy. The opposition has stopped short of calls for either the use of violence or the overthrow of the CCP.

The official press has taken pains to present the post-June 4 democratic movement in exile as consisting of revolutionaries who seek to overthrow the Chinese government by armed action. This assertion is made to legitimate condemning the movement's foreign support as interference in China's internal affairs, and hence a violation of international law.[35] However, these charges can only be made plausible by selective quotation and quotation out of context. No major democratic organization in exile so far has called for either armed rebellion or terrorism, or, for that matter, for the overthrow of the CCP.

Yan Jiaqi, who has emerged as the main spokesman of the democratic exiles, has predicted that Deng Xiaoping, Li Peng, and Yang Shangkun will "reap the storm" that their violence has sown and will be publicly tried for their crimes.[36] However, such statements merely describe the fragility of a coercive regime, and do not constitute a call for violence or a declaration of anti-socialism. The program of the Democratic Chinese Alliance (*Minzhu Zhongguo zhenxian*), which Yan established with Uerkesh Daolet (Wuerkaixi), Liu Binyan, Su Shaozhi, and Wan Runnan in Paris on July 20, makes "reason, peace, and nonviolence our standards for action" and "freedom, democracy, rule of law, and human rights" its goals.[37] The organization's strategy, according to Yan, envisages four stages. First will occur the inevitable fall of Li Peng, which will come about through his own weakness and unpopularity at home and abroad; second, the alliance will press for reversal of the verdict on the democratic movement; then, its members will return home to participate in revising the constitution so as to establish an open, pluralistic political system similar to the ones that the Soviet Union, Poland, and Hungary are now moving to establish; and finally, it will work to establish a federal system in China within which the Hong Kong, Taiwan, and Tibet problems will be amenable to resolution. At the end of this process, the CCP will be competing peacefully in elections with the Kuomintang and the Democratic Alliance. Yan estimates that the entire process will take 10 years or longer.[38] He argues that democracy cannot be achieved by violent means and that the democracy movement itself must begin the democratization process, by relying on dialogue and the power of ideas rather than on force.

The Association of Chinese Students and Scholars in the United States established itself in Chicago in late July 1989 on a platform of moderation. It is a loosely organized liaison group rather than a political movement or party. It intends to work for democratization chiefly through the dissemination of information to China. As citizens of the PRC, its members seek to maintain normal relations with China's officials and missions abroad.[39]

Even the organization that the Beijing authorities deem the most radical and dangerous, the Chinese Alliance for Democracy or China Spring, has not crossed the line separating reformism from revolution. At its Fourth National Congress, held in Los Angeles from June 23–26, 1989, China Spring debated a motion to include "overthrow of the Chinese Communist Party in its constitution." It also examined a proposal to abandon exclusive reliance on nonviolent tactics in favor of "revolutionary" methods, which included the formation of suicide squads to conduct "secret armed struggle on the mainland" and the use of terrorism abroad against PRC officials and their children in order to deter the authorities from arresting and executing leaders of the democratic movement. Both of these proposals were rejected.[40]

To say that the major dissident organizations in exile have eschewed anti-communism and the use of violence is not to say that

188

these issues are not debated among exile democrats,[41] or that there is no armed resistance in China or assistance for it from abroad. Scattered shooting has been reported in Beijing, a train wreck occurred that might have been due to sabotage, some democratic movement leaders have been spirited out of the country, and others have somehow found ways to evade capture. Money is being collected by individual activists abroad for unspecified purposes and some individual Chinese do speak of the need to resort to violence. It is hard to gauge the prevalence and impact of such activities, which are by nature secretive, and obviously the advocacy and use of violence may increase. But so far, violence remains a minor thread in the movement as a whole, and it is not publicly advocated by any major democratic organization.

Regime Monopoly of Force

Besides intellectual reasons for nonviolence, practical concerns have dictated a nonviolent approach as well. The regime still controls overwhelming military and police force, and recent events have confirmed the importance of this factor. The events of June showed that the instruments of proletarian dictatorship—the least-mentioned but perhaps the most important of Deng's four cardinal principles—are still firmly in the hands of the senior leaders. It is hard to say whether their control is due to ordinary military discipline, the effectiveness of the political commissar system, or the reinforcement of the control system with personal networks. Whatever the reason, the army and police forces have stood firmly with the regime.

Their support explains why it would be unrealistic for the democratic movement to take to the hills as Mao did in the 1930s. Conditions today are very different from those encountered by the Jiangxi Soviet when it faced Chiang Kai-shek's army. The total Nationalist forces were less than half the size of the PLA today, and much more poorly trained and armed. Chiang Kai-shek controlled only about one-fifth of the Nationalist Government's military forces, and he controlled even those forces through factional allies rather than directly. Chiang had to allocate proportionally more military resources to national defense than the PLA does today and had correspondingly fewer resources to spare for internal security. Communications and transport were primitive and the Soviet Union was willing to help the insurgents. Despite all these advantages, the CCP barely survived Chiang's extermination campaigns of the early 1930s.[42]

The democrats say that if violence is to play a role in China's future, it will have to come from within the Chinese military and not from the democratic movement abroad or the democratic underground in China. In a debate over the use of violence at the recent Fourth Congress of the China Spring, Chairperson Hu Ping stated: "When the 'Gang of Four' was arrested in 1976, this certainly wasn't a peaceful change, but nobody complained about it. If somebody comes forward now to arrest the group of people who are holding power, there certainly won't be anyone to complain that they did not use peaceful methods. . . . However, our organization does not have the power to carry out a military coup."[43] According to Wan Runnan of the Chinese Democratic Alliance: "Our principle of nonviolence doesn't mean that no blood will flow. There is a division of roles. Our role is to carry out activities that are peaceful, rational, and nonviolent. But others will play other roles."[44]

With violence ruled out as an option, nonviolence and support for socialism offer the best possibility of building a broad anti-regime coalition and maximizing official and unofficial foreign support. As a China Spring leader stated during the Fourth Congress debate, "only the flag of peaceful methods can get wide popular acceptance. . . . If anybody here asks me for money for guns [to use against the communists], I would certainly claim to be giving you the guns to use for hunting birds."[45]

Social Composition of the Movement

The last factor that has argued for peaceful methods is the social composition of the democratic movement. The demonstrators in Beijing and other cities this spring were overwhelmingly urbanites (*shimin*)—students, peddlers, office workers, teachers, shop and factory workers. In exile, the class basis of the movement has become even narrower. It is now composed almost exclusively of students and intellectuals and a few ex-officials, with financial support from overseas Chinese in Hong Kong and elsewhere (including Taiwan). The intellectuals are in no position to take up arms without the support of other classes, if only because their numbers are so small—less than half of 1 percent of the Chinese population is college-educated.[46]

It is difficult to imagine an insurrection in China that is not based in the countryside. So far as I know, the democratic movement did not enjoy much active support in the rural areas. The rural dwellers may have lacked information about the democratic movement; if they participated in it, they would not have enjoyed the same anonymity as did urban crowds; they were busy earning a living; and, perhaps most importantly, although the farmers were dissatisfied with the regime, they have not been as severely affected by inflation as urban dwellers and have greater possibilities for making do economically. As Wan Runnan has said, "When the economy worsens, the peasants will suffer. This is what is needed to change their political stance. For now, they still hope to muddle through; they still think they can make it."[47]

Of course, the social makeup of the countryside is becoming increasingly complex. Rural dwellers include not only farmers but also industrial workers, shop clerks, peddlers, fishermen, teachers, monks, and local officials. Members of some of these groups have evidently been willing to help the democratic activists go underground or escape. But this scattered assistance does not provide the critical mass for a peasant uprising.

Conclusion

Although the democratic movement has maintained its tradition of moderation, a fundamental conflict over the nature of socialism in China reached a climax in 1989. Mikhail Gorbachev was so popular with the Chinese demonstrators not because he was seen, as so many Americans see him, as leading a retreat from socialism, but because the Chinese saw him as symbolizing the hope that a communist regime can permit a free press, a dialogue with society, and an independent political opposition, and can thrive under the stimulus of such challenges. Deng and the surviving senior revolutionaries, by contrast, have remained orthodox Stalinists on the question of power. To Deng, "the key point is that [the demonstrators] wanted to overthrow our state and the party. Failing to understand this means failing to understand the nature of the matter. . . . Their goal was to establish a bourgeois republic entirely dependent on the West."[48]

Deng has a point: if his four principles are the standard of true socialism, then the democrats did want to overthrow the socialist system. If open, competitive democracy and political freedom are the monopoly of the bourgeoisie, they did want to establish a bourgeois republic. If the exercise of free speech that is guaranteed by the Chinese constitution is illegal, then the students and intellectuals denounced by Chen Xitong did commit subversion. But the democrats continue to see their relation to the regime differently. In the words of the biographer of China's first remonstrator, Qu Yuan: "It was his fate to be faithful and yet doubted, to be loyal and yet suffer slander—can one bear this without anger?"[49]

ELEVEN

Conclusion: Prospects for Chinese Democracy

The Chinese communist regime has always claimed that the kind of democracy China already has is, in the words of Deng Xiaoping, the "broadest democracy that has ever existed in history," and that Western-style "bourgeois democracy" is not worth having anyway. But a contradictory theme lies beneath the surface of such defensive rhetoric. Deng has often argued that China's "national conditions" (*guoqing*)—a code word for backwardness—do not allow the country to have as much democracy as it would like. "In our construction today," he said in 1979, explaining why China must adhere to the four basic principles, "we must do things in accordance with Chinese conditions and find a Chinese-style path to modernization. . . . Departure from the four basic principles and talk about democracy in the abstract will inevitably lead to the unchecked spread of ultra-democracy and anarchism." To George Bush in February 1989, just before the Chinese government interfered with Fang Lizhi's attendance at the U.S. President's banquet, Deng said, "If we were to run elections among China's one billion people now, chaos . . . would certainly ensue. . . . Democracy is our goal, but the state must maintain stability."[1]

People's Daily gave the backwardness argument full Marxist form after the repression of the democratic movement:

> Some students and members of the masses blindly worshipped the Western democratic system and imagined that we could bring the Western general election or parliamentary systems into China as easily as imported factory machinery. These were unrealistic fantasies. From a Marxist viewpoint, the democratic system is part of the superstructure and is constantly limited by the economic base and other aspects of the superstructure. In no way can it exist or develop in isolation from the material and cultural conditions of society. . . . [In our country,] the economy and cul-

193

ture are quite backward; history has given us little democratic tradition; the influence of feudal ideology is very deep; and many people have a superficial understanding of law and democracy. These national conditions (*guoqing*) determine the fact that the establishment of socialist democratic politics can only be a gradual, step-by-step process.

Driving the point home with a phrase from the classics, the author concluded that people who try to accelerate the growth of democracy in China are like the famous simpleton in Mencius, who tried to help the wheat grow by pulling up the shoots.[2]

The events of 1989 raise the question of whether this self-critical view of Chinese national character, which is widespread among Chinese of all political persuasions, has become outdated. After nearly a century of struggling for democracy, have the Chinese created the conditions for it? How might the transition occur? What would Chinese democracy be like?

The theme of China's backwardness as a limit on democracy is as old as the Chinese desire for democracy,[3] and in the beginning it may have been justified. In the country's first elections, held in 1909 for provincial assemblies, voters had little idea what sort of body was being chosen, and they bought and sold votes openly, even though only the wealthiest and best educated .25 percent of the population were enfranchised. Several years later, after the Republic had been established, when 10 percent of the population were allowed to vote for electoral colleges who were to chose delegates to the national parliament, hired thugs stuffed purchased ballots into voting boxes in wads of a hundred or more, fistfights broke out at the voting places, and ballots were stolen. Five years later, in 1918, another parliamentary election was held with a smaller, more elite, franchise; this time, according to a British observer, "The quotations for votes and the daily market fluctuations were chronicled in the native press as that of a marketable commodity, on the same footing as rice or beancake or other articles of commerce."[4]

In the early twentieth century China had no radio or television. The printed press reached an audience estimated at 1 percent of the population. As late 1952, shortly after the PRC was established, China had only about 14,000 miles of railway and 80,000 miles of highway; its post office handled an average of one and one half letters per person per year, and the country had a total of about 350,000 telephones for over 500 million people.[5] The 1964 national census uncovered an illiteracy rate of 38.1 percent.[6] Land reform teams entering the villages encountered peasants who were surprised to hear that the Manchu emperor was no longer their ruler.

China today, however, although poor, is in many ways quite developed, as I suggested in chapter 7. GNP per capita in 1980 was already above the level found in the three poorest stable democracies of the 1970s. If the goal of quadrupling national income by the year 2000 is achieved, GNP per capita will match or exceed the level enjoyed by the eight poorest democracies in the early 1970s (India, Sri Lanka, the Philippines, Turkey, Costa Rica, Jamaica, Chile, and Uruguay in ascending order of wealth).[7] China is far more industrialized than the other poor and lower-middle income countries as measured by the proportion of gross domestic product attributable to industry (nearly 50 percent).[8] China's urbanites constitute 12 to 32 percent of the population, depending on the definition used.[9] Even the higher of these figures understates the mobility and sophistication of the populace, because tens of millions of peasants go the cities and small towns to do short-term business or to live for years, and the countryside itself is for the most part densely populated, crisscrossed with boat and bus routes, closely tied into the national administrative system, and active in a commercial network that extends in many cases into the international market.

Most of China's villages have schools, however rudimentary. The level of literacy in the 1982 census was as high or higher than that of India and Turkey.[10] In 1985 the government extended compulsory education to nine years, which when gradually implemented should further increase the average level of education. Mass communication in the form of wired loudspeakers, radio, television, and newspapers penetrates into virtually every village and effectively reaches illiterates and people living on deserts, steppes, and rivers.[11]

Social scientists have identified no absolute threshold of development required to qualify a people for democracy, but China is now clearly above the minimum level in simple economic terms and far above it in social development and communication facilities.[12] In addition, despite increasing polarization of wealth in recent years, China still has a relatively equitable distribution, which is generally considered a helpful condition for democracy. It has strong police and military institutions, which are as necessary in a democracy as in a dictatorship to keep the peace.

Chinese doubts about their own capacity for democracy, however, center not on communications facilities or literacy but on political culture. The popular 1988 television series *River Elegy*, described in chapter 7, typified this view. It argued that China's ancient, peasant-based civilization would doom it to poverty and autocracy until it was replaced by a modern culture. "This broad yellow earth of ours cannot teach us what is the true spirit of science; the devastating Yellow River cannot teach us what is the true mentality of democracy," the narrator states. China is an example of Marx's "Asiatic mode of production."

> Myriad unmentionably insignificant individuals, ranked and amalgamated into a unity by a certain order, bearing up that ultimate supreme entity—doesn't this monolithic social structure resemble a massive pyramid? Therefore such things as democracy, freedom and equality could hardly come to belong to an 'Asiatic' [civilization like China].

According to Su Xiaokang, the main author of the screenplay, "What is needed is a reconstruction of the Chinese people's cultural-psychological structure." [13]

After the suppression of the democracy movement, *People's Daily* denounced *River Elegy* for insulting the Chinese people and belittling their achievements under socialism.[14] Yet the view of national character as the seedbed of dictatorship was shared by the regime. For example, the party's official inquest into the Mao era, published in 1981, laid the blame for Mao's errors mainly on the national characteristic of feudalism:

> Our party fought in the firmest and most thoroughgoing way against [feudalism], and particularly against the feudal system of land ownership and the landlords and local tyrants, and fostered a fine tradition of democracy in the anti-feudal struggle. But it remains difficult to eliminate the evil ideological and political influence of centuries of feudal autocracy. .... This meant that conditions were present for the overconcentration of party power in individuals and for the development of arbitrary individual rule and the personality cult in the Party. Thus, it was hard for the Party and state to prevent the initiation of the "cultural revolution" or check its development.[15]

In placing the responsibility for authoritarianism on Chinese national character, both the party and the democratic intellectuals transferred much of the onus for an acknowledged catastrophe

196

from the shoulders of those who wrought it to the backs of those who suffered it. They perpetuated the belief that the Chinese people need to undergo a transformation before they will be qualified for democracy. What outraged the party elders about *River Elegy* was not its pessimism about Chinese culture; it was its writers' intrusion on the Party's self-assigned mission of enlightening the Chinese people, as well as the Westernizing character of the enlightenment they wanted to offer.

No one has ever drawn up an authoritative list of cultural requirements for democracy. One scholar argues that democracy requires widespread acceptance of such values as dignity, autonomy, and respect for persons; belief in individual rights; trust, tolerance, and willingness to compromise; commitment to democratic procedures and values; public spirit; and nationalism, among others.[16] An influential study of the political cultures of five democracies identified a number of attributes that are helpful for stable democracy, including a relatively high degree of consensus on some basic political values (including nationalism, modernization, and the desire for order); widespread acceptance of the present constitutional order as legitimate; and a certain degree of alienation from politics which reduces expectations directed at the political system.[17]

The Beijing demonstrations of 1989 put many of these attributes on display. The people of Beijing evidently desire democracy and freedom. They are nationalistic and concerned about politics. They are wary of government. They showed a capacity for public spiritedness, spontaneous public order, and tolerance.

These are only impressions, but some scientific evidence exists to support them. In December 1988, four months before the Tiananmen Square demonstrations, a pilot study for a national scientific sample survey was conducted in Beijing by Shi Tianjian, a Columbia University graduate student. The study was designed, among other purposes, to collect the first set of reliable data on the political attitudes of Chinese citizens.[18] In the pilot study, Shi's respondents showed extremely high levels of attention to political news in newspapers and on radio and television. Seventy-seven percent of the respondents said they were interested in politics.

The respondents demonstrated strong aspirations for more democracy. In a question on the role that the National People's Congress ought to play, 65 percent felt it should either "convey the masses' opinions to the government" or "set laws and represent the citizens in supervising government," while only small numbers assigned it more passive roles or felt unable to comment. Seventy-two percent agreed with the statement that "democracy is the best form of government" and 79 percent disagreed with the proposition, "If we implement democracy in our country now it will lead to chaos." Sixty-two percent disagreed with the statement, "A country can't be run well if it has too many political parties," and 55 percent did not agree that "If people's thinking isn't unified, society will be turbulent." At the same time, the questionnaire revealed a reservoir of trust in the government; for example, nearly half the respondents said they would expect to receive fair treatment if they sought the help of a government organ.

Political culture is best understood as a distribution of attitudes and values among a national population, and the population of Beijing is untypical of China. Seventy-eight per cent of Shi's respondents were employees of government organs or state-owned enterprises, among the most privileged and politically sophisticated Chinese. Studies in many countries have shown that some democratic values like knowledge of and interest in politics, tolerance, and political self-confidence vary with, among other things, class, education, age, and gender.[19] In China, we might expect peasants to be less interested in politics and more impatient with democratic procedures than urban residents; small individual enterpreneurs to be more impatient with government bureaucracy than factory workers, and so on. Shi Tianjian's national survey, scheduled to take place in July 1989, was designed to test hypotheses like these. It would have shown whether the political culture of the vast majority of Chinese is really as unsuited to democracy as so many Chinese intellectuals believe, and it would have identified those segments of the population more and less hospitable to democratic modes of poltitics. However, the national survey did not go off on schedule because of political events.

So far as I know, only one survey has been publicly reported which serves to supplement Shi's figures with nationwide data, a study conducted in 1987 by the Group for the Investigation and Study of the Political Psychology of Chinese Citizens. The scientific quality of the sample is not clear and the published report does not provide breakdowns by population sectors. In this survey, high percentages of citizens expressed pride in living in a socialist country and supported the notion that the party should take the lead in all things. At the same time, 94 percent of the respondents felt that

198

"every person has a share of responsibility for the fate of the country," 58 percent agreed with the statement "China now has a certain amount of democracy, which needs to be further perfected," and a strong majority believed that people should be permitted to speak up when the party makes mistakes.[20]

The picture created by the two surveys together and by the events in Beijing is that the Chinese people are proud of their country, have a strong sense of political interest and knowledge, and retain considerable faith in socialism and the Communist Party. They strongly desire more freedom and democracy, although their ideas of democracy are not very specific, are cynical about how much their own voices count in their local unit or in politics generally, and are normally reluctant to buck the system by demonstrating or appealing vigorously for their rights when these are abused. This pattern of attitudes combines elements of what have been described as "aspirant" and "deferential" political cultures. If these attributes characterize Chinese political culture, they bode well for the functioning of a future democratic politics in China.[21]

The major cleavage in Chinese political culture today may not be between the advanced intellectuals and the backward masses, but between a people ready for more freedom and political leaders afraid to grant it. Zhao Fusan, vice president of the Chinese Academy of Social Sciences, suggested that China is now "torn between two cultures. . . . The leadership class is locked in China's traditional culture—a kind of benevolent despotism. Young people, however, have become Westernized and dream of dialogue."[22]

Democracy has been defined as a system of institutionalized uncertainty; and "it is the act of alienation of control over outcomes of conflicts that constitutes the decisive step toward democracy."[23] Such a transition begins when the ruling elite, or a substantial section within it, perceives that the potential advantages of giving up some control over outcomes outweigh the risks. To identify the conditions under which this may happen in China, it may be useful to look at democratizing transitions in the Soviet Union and Taiwan, neighboring systems that are similar to China, although in different ways.

In the Soviet Union, even though economic reform lags behind that in China, political reform is more advanced. To be sure, one reason for the contrast is that the Soviet Union stands at a higher level of social and political development than China. The Soviet population is predominantly urban. The great majority of Soviet

199

citizens have at least some secondary education. Since the death of Stalin, Soviet citizens have had regular experience of participating in political campaigns and volunteer community organizations. Even though there was no real political competition, these activities gave the Soviet population a high level of political knowledge. The development of Soviet society more closely resembles that of the East Asian NICs like Taiwan or South Korea than that of mainland China. Although the Soviet people were not actively clamoring for democracy when Gorbachev came to power in 1985, they were ready for a relaxation of authoritarianism.

The key to the difference between Soviet and Chinese political reform, however, lies in the different calculations of each leadership about how much political change was necessary to achieve economic reform in its country. Both Gorbachev and Deng were motivated to reform primarily by their countries' economic backwardness. But the case for economic reform in the Soviet Union was not as clearcut as it was in China. In China, at the beginning of the reform period agriculture was stagnant, industrial productivity was low, and the people's living standards had not increased in twenty years. There was virtually total political consensus on the need for economic reform, even though opinions differed as to the specific nature of the reforms needed. With only a small amount of political opening-up, Deng was able to create enough political pressure to persuade the party leaders to go ahead with reform. Because of the low starting point of the reform, relatively simple reform measures brought rapid gains in output and living standards. This constant advance helped Deng to consolidate and maintain support for reform among both the people and the leaders for ten years. Even in 1989, when the far-reaching, and from the leadership's viewpoint negative, political and social consequences of reform stood fully revealed, there appeared to be no important voice calling for abandonment of economic reform, because there seemed to be no other way out for China.

By contrast, the Soviet Union, although facing an economic slump when Gorbachev came to power, had the second largest economy in the world. It was the world's second military superpower. Its people, especially the white-collar and industrial workers, enjoyed a fairly high standard of living. All segments of the Soviet population, not only the bureaucracy, were initially resistant to reform. Gorbachev, unlike Deng, enjoyed no ready-made consensus on the need for reform; he was more radical than most of his people.

Under Deng there was no attractive argument for solving China's problems by reverting to a neo-Stalinist planned system, because the infrastructure for a proper planned economy had never been built. In the Soviet Union, where the planning apparatus was much bigger and worked better than the Chinese planning bureaucracy ever had, economic conservatives were able to argue that the answer to the flaws of planning was more and better planning. Moroever, the planning apparatus in the Soviet Union is a major bureaucratic constituency with political influence, while that in China is small and weak. In China, popular resistance to reform was gradually generated by inflation and corruption, but in the Soviet Union it was generated as soon as reform began by the effort to make people work harder. In the Soviet Union, there was no sector of the economy where resources were so badly underutilized as to make possible a rapid spurt of growth that could purchase support for reform among skeptical sections of the population.

Gorbachev's strategy was to use political reform to generate support for economic reform. He offered a reform package that sweetened measures of economic reform the public viewed skeptically with measures of political relaxation that they liked. He encouraged a pro-reform minority in the party and in the public to express its opinions vociferously and to create a somewhat illusory appearance of public demand for reform. Unable to find quick economic payoffs to consolidate the pro-reform forces, Gorbachev has had to continue with ever more risky measures of political liberalization to keep up the pressure for economic reform on a recalcitrant bureaucracy and ambivalent working class.

In short, it was precisely because the Maoist experience was economically much more disastrous than that under Stalin, Khrushchev and Brezhnev that post-Mao economic reform has required less innovative political coalition-building than post-Brezhnev reform. Even so, the Chinese leaders did see significant disadvantages in reform, as I argued in chapter 3. But their economic situation was so parlous that they saw no choice but to risk those disadvantages; they are now paying the price that they feared but still see no alternative to maintaining most of the reform policies. Gorbachev's reform strategy entails even greater and more direct risks because he has to reach outside the party for support. Nonetheless, it is only by taking these risks that Gorbachev sees a chance to rescue the Soviet economy from stagnation.

In Taiwan, as described in chapter 8, Chiang Ching-kuo also took risks in embarking on political reform in 1986. Taiwan, like the Soviet Union, had reached a high level of economic and social development and had a highly educated and politically sophisticated public. These conditions created a demand for political reform. But Chiang's decision to shift from slow liberalization to more rapid and fundamental democratization was based on the calculation that it was worth taking the chance of losing control over the pace of change in order to improve his regime's ability to deal with threats to its international survival and internal stability.

Internationally, in the early 1980s Taiwan was becoming increasingly isolated and seemed to have no effective way to respond. The PRC's peaceful unification offensive, described in chapter 9, had placed Taiwan's diplomacy on the defensive. In 1982 President Ronald Reagan, viewed by Taiwan as a staunch friend, agreed to a joint communique with the PRC committing the U.S. gradually to reduce arms sales to Taiwan. Taiwan's major ally in Asia, South Korea, showed increasing interest in establishing ties with Beijing. In early 1986 Beijing gained admission to the Asian Development Bank, presenting Taiwan with the riddle of how to maintain its own participation without accepting the status of a local government.

At home, a series of incidents suggested that the ruling party and the security apparatus were becoming inbred and complacent. Relatives of a jailed opposition leader were murdered in 1980 (the murder has never been solved); a visiting Taiwanese-American professor died in police custody in 1981; and in 1984 Taiwanese gangsters in California assassinated a U.S. citizen, Henry Liu, who had written a controversial biography of Chiang Ching-kuo. During the assassins' American trial the following year it was revealed to the embarrassment of the ROC government that the assassination had been ordered by its chief of military intelligence. Also in 1985 the financial collapse of the large Tenth Credit Cooperative and the related Cathay investment company was linked to government officials, leading to the resignation of the Minister of Finance. All these developments caused a loss of international prestige that the regime could ill afford, and fed popular support for the opposition. The opposition criticized the ruling KMT more and more aggressively in the press and in the Legislative Yuan. The Garrison Command responded by using its martial law powers to ban many opposition magazines, which made the regime increasingly unpopular. Against this background it was not certain the KMT could perform well in important national elections scheduled for December 1986.

The most serious threat, however, came from the unsettled succession. President Chiang turned 70 in 1979 and suffered from diabetes. In the mid-1980s he was visibly weakened, making fewer public appearances, going out in a wheelchair, and limiting himself to short speeches. His heir apparent, the popular and able Prime Minister Sun Yun-hsuan, suffered a cerebral hemorrhage in 1984. As matters stood, the ability of Chiang's successor to consolidate power and to take initiatives to solve the country's problems would be hampered by conservative party elders and by the powerful mainlander-dominated military and security bureaucracies, groups that all retained much power.

In the 1980s Chiang Ching-kuo began to make succession arrangements, and political reform became part of them. In 1983, he demoted the second most powerful man in his regime, Wang Sheng, head of the military's political warfare department, to the post of Ambassador to Paraguay. The following year he chose Lee Teng-hui, a native Taiwanese, as his Vice President and constitutional successor should he die in office. He appointed several new Taiwanese members to the ruling party's Central Standing Committee. He removed his son, Chiang Hsiao-wu, a potential dynastic successor, from the political scene by sending him to a diplomatic post in Singapore. On the Republic of China's Constitution Day in 1985, Chiang placed his personal prestige strongly behind a constitutional succession, stating that the succession must be handled according to the constitution, and that so far as he was concerned neither a military man nor a member of his own family could conceivably succeed him in office.[24]

While providing his successor with political resources to consolidate power, by initiating reforms Chiang also endowed the new leader with needed flexibility in policy matters. As probably the last mainlander president of Taiwan and the last national leader in the Chiang family line, Chiang Ching-kuo was the only person able with the unchallengeable legitimacy within the Kuomintang to make changes which, as I argued in chapter 9, move Taiwan in the direction of Taiwanese rule and prolonged political separation from the mainland.

If these were Chiang Ching-kuo's calculations, his gamble paid off handsomely. The KMT performed well in the 1986 elections. Upon Chiang's death in January 1988 the constitutional succession went smoothly, and Lee Teng-hui was subsequently able to make himself a fairly strong president. In 1989 Taiwan enhanced its profile in the international arena by participating in the Asian Bank meetings in Beijing, establishing new formal economic ties with a number of Western European and European socialist countries, and gaining diplomatic recognition from the Bahamas, Grenada, Liberia, and Belize. As a result of giving up some of its control over the political system, the KMT has strengthened its domestic authority and international flexibility and prestige.

In May 1989, Deng Xiaoping could have enjoyed benefits similar to those gained by Gorbachev and Chiang Ching-kuo by taking smaller risks. Deng could have authorized Zhao Ziyang to enter into dialogue with the students, allowed Zhao to renounce the controversial April 26 *People's Daily* editorial that labeled the demonstrations a "turmoil," directed the NPC to adopt the relatively liberal press and demonstrations laws that were already in draft, and ordered vigorous persecution of corruption among the relatives of the top leaders. Deng could then have handed power over to Zhao—as he had stated repeatedly he intended to do—and retired in glory, bringing the other elderly leaders into retirement with him. These actions might have ended the demonstrations, solved the long-pending succession crisis, bequeathed his countrymen a strong, popular leader with an unambiguous mandate, established a precedent for resolving social conflicts through peaceful legal procedures, ameliorated at least temporarily the legitimacy crisis that was the immediate cause of the 1989 troubles, and provided his successor with a surge of popular support that he could have used to push economic reform through its next, most difficult phase: price reform. These actions would have strengthened confidence in China's stability abroad, and would have improved the prospects for successful integration of Hong Kong into the PRC and for peaceful reunification with Taiwan.

Instead, as the crisis worsened, Deng and a group of his octogenarian colleagues came together for the first time in many years. As explained some days later to a meeting of military cadres by Deng's top military ally Yang Shangkun,

> Xiaoping, Chen Yun, Peng Zhen, Big Sister Deng [Deng Yingchao, the wife of the late Zhou Enlai], and Wang Zhen all felt that there was no way to retreat, because a retreat would indicate our collapse and the collapse of the PRC, and this would mean a comeback for capitalism, just as former U.S. Secretary of State

Dulles—who said that our socialism would become liberalism through a number of generations—had hoped. Comrade Chen Yun made a very important statement. He said that the People's Republic was built through decades of war, and that the achievements won with the blood of tens of millions of revolutionary martyrs could be ruined overnight, and that this would be equal to the negation of the Chinese Communist Party.[25]

The old soldiers referred to the student demonstrators as *"wawa,"* babies. It was unthinkable to share power with children, and their Westernized clothing and language confirmed the leaders' fears of capitalist subversion, which as I argued in chapter 3 they had harbored since the start of the open-door policy in the late 1970s. Moreover, compared to the situations faced by Gorbachev and Chiang Ching-kuo, the crisis of the regime's relations with its people intersected in an unfortunate way with the succession crisis within the regime. Had Zhao Ziyang been allowed to turn the turmoil in the streets outside Zhongnanhai to his advantage in the power struggle inside Zhongnanhai, he would promptly have eased the old leaders out and demoted rivals like Li Peng who based their positions in the crisis on loyalty to them.

The feudalism the leaders were fond of denouncing revealed itself among them—in the assumption that their victory in the civil war gave them the state as a personal possession for them and their favorites, in the condemnation of Zhao's position as a personal betrayal of his patron Deng, in the perception that opposition was equivalent to rebellion and compromise equivalent to defeat, in the idea that they knew best what China needed and that what China needed was order, and in the notion that their people ultimately understood only the language of force. It was this style of thinking which justified the threatening words of the new party general secretary Jiang Zemin after the crackdown, "If we let [the perpetrators] wiggle out of the hands of the law, there will be endless calamities and no peace for the state or the people. Towards these cruel enemies there must not be even one percent of forgiveness. If we go easy on them, we shall commit an error of historic proportions."[26]

Deng said it was fortunate that the old cadres were still around and able to step in. "We still have a group of senior comrades who are alive," he observed with satisfaction, "we still have the army, and we also have a group of core cadres who took part in the revolution at various times. That is why it was relatively easy for

205

us to handle the present matter."[27] An alternative view is that the "gang of oldies" (*laoren bang*, as Chinese called them after the repression) lacked the imagination or energy to take risks that might have turned the crisis to the country's advantage. Instead, their rigidity left the regime much weakened.

The repression of June 1989 has bequeathed a regime that is the weakest in PRC history. Its most powerful leaders are elderly, unable to work long hours, and lack intellectual flexibility. There is no clear successor. All the most powerful younger men in the regime—Li Peng, Jiang Zemin, Qiao Shi—are compromised by the role they played in Deng's repression to the point that maintaining them in power will be costly to the regime. The mix of personnel under the top leaders reveals severe factionalization. Politicians formerly associated with Hu Yaobang and Zhao Ziyang are still numerous in the central government and in the provinces, as are others whose careers were patronized by the elderly men who are about to die off. At a moment when the nation is wedged between the old system and the new and needs strong leadership, the political structure promises policy paralysis and frequent, unpredictable political realignments.

The repression has done nothing substantial to reverse the decay of social control which helped bring on the crisis of spring 1989. Propaganda about the "counterrevolutionary rebellion" seems unable to persuade many people. Coercive measures to reform the thinking of students are likely to make them more dissatisfied. The regime has arrested large numbers of participants in the April-June demonstrations, but it cannot restore the ideological fervor or the tight system of social controls which used to make possible Mao-style campaigns of mutual persecution. Control mechanisms that rely primarily on the police and cannot draw on voluntary cooperation are costly and relatively ineffective.

The crackdown is likely to make the economic situation worse. The regime is more divided than ever about the solutions to its economic problems, and even if it could formulate a clear policy it would not have the power to carry it out. Political demoralization makes it even more likely that enterprises and individuals will evade government policies whenever it seems to be in their interest to do so. The rate of foreign investment is likely to decline, not only because of economic sanctions but because of concern about political risk. Inflation, one of the proximate causes of the 1989 crisis, is likely to increase because the regime lacks means to control the

206

rate of investment, the money supply, or prices. And corruption, another major cause, will probably worsen because the government can neither move back to a planned system or forward to a market system. The trend toward economic federalism is likely to accelerate as the central government is increasingly unable to provide anything of economic value to the provinces in exchange for the taxes and regulations it imposes on them.

In short, all the problems that brought on the crisis are still there and are worse than before; the means to deal with them are weaker than before. In addition, the government's international prestige has been damaged, and the prospect of obtaining Taiwan's reunification with the mainland is more remote than ever.

A weak regime facing so many problems is bound to be tempted by an authoritarian solution. The conditions for Mao-style popular mobilization no longer exist; the most an authoritarian regime can achieve is repression. Chinese authoritarianism would involve reasserting direct control over foreign trade, financial institutions, major enterprises, and the grain supply, suppressing incomes and consumption, tightly controlling the propaganda media, concealing intra-regime conflicts, and deterring autonomous political discussion. There is probably no limit to the number of years an unpopular, inefficient, coercive regime can survive as long as it retains control of the armed forces. But it seems unlikely such a regime can solve China's economic problems or win popular legitimacy. So it cannot be considered stable.

It is not easy, but it is possible and sometimes necessary for a weak regime to begin a transition toward democracy. Given the existence of a strong social demand for liberalization, factionalism at least makes it probable that some groups within the regime will see sponsoring change in the direction of democracy as a way of improving their power position against other factions. Even if it were not the case that many of Zhao's followers remain high in the regime which Deng Xiaoping cobbled together after the repression, from now on democratic reform will always present itself as a possible tactic to factions seeking to improve their power positions.

The opening for a new attempt could be created by Deng's death, by renewed social disorder, or by the fall of Li Peng as a result of rivalries within the regime. The chances for success will be greatest if it is a dominant faction which uses democratization to try to solidify its power against weaker rivals. But since the rival factions are sure to lose from such a change they will try to form a veto

207

bloc, and the weakness of authority in the regime always makes it possible that such a bloc can succeed. Devolution of power is easier for a strong leader like Chiang Ching-kuo whose personal authority overrides opposition in all sectors of the party and government, or for a new, legally elected, and popular leader like Gorbachev who enjoys a political honeymoon during which he is able to make policy innovations.[28] But there is little likelihood that China will have such a strong leader after Deng dies.

A weak regime that tries to democratize under the pressure of economic stagnation and popular dissatisfaction faces a larger risk than a stronger regime that political reform will spin out of control and lead to a rapid "deflation" of power.[29] To make a successful transition under these circumstances, it is helpful to have a powerful external force to guarantee stability. Poland in 1989 enjoyed the benefit of a distant, silent, ambiguously threatening Soviet Union to persuade the factions in both government and opposition to work together for a smooth transition. It is possible that China's army will play the silent guarantor in its own country, just as in 1989 it emulated the repressive role which the Soviet army played decades earlier in Eastern Europe. It may be just as well, then, that the Chinese army shows no sign of splitting. Also, the patience and nonviolence of the democratic opposition in China, even if it is a product of weakness, may help the regime navigate a democratizing reform as did the cautiousness of Solidarity in Poland.

Such an attempt at transition can occur at any time, but it is impossible to set a deadline for it. The Chinese communist regime is too entrenched to collapse: the ruling party and its army are still the only two large organized political forces in society. They have enormous vested interests to defend, and the struggles within them are over the distribution of power, not the regime's survival. The exile democratic movement is unarmed and divided on both goals and strategy. Even if it took up arms, which is unlikely, no foreign power is likely to offer assistance on the scale needed to overthrow the government. In fact, any foreign threat to China's perceived national security will make it less rather than more likely that those in power will be willing take the risks of democratizing. Thus there seems to be little likelihood that democratization will be forced on China from outside. The transition to democracy is likely to come from above when it comes, and to be hard, prolonged, complex—and inconclusive.

For when Chinese democracy begins to take shape, it may turn out to be a mixture of democratic and authoritarian elements, openness and secrecy, idealism and selfishness, turbulence and stability, hard for Western and especially American observers to recognize as democracy, and far from satisfactory to the Chinese themselves as an end point of their political development. Democratic politics in China will have many characteristics of Chinese politics in the past, only they will occur in the open rather than in secret. Such politics may be characterized by moral and symbolic posturing, stress on personal loyalty in politics, frequent betrayals, extreme rhetoric, emotional intensity, fractionalization of viewpoints and organizations, moralization of political issues and consequent difficulty in pragmatic compromise. The issues in a democratic China may not be all that different from those that have agitated Chinese politics earlier in this century—national pride and independence versus openness to the world, the clashing interests of rural residents and urbanites, the degree of freedom to be allowed individuals who offend the mores of the national community in pursuit of selfish gain or notoriety, and the permissible degree of interference by the ruling party in administrative affairs, education, and the military.

To some extent the politics of Taiwan may serve as a preview, even though Taiwan and the mainland have very different political traditions and face different issues. Since political liberalization occurred in Taiwan there have been carnival-like rallies and demonstrations, some featuring the throwing of rocks at the police; an opposition politician jumped on tables in the Legislative Yuan to grab the microphone and the neckties of elderly politicians of the ruling party; numerous small opposition parties have been formed and there have been constant joinings and defections from the opposition groups. Although self-immolation is not a Chinese tradition, in 1989 two Taiwan independence activists burned themselves to death in political protests. During the May 1989 demonstrations in Beijing, similarly, more than a dozen demonstrators registered to burn themselves in protest against the government's failure to enter into dialogue, although none actually did so.[30] It is not likely that democratic politics in China will be any less turbulent than those in Taiwan.

The institutions of a democratic China will probably evolve from the present structure. The system will probably have a single supreme legislature like the National People's Congress, unicameral and not subject to judicial review. It may have a single dominant party like those in Taiwan and Japan that stays in office permanently. This is most likely to be the Communist Party, because they will enter the democratizing transition with enormous advantages —size, organizational sophistication, control over resources—and will use them to fight and win elections. Protecting the vested interests of party members and party-chosen bureaucrats will be high on the agenda of the politicians who engineer the transition.

The factionalized opposition will probably develop out of the existing satellite parties as well as some exile democratic organizations acceptable to the communists. Elections will be short and hard-fought, with manifestoes and personal attacks, and will draw high participation rates, but many of the voters will be mobilized on the basis of personal ties to the candidates or payoffs from political machines rather than issues. Some broad version of socialism will continue to be the official ideology and few politicians will question it. The press, freed from government control, will be intensely partisan, with every journal serving the interests of some party, party faction, or social group. Readers will still have to read between the lines, and much of what they read will not be true. The military will continue to serve as a silent arbiter, its interventions kept as much as possible from the public eye, and will continue for a long time to owe its primary loyalty to the ruling party.

Although some of the exile democrats advocate that China adopt American-style federalism and separation of powers, I suspect that neither will be adopted because they are unfamiliar and would tend to divide power that will already be fragmented. China will continue to seek governmental efficiency through an ostensibly centralized system of undivided sovereignty. But the tug-of-war between the central government and provinces as big as European states will continue, and the center will probably weaken as the provinces prosper.

The international stake in China's course of development is large. In both Cambodia and Korea, the danger of war is substantial if China fails to play a constructive role, and war in either place, especially Korea, could involve other powers including the Soviet Union and the U.S. As one of the world's nuclear powers and a major arms supplier, China must participate in any successful disarmament arrangements. With one-quarter of the world's population, China has an enormous potential impact on world food markets, on the population problem, and on the environment. If China does well, it can make a large positive contribution to world

210

prosperity both as a producer and as a market. Otherwise, China will continue to pollute the earth and the atmosphere, will stunt the development of a quarter of humankind, and will be an unreliable partner in world security issues.

Although many countries fear a strong China, a weak China is even more threatening because of the damage it can do to itself and to the world. From now on, it is doubtful that an undemocratic China can be stable and strong. A more democratic system may give China more real stability than the cycles of repression and popular outrage that have shaken the country throughout the twentieth century. To be sure, clashes of interest and personality that had been hidden would be visible, and no one would be in full control. But democratic institutions might provide peaceful and legitimate channels for resolving issues of power and policy, ways of forming a national consensus on important issues and of changing policies to serve it, a political environment that fosters economic growth, protection for dissent, and means for the political system to continue to evolve without mass violence.

NOTES

1. Setting the Scene

1. *Beijing zhi chun*, no. 5 (May 16, 1979); summarized in Andrew J. Nathan, *Chinese Democracy*, paperback ed. (Berkeley, Calif.: University of California Press, 1986), pp. 87–89.

2. Deng's talk of June 9, 1989, in *Beijing Review* 32:28 (July 10–16, 1989), p. 18.

3. "Li Peng, Yang Shangkun, Qiao Shi, Yao Yilin tongzhi zai 5 yue 22 ri huiyishang de jianghua yaodian," inner-party document, reprinted in *Huaqiao ribao* (New York), June 14, 1989, pp. 4–5.

4. Nathan, *Chinese Democracy*, pp. 206–209.

5. A short biography of Hu is carried in *Zhongguo zhi chun* no. 58 (February 1, 1988), pp. 29–30.

6. *Zhongguo zhi chun* no. 60 (April 1, 1988), pp. 32–33.

7. R. Randle Edwards, Louis Henkin, and Andrew J. Nathan, *Human Rights in Contemporary China* (Columbia University Press, 1986), p. 177, n. 25.

8. From my notes of Wang's talk at the East Asian Institute, Columbia University, April 14, 1989. He has made the same points in his many published works. They are, of course, not unique to him but common in Western Marxist circles.

9. Wang Ruoshui, "The Pain of Wisdom," Hong Kong *Ching Pao* no. 94, May 1985, translated in Joint Publications Research Service, *China: Political and Social Affairs*, JPRS-CPS-85-083, 16 August 1985, pp. 147–151.

10. Yan Jiaqi, "Zongjiao, lixing, shijian," *Guangming ribao*, September 14, 1978, p. 3.

11. Many of the articles are collected in Yan's *Quanli yu zhenli* (Beijing: Guangming ribao chubanshe, 1987). The study of leaders is *Shounao lun* (Shanghai: Renmin chubanshe, 1986); the history of

1. Setting the Scene

the cultural revolution is Gao Gao and Yan Jiaqi, *"Wenhua dageming" shinian shi, 1966–1976* (Tianjin: Renmin chubanshe, 1986).

12. Zhao Ziyang, "Advance Along the Road of Socialism with Chinese Characteristics," *Beijing Review* 30:45 (November 9–15, 1987), p. 37.

13. Text in *Baixing* no. 193 (June 1, 1989), p. 8.

14. Leo A. Orleans, *Chinese Students in America: Politicies, Issues, and Numbers* (Washington, D.C.: National Academy Press, 1988), p. 110.

15. "Di'erhzhong zhongcheng," originally published in *Kaituo*, no date given, reprinted in *Zhengming* 96 (October 1, 1985), pp. 48–61; Wu's speech at the Fourth Writers' Congress of December 1984, in *Zhengming* no. 89, March 1, 1985, pp. 11–12; Wang Ruoshui, *Wei rendaozhuyi bianhu* (Beijing: Sanlian shudian, 1986), esp. 239–274; Li Honglin, *Lilun fengyun* (Beijing: Sanlian shudian, 1985).

16. Bo Yibo, "Unforgettable Memory—Recalling Peng Dehuai," *Renmin ribao*, 23 October 1988, in FBIS-CHI-88-216, 8 November 1988, p. 39.

17. *People's Republic of China: Preliminary Findings on Killings of Unarmed Civilians, Arbitrary Arrests and Summary Executions Since June 3, 1989* (New York: Amnesty International USA, August 1989); "Massacre in Beijing: The Events of 3–4 June 1989 and Their Aftermath," A Report Prepared by the International League for Human Rights and the Ad Hoc Study Group on Human Rights in China, New York, undated [September 1989].

18. This and the next few paragraphs are drawn from Andrew J. Nathan, "Scholars Must Keep Their Vision of China Unclouded by Politics," *The Chronicle of Higher Education*, July 26, 1989, p. A36.

2. A Factionalism Model for CCP Politics

1. Franz Schurmann, *Ideology and Organization in Communist China* (Berkeley: University of California Press, 1966), pp. 55–57.

2. Michel C. Oksenberg, "Policy Making Under Mao, 1949–1968: An Overview," in John M. H. Lindbeck, ed., *China: Management of a Revolutionary Society* (Seattle: University of Washington Press, 1971), pp. 79–115.

3. George M. Foster, "The Dyadic Contract: a Model for the Social Structure of a Mexican Peasant Village," in Jack M. Potter, May N. Diaz and George M. Foster, eds., *Peasant Society: A Reader* (Boston: Little, Brown, 1967), pp. 213–30; James C. Scott, "Patron

Client Politics and Political Change in Southeast Asia," *American Political Science Review* (APSR) 66:1 (March 1972), pp. 91–113; and Carl H. Landé, "Networks and Groups in Southeast Asia: Some Observations on the Group Theory of Politics," APSR 67:1 (March 1973), pp. 103–127.

4. J. A. Barnes, "Networks and Political Process," in Marc J. Swartz, ed., *Local-Level Politics: Social and Cultural Perspectives* (Chicago: Aldine, 1968), pp. 107–30; Adrian C. Mayer, "The Significance of Quasi-groups in the Study of Complex Societies," in Michael Banton, ed., *The Social Anthropology of Complex Societies,* A.S.A. Monograph 4 (London: Tavistock, 1966), pp. 97–122.

5. This conception of a faction is similar to that offered by Ralph Nicholas, "Factions: a Comparative Analysis," in Michael Banton, ed., *Political Systems and the Distribution of Power,* A.S.A. Monograph 2 (London: Tavistock, 1965), pp. 27–29.

6. Each structural characteristic discussed is not necessarily unique to factions (for example, guerrilla bands may be equally flexible, and for some of the same reasons), but none of them is universal and the combination of characteristics is distinctive.

7. Nathan Leites, *On the Game of Politics in France* (Stanford: Stanford University Press, 1959), pp. 23 and 45.

8. Leites, *On the Game,* Ch. 4, esp. pp. 97–98.

9. Bernard J. Siegel and Alan R. Beals, "Pervasive Factionalism," *American Anthropologist,* 62 (1960), pp. 394–417. For a critique, see Nicholas, "Factions," pp. 56–57.

3. Political Risk in China

1. "Li Renjun Reports on Economy to the NPC Standing Committee," Beijing Xinhua Domestic Service in Chinese, April 8, 1980, in Foreign Broadcast Information Service, *Daily Report: China* (hereafter referred to as FBIS), April 9, 1980, pp. L1–L4; abridged version in *Beijing Review* (hereafter referred to as BR) 16, April 21, 1980, pp. 17–18.

2. "CBR Forecast: China's Trade Through 1985," *The China Business Review* (hereafter referred to as CBR), May-June 1979, pp. 10–14.

3. "Rating Country Risk," *Institutional Investor* 13:9, September 1979, p. 244.

4. Central Intelligence Agency, National Foreign Assessment

Center, "China: The Continuing Search for a Modernization Strategy," April 1980, p. v.

5. Quoted in Robert Trumbull, "China Asks Japan for $5.5 Billion Loan for 8 Rail, Port and Power Projects," *The New York Times* (hereafter referred to as NYT), September 7, 1979, p.D5.

6. Frank Vogl, "Protection Against Political Upheaval," NYT, January 18, 1979, section 3, page 1.

7. "OPIC: Three Steps Remain," CBR, September-October 1979, p. 20.

8. "The National Council Meets with Vice Premier Deng Xiaoping," CBR, July-August, 1979, p. 14.

9. BR 16, April 21, 1980, p. 4, with a grammatical correction.

10. Beijing Xinhua in English, January 11, 1980, in FBIS, January 15, 1980, p. L3.

11. Nicholas Schweitzer, "Bayseian Analysis: Estimating the Probability of Middle East Conflict," in Richard J. Heuer, Jr., ed., *Quantitative Approaches to Political Intelligence: The CIA Experience* (Boulder, Colo.: Westview Press, 1978), p. 23.

12. Hong Kong *Wen Wei Po* in FBIS, March 13, 1980, p. U2, and *Wen Wei Po* editorial in ibid., p. U3; I have combined an indirect quotation from the report with a direct quotation from the editorial.

13. "Communiqué of the Fifth Plenary Sesson of the 11th Central Committee of the Communist Party of China," February 29, 1980, in BR 10, March 10, 1980, p. 8.

14. Quoted in NYT, March 5, 1980, p. A2.

15. NYT, April 18, 1980, p. A4. The Cabinet, or State Council, is the top administrative organ of the governmental hierarchy.

16. Hong Kong Agence France Press report in FBIS March 17, 1980, p. L27; Tokyo Kyodo report in FBIS, March 21, 1980, p. 42.

17. The following argument is based on Andrew J. Nathan, *Peking Politics, 1918–1923: Factionalism and the Failure of Constitutionalism* (Berkeley: University of California Press, 1976); and "A Factionalism Model for CCP Politics," *China Quarterly* 53, January-March, 1973, pp. 34–66.

18. For example, see *Hongqi* No. 5, March 5, 1980, in FBIS, March 17, 1980, p. L23.

19. "Chairman of Delegation of People's Republic of China Deng Xiaoping's Speech at Special Session of U.N. General Assembly," *Peking Review* Supplement to 15, April 12, 1974, p. IV.

20. "Deng Xiaoping Writes on Four Modernizations," Bangkok

Post in English, February 10, 1980, in FBIS, February 12, 1980, p. L1.

21. Quoted in Alexander Eckstein, *China's Economic Revolution* (Cambridge: Cambridge University Press, 1977), p. 242.

22. "A Vigorous and Cautious Approach is Required," *Renmin ribao* editorial, May 8, 1979, in FBIS, May 15, 1979, p. L3.

23. Yao Zhuang, "The Positive Role of the Law on Joint Ventures Using Chinese and Foreign Investments," *Renmin ribao*, July 24, 1979 in FBIS, August 8, 1979, p. L9.

24. "Beware of Getting Duped When Developing Foreign Trade," Hong Kong *Wenhui bao* (*Wen wei po*), March 7, 1979, cited in CBR, March-April 1979, pp. 68–69.

25. BR 29, July 20, 1979, p. 25.

26. Li Yongji, "A New Law Favorable to the Four Modernizations," *Jiefangjun bao*, July 21, 1979, in FBIS, July 23, 1979, p. L21.

27. See CBR, November-December 1978, p. 57.

28. On Chinese reluctance to accept long-term outside experts, see Bernard D. Nossiter, "U.N. Agency to Help China Curb Population Growth," NYT, March 16, 1989, p. 12.

29. State Statistical Bureau, "Communiqué on Fulfillment of China's 1979 Economic Plan," BR 20, May 19, 1980, p. 22

30. Guangdong Provincial Service, April 5, 1989, in FBIS, April 7, 1980, p. P4.

31. Beijing Xinhua Domestic Service, May 26, 1979 in FBIS, May 21, 1979, p. L3.

32. BR 19, May 12, 1979, p. 6. The speaker was Hu Qiaomu, a member of the Central Committee Secretariat.

33. See Stanley B. Lubman, "Trade Between the United States and the People's Republic of China: Practice, Policy, and Law," *Law and Policy in International Business* 8:1 (1976), p. 22; CBR, March-April 1979, p. 52.

34. CBR, July-August 1979, p. 55.

35. Based on remarks of Alexander Tomlinson at the conference on "Business with China: An International Reassessment," April 10, 1980, New York City.

36. Deputy Minister of Foreign Trade Chen Jie, quoted in NYT, May 15, 1979, p. D11.

37. "An Interview with the Bank of China," CBR, November-December, 1979, p. 36.

38. *Ibid.*; also see James B. Stepanek, "China, the IMF, and the World Bank," CBR, January-February, 1980, pp. 55–62.

39. *China Newsletter* (Jetro) 23, October 1979, p. 1; CBR, January-February 1980, pp. 66–67.

40. Guangdong Province Economics Society Chairman Sun Ru, quoted in John Kam, "Importing Some of Hong Kong . . . Exporting Some of China," CBR, March-April 1980, p. 31.

41. Shen Xiaoming, "Is the Law of Joint Ventures with Chinese and Foreign Investments Beneficial to the Realization of the Four Modernizations?", *Gongren ribao*, July 17, 1979, in FBIS, August 7, 1979, p. L7.

42. Eckstein, *China's Economic Revolution*, pp. 236–245.

43. Kevin Fountain, "The Development of China's Offshore Oil," CBR, January-February 1980, p. 24.

44. Quoted in Tao-tai Hsia, "China's Foreign Trade and the 'Gang of Four,' " in Shao-chuan Leng, ed., *Post-Mao China and U.S.-China Trade* (Charlottesville: University Press of Virginia, 1977), p. 102.

45. On the housing shortage, see BR 6, February 11, 1980, p. 7; on luxury hotels see "Tourism: The Hotel Deals" in CBR, March-April 1979, pp. 21–27.

46. "CBR Forecast," CBR, May-June, 1979, p. 10.

47. CBR, March-April 1980, p. 42.

48. Mao Jiashu, Liu Shuyou and Zhang Zhixiang, "Do Not Be Deceived by Superficial, Temporary Phenomena—Is Socialism Not as Good as Capitalism?" in *Zhongguo qingnian bao*, April 14, 1979, in FBIS, May 9, 1979, p. L3–L6.

49. Xu Dixin, "Skimming Over the U.S. Economy," *Beijing ribao*, March 28, 1980, in FBIS, April 15, 1980, p. B4.

50. Beijing Domestic Service, March 3, 1980, in FBIS, March 5, 1980, p. B1.

51. Liu Zhenchan, " 'Imitate Others' Manner of Walking' and 'Mimic Others' Manner of Knitting the Brow,' " *Renmin ribao*, April 5, 1980, in FBIS, April 7, 1980, p. L9.

52. Dai Yongxia, "The Focal Point of Learning From Foreign Countries," *Zhongguo qingnian bao*, March 15, 1979, in Joint Publications Research Service, *Translations on People's Republic of China*, No. 515, May 1, 1979, p. 28.

53. Guangzhou Guangdong Provincial Service, November 27, 1979, in FBIS, November 30, 1979, p. P1.

54. "China's New Engineering and Manpower Service Companies," CBR, March-April 1980, pp. 36–37; "China's Labor Exports," *China Newsletter* (Jetro) 24, December 1979, pp. 24–26. Previously

the PRC exported labor only in connection with foreign aid—for example, to Laos and Tanzania.

55. John Kamm, "Importing Some of Hong Kong," CBR, March-April 1980, pp. 28–35.

56. As Eckstein puts it, "Self-reliance never meant complete autarky, but rather a deliberate pursuit of an import substitution and import minimization policy." *China's Economic Revolution*, p. 238.

57. *Jilin ribao*, September 2, 1979 in FBIS, September 6, 1979, p. S8.

58. Shenyang Liaoning Provincial Service, August 29, 1979, in FBIS, September 7, 1979, p. S2

59. Hong Shu, "The Whole Party Obeys Its Central Committee," *Hongqi* 4, February 16, 1980, in FBIS, March 19, 1980, p. L19

60. Richard E. Batsavage and John L. Davie, "China's International Trade and Finance," in Joint Economic Committee, Congress of the United States, *Chinese Economy Post-Mao, Volume 1* (Washington, D.C.: Government Printing Office, 1979), p. 725.

61. Editorial, "Take a Clear-Cut Stand in Upholding the Four Cardinal Principles," *Renmin ribao, Overseas Edition*, 23 June 1989, in FBIS-CHI-89-120, 23 June 1989, p. 14.

4. Americans Look at China

1. *New York Times*, December 10, 1984, p. A23.

2. *Christian Science Monitor*, December 4, 1984, p. 3.

3. *National Review*, December 14, 1984, p. 53.

4. "China's official attack on Marxist orthodoxy as outdated . . . is a historic watershed that can have far-reaching, dramatic consequences." *New York Times*, December 11, 1984, p. A31.

5. Kenneth Lieberthal, "Domestic Politics and Foreign Policy," in Harry Harding, ed., *China's Foreign Relations in the 1980s* (New Haven: Yale University Press, 1984), p. 68.

6. *The New York Times*, December 24, 1984, p. 18.

7. For example, see Michael H. Hunt, *The Making of a Special Relationship: The United States and China to 1914* (New York: Columbia University Press, 1983).

8. See Harold R. Isaacs, *Images of Asia: American Views of China and India* (originally published as *Scratches on Our Minds*) (New York: Capricorn Books, 1962), pp. 140–176.

9. Quoted in Foster Rhea Dulles, *American Foreign Policy Toward Communist China, 1949–1969* (New York: Thomas Y. Crowell Company, 1972), p. 6.

10. Richard M. Nixon, "Asia After Viet Nam," *Foreign Affairs* 46:1 (October 1967), p. 121; quote below, p. 123.

11. *Experience Without Precedent: Some Quaker Observations on China Today*, Report of an American Friends Service Committee Delegation's Visit to China, May, 1972 (Philadelphia: AFSC, 1972), p. 52; earlier quotation from p. 7.

12. For a survey of these trends of thought, see Harry Harding, "From China, With Disdain: New Trends in the Study of China," *Asian Survey* 22:10 (October 1982), pp. 934–958.

13. Ken Ling, *The Revenge of Heaven* (New York: Putnam, 1972).

14. Simon Leys, *Chinese Shadows* (New York: Viking Press, 1977).

15. For example, A. Doak Barnett, *Uncertain Passage: China's Transition to the Post-Mao Era* (Washington, D.C.: The Brookings Institution, 1974), pp. 154–165, 179–184; Lucian W. Pye, "Mass Participation in Communist China: Its Limitations and the Continuity of Culture," in John M. H. Lindbeck, ed., *China: Management of a Revolutionary Society* (Seattle: University of Washington Press, 1971), pp. 22–33.

16. For expressions of this view see, among other sources, various issues of the *Bulletin of Concerned Asian Scholars*.

17. Boston: Little, Brown, 1982, and New York: Times Books, 1982.

18. See, for example, the diverse attitudes expressed in Mark Selden and Victor Lippit, eds. *The Transition to Socialism in China* (Armonk, N.Y.: M.E. Sharpe, Inc., 1982).

19. *Images*, p. 66.

20. Hunt, *Making*, pp. xi, 302.

21. *The U.S. and China*, New Ed. (New York: Viking, 1962), p. 251.

22. "Intellectuals, Estrangement, and Wish Fulfillment," *Society* (July/August 1983), pp. 16–24.

23. *Washington Post*, May 2, 1984, Section A, p. 8.

6. Reform at the Crossroad

1. See Anne F. Thurston, "Year of the Dragon Ends on Note of Malaise," *Christian Science Monitor*, February 3, 1989, p. 19.

2. Articles by or about Wang Jian include Wang, "Choosing a

Correct, Long-Term Strategy for Development—an Idea on the 'Big International Cycle' Strategy for Economic Development," *Jingji ribao* 5 January 1988, in FBIS-CHI-88–044, 7 March 1988, pp. 50–54; Wang, "Several Questions Concerning Strategy for Economic Development of the Great International Circle," *Shijie jingji daobao* 28 March 1988, in JPRS-CAR-88-020, 25 April 1988, pp. 3–6; Wang, "Several Considerations on the Strategy for Export-Oriented Development of the Coastal Areas," in *Hongqi* No. 7, 1 April 1988, in JPRS-CRF-88-014, 7 June 1988, pp. 23–25; and Cheng Wanquan, "The Resourceful Young Scholar—on Wang Jian Who Struck the Idea of the 'Great International Circle,' " in *Ban yue tan*, No. 4, 25 February 1988, in FBIS-CHI-88-056, 23 March 1988, pp. 26–27. Also see Huang Fangyi, "China's Introduction of Foreign Technology and External Trade," *Asian Survey* 27:5 (May 1987).

3. Li Peng, "Report on the Work of the Government," *Beijing Review* 31:17 (April 25–May 1, 1988), pp. 22–47.

4. *Renmin ribao, haiwaiban,* October 11, 1988, p. 1.

5. For the rise of technocracy in the Thirteenth Party Congress in late 1987, see Li Cheng and Lynn White, "The Thirteenth Central Committee of the Chinese Communist Party: From Mobilizers to Managers," *Asian Survey* 28:4 (April 1988), pp. 371–399.

6. Lowell Dittmer, "China in 1988: The Continuing Dilemma of Socialist Reform," *Asian Survey* 29:1 (January 1989), p. 16.

7. See Kenneth Lieberthal and Michel Oksenberg, *Policy Making in China: Leaders, Structures, and Processes* (Princeton: Princeton University Press, 1988), pp. 51–58.

8. See State Economic Restructuring Institute, "Only Through Tackling Difficult Problems in Reform Can Society Be Stabilized," *Shijie jingji daobao* 29 August 1988, in FBIS-CHI-88-194, 6 October 1988, pp. 17–19.

9. For a perceptive Western analysis of this phenomenon, see Christine P.W. Wong, "Ownership and Control in Chinese Industry: The Maoist Legacy and Prospects for the 1980s," in Joint Economic Committee, Congress of the United States, *China's Economy Looks Toward the Year 2000* (Washington, D.C.: Government Printing Office, May 21, 1986), Vol. 1, pp. 571–603.

10. *Renmin ribao, haiwaiban,* June 23, 1988, p. 1.

11. Zhao, "Report to the Third Plenary Session of the 13th CPC Central Committee," *Beijing Review* 31:46 (November 14–20, 1988), center section; quotation is from p. iv, but I have used my own translation here and in other quotes from this speech.

12. *Renmin ribao, haiwaiban*, January 24, 1989, in FBIS-CHI-89-105, 25 January 1989, p. 16.

13. *Renmin ribao, haiwaiban*, July 6, 1988, p. 1 and July 7, 1988, p. 4.

14. "According to incomplete statistics, over the last five weeks almost 100 serious criminals in Guangdong have been executed," reported a pro-PRC news agency in Hong Kong on January 26, 1989; *Zhongguo tongxunshe*, January 26, 1989, in FBIS-CHI-89-018, 30 January 1989, p. 61.

15. *Renmin ribao, haiwaiban*, July 4, 1988, p. 1.

16. "Essay by Ren Wanding" in *South China Morning Post*, 29 November 1988, in FBIS-CHI-88-229, 29 November 1988, pp. 24–26.

17. *Renmin ribao, haiwaiban*, November 10, 1988, p. 2.

18. See Frederic Wakeman, Jr., "All the Rage in China," *The New York Review of Books*, March 2, 1989, pp. 19–21.

19. See, e.g., Wu Jiaxiang, "Xin quanweizhuyi shuping," *Shijie jingji daobao* January 16, 1989, reprinted in New York *Huaqiao ribao*, February 16, 1989, p. 10. In an interview, Huntington himself disclaimed the applicability of his theory to China. See *Shijie jingji daobao*, March 27, 1989, p. 13.

20. Zhao Ziyang, "Guanyu dang de jianshe de jige wenti," speech given January 28, 1989, *Renmin ribao, haiwaiban*, March 17, 1989, pp. 1–2.

21. Chi Hsin, "Behind-the-Scene Maneuvers in Stopping the Price Reform," *Chiu-shih nien-tai*, 1 November 1988, in JPRS-CAR-89-005, 13 January 1989, pp. 1–3.

7. Paradoxes of Reform and Pressures for Change

1. *Chinese Democracy*, paperback (Berkeley: University of California Press, 1986).

2. *Chinese Democracy*, pp. 98–100.

3. World Bank, *World Development Report 1987* (New York: Oxford University Press, 1987), Table 3; 1953 figure from Judith Banister, *China's Changing Population* (Stanford: Stanford University Press, 1987), p. 352.

4. State Statistic Bureau, *Statistical Yearbook of China 1983* (Hong Kong: Economic Information and Agency, 1983), p. 23. Six percent

is the figure for average annual increase in national income from 1953 to 1982.

5. *China Daily* 19 February 1988 in Foreign Broadcast Information Service, *Daily Report: China,* FBIS-CHI-88-034, 22 February 1988, p. 19.

6. See Vaclav Smil, *The Bad Earth: Environmental Degradation in China,* paperback (Armonk: M.E. Sharpe, Inc., 1984).

7. The gross value of agricultural output rose from about 140 billion yuan in 1978 to about 468 billion in 1987; this figure reflects the impacts both of increased output and of inflation. Employment in rural township enterprises was over 47 million persons in 1987, and their output was 293 billion yuan; these figures presumably do not include individual enterprises, some of which are quite large. *Zhongguo tongji nianjian,* Guojia tongjiju, ed. (Beijing: Zhongguo tongji chubanshe, 1988), pp. 44, 287.

8. Foreign investment: State Statistical Bureau, "Utilization of Foreign Capital: 1979–88," in *Beijing Review* 32:10 (March 6–12, 1989), p. 26; actually used capital was $47 billion. Foreign trade as a percentage of GNP (in 1987): State Council Research Office, "Bridging the Economic Gap", *Beijing Review* 32:5 (January 30–February 5, 1989), p. 24.

9. *Statistical Yearbook of China 1983,* p. 220.

10. Seattle: University of Washington Press, 1986.

11. *Discriminate Deterrence: Report of The Commission on Integrated Long-Term Strategy* (Washington, D.C.: Government Printing Office, 1988), p. 6.

12. Su Xiaokang, Wang Luxiang, chief writers, *Heshang* (Beijing: Xiandai chubanshe, 1988).

13. For an excellent anthology of such writings in translation, see Geremie Barmé and John Minford, *Seeds of Fire: Chinese Voices of Conscience* (New York: Hill and Wang, 1988).

14. See the articles collected in Guillermo O'Donnell, Philippe C. Schmitter, and Laurence Whitehead, eds., *Transitions from Authoritarian Rule: Comparative Perspectives,* paperback (Baltimore: The Johns Hopkins University Press, 1986).

8. Democratizing Transition in Taiwan

1. *Shih-pao chou-k'an,* No. 86 (October 18–24, 1986, pp. 8–13. Hereafter abbreviated SPCK. This is the New York edition of the

popular Taiwan newsweekly, *Shih-pao hsin-wen chou-k'an*. Also see Hungdah Chiu and Jyh-pin Fa, "Law and Justice since 1966," in James C. Hsiung and others, eds., *Contemporary Republic of China: The Taiwan Experience, 1950–1980*, paperback ed. (New York: The American Association for Chinese Studies, 1981), pp. 314–330.

2. *Taiwan Statistical Data Book* (Taipei: Council for Economic Planning and Development, 1986), p. 33.

3. *Chung-kuo lun-t'an* (Taipei), No. 262 (August 25, 1986), p. 39.

4. SPCK, No. 82 (September 20–26, 1986), p. 54.

5. *Taiwan Statistical Data Book*, p. 60.

6. *Chung-hua min-kuo t'ung-chi t'i-yao* (Taipei: Hsing-cheng yuan, 1983), pp. 16–18.

7. SPCK, No. 82 (September 20–26, 1986), p. 54.

8. See, e.g., SPCK, No. 60 (April 20–26, 1986), pp. 6–7.

9. SPCK, No. 81 (September 14–20, 1986), pp. 40–41.

10. Edwin A. Winckler, "Institutionalization and Participation on Taiwan: From Hard to Soft Authoritarianism?" *The China Quarterly* 99 (September 1984), pp. 481–499.

11. Interview, K'ang Ning-hsiang, Taipei, January 2, 1987.

12. *Shih-pao hsin-wen chou-k'an*, No. 6 (June 22–28, 1986), pp. 4–7.

13. *Chung-kuo lun-t'an*, No. 228 (March 25, 1985), pp. 8–24, and No. 238 (August 25, 1985), pp. 12–15.

14. Samuel P. Huntington, *Political Order in Changing Societies* (New Haven: Yale University Press, 1968), p. 344.

15. SPCK, No. 86 (October 18–24, 1986), pp. 8–9.

16. SPCK, No. 85 (October 11–16, 1986), p. 12.

17. Interview, Professor Hu Fo, Taipei, January 1, 1987.

18. SPCK, No. 64 (May 18–24, 1986), pp. 6–11.

19. SPCK 81 (September 14–20, 1986), pp. 38–39.

20. SPCK, No. 81 (September 14–20, 1986), pp. 38–39.

21. SPCK, No. 84 (October 4–10, 1986), p. 7, and interviews, Taipei, January 2, 1987.

22. Interview, Taipei, January 1, 1987.

23. SPCK No. 86 (October 18–24, 1986), p. 6.

24. E.g., *Chung pao* (New York) (October 31, 1986, p. 2; *Pei-Mei jih-pao* (New York) (December 17, 1986), p. 1.

25. SPCK, No. 90 (November 15–21, 1986), p. 8.

26. *Chung-kuo shih-pao* (Taipei), November 7, 1986, p. 2.

27. *Chung-kuo lun-t'an*, No. 268 (November 25, 1986), pp. 30–33.

28. See especially his series, "Ke-ming wan-sui," in *Mei-li-tao chou-k'an* (Los Angeles), Numbers 91–95 (May 29–July 3, 1982), and his preface to the series, "Tu-shih you-chi-tui shou-ts'e," *Mei-li-tao chou-k'an*, Nos. 105–108 (September 18–October 9, 1982).

29. See the series of reports in SPCK, Nos. 91–93 (November 22–December 12, 1986).

30. SPCK, No. 93 (December 6–12, 1086), p. 19.

31. SPCK, No. 94 (December 13–19, 1986), pp. 3–25.

32. See "Elections in Taiwan, December 6, 1986: Rules of the Game for the 'Democratic Holiday'," An Asia Watch Report, Washington, D.C.: Asia Watch, November 1986.

33. *Chung-yang jih-pao* (International Edition), December 8, 1986, p. 1.

34. *Chung-pao* (New York), November 8, 1986, p. 2.

35. SPCK, No. 95 (December 20–26, 1986), p. 28.

36. *Chung-pao* (New York), November 1, 1986, p. 1.

37. *Chung-pao* December 20, 1986, p. 1, reporting material carried in *Kuang-chiao-ching* (Hong Kong), December 16, 1986.

38. *The New York Times*, December 14, 1986, p. 14.

39. *Beijing Review*, No. 46 (1986), p. 23.

40. Cf. editorial in the *Washington Post*, December 4, 1986.

41. *Chung-pao* (New York), October 8 and 9, November 11 and 20, all on p. 2.

42. Amnesty International, "Republic of China (Taiwan), Political Imprisonment in Taiwan," Amnesty document ASA 38/11/86, dated August 1986.

43. See Andrew J. Nathan, *Chinese Democracy* (New York: Alfred A. Knopf, 1985), chapter 5.

44. *Political Science Quarterly*, 99:2 (September 1984), pp. 193–218.

45. See, for example, Guillermo O'Donnell, "Tensions in the Bureaucratic-Authoritarian State and the Question of Democracy," in David Collier, ed., *The New Authoritarianism in Latin America* (Princeton, N.J.: Princeton University Press, 1979), pp. 285–318, and Adam Przeworski, "Some Problems in the Study of the Transition to Democracy," in Guillermo O'Donnell et al., eds., *Transition From Authoritarianism: Comparative Perspectives* (Baltimore: Johns Hopkins University Press, 1986), pp. 47–63.

9. *The Effect of Taiwan's Political Reform on Taiwan-Mainland Relations*

1. Henry Kissinger, *White House Years* (Boston: Little, Brown, 1979), p. 1062.

2. "The Present Situation and the Tasks Before Us," in *Selected Works of Deng Xiaoping (1975–1982)* (Beijing: Foreign Languages Press, 1984), p. 225.

3. The significance of this is explained by Thomas E. Stolper, *China, Taiwan, and the Offshore Islands* (Armonk, N.Y.: M.E. Sharpe, Inc., 1985).

4. See, e.g., "Yao Chia-wen on Taiwan's Legal Status," in *Chiu-shi nien-tai* (Hong Kong), 1 July 1988, in JPRS-CAR-88-058, 23 September 1988, pp. 44–45.

5. An informative discussion (and refutation) of these and additional proposals may be found in Li Jiaquan, "Again on Formula for China's Reunification," in *Beijing Review* 31:13 (March 28–April 3, 1988), pp. 23–27.

6. Proposed in a Taiwan magazine by John Quansheng Zhao, a scholar from mainland China teaching in the U.S.: "Yi-ke 't'ung-yi-tuo-yuan cheng-chih' mo-shih de t'i-ch'u," *Chung-kuo lun-t'an* 26:5 (June 10, 1988), pp. 47–57.

7. For the comments to this effect of the PRC Foreign Ministry spokesman, see *Jen-min jih-pao, hai-wai pan*, December 20, 1988, p. 1.

8. Among numerous sources, see *Shih-pao chou-k'an* (New York), No. 182, August 19–25, 1988, pp. 22–26 and Professor Hsiung's own account of the incident in *Shih-pao chou-k'an* (New York), No. 185, Sept. 9–15, 1988, pp. 54–55.

9. *Beijing Review* 31:30 (July 25–31, 1988), pp. 9–10.

10. Reported in *Hua-ch'iao jih-pao* (New York), September 14, 1988, p. 10, as reprinted from *Ch'ien-chin chou-k'an* (Taiwan), August 27, 1988.

11. Chen Bing, "Thoughts Associated with 'Chen Li-fu's Proposal,'" *Liaowang Overseas Edition*, 12 September 1988, in FBIS-CHI-88-177, 13 September 1988, p. 64.

12. E.g., most recently, President Lee's interview with *Reader's Digest* editors, reported in *Lien-he pao*, overseas airmail edition, October 27, 1988, p. 1.

13. *Jen-min jih-pao, hai-wai pan*, December 31, 1988, p. 1.

14. See Kao Ying-mao, " 'K'ai-fang' yü 'cheng-t'i li-yi' ping-chin ti da-lu cheng-ts'e" and T'ien Hung-mao, "Chung-kung 't'ung-chan ts'e-lüeh tui T'ai-wan an-ch'üan ti wei-hsieh" (papers presented at the conference on "Ta-lu cheng-ts'e wang he-ch'u ch'ü?", Taipei, December 29–30, 1988), p. 11.

15. Zhang Jingxu, "U.S.-Taiwan Relations and Peaceful Reunification Across the Strait," *Liaowang Overseas Edition*, No. 45, 7 November 1988, in FBIS-CHI-88-216, 8 November 1988, pp. 5–8; I have corrected the translation.

16. Cited in Dennis Van Vranken Hickey, "America's Two-Point Policy and the Future of Taiwan," *Asian Survey* 28:8 (August 1988), p. 889.

17. Gaston J. Sigur, Jr., "U.S. Policy Priorities for Relations With China," address at the Brookings Institution, April 22, 1987, Department of State "Current Policy No. 948."

18. Cf. Andrew J. Nathan, "Ch'iu-t'ung ts'un-i: shih wei Hai-hsia liang-an kuan-hsi hsun i ch'u-lu," *Lien-he pao* (Taipei), June 14, 1988.

19. E.g., Yao Yiping, "Improve the Relations Between the Two Shores of the Taiwan Strait with Sincerity," *Liaowang Overseas Edition* No. 34, 22 August 1988, in FBIS-CHI-88-173, 7 September 1988, pp. 53–56.

10. Chinese Democracy in 1989

1. Interviews, New York City, August 12, October 25, and November 20, 1987; *Zhonggong nianbao* (Taibei: Zhonggong yanjiu zazhi she), 1969 and 1971 issues.

2. *Chinese Law and Government* 10:3 (Fall 1977), pp. 15–62.

3. Andrew J. Nathan, *Chinese Democracy*, paperback (Berkeley: University of California Press, 1986), chs. 1 and 2.

4. Deng's August 18, 1980, speech, "On the Reform of the System of Party and State Leadership," in *Selected Works of Deng Xiaoping (1975–1982)* (Beijing: Foreign Languages Press, 1984), pp. 302–325.

5. Liao Gailong, "The '1980 Reform' Program of China," *Jiushi niandai* No. 134, 1 March 1981, in Foreign Broadcast Information Service, *Daily Report: People's Republic of China* (hereafter FBIS), 16 March 1981, pp. U1-U19.

6. Nathan, *Chinese Democracy*, ch. 10.

7. Nathan, *Chinese Democracy*, chs. 4, 6.

8. Wei Shiqing, "Lishi buhui wangji zheci huiyi—jinian lilun gongzuo wuxu hui shizhounian," *Huaqiao ribao*, February 1, 1989, pp. 2, 10.

9. Yan Jiaqi wrote "Xiandai zongjiao de mijue" under the pseudonym Bu Shuming in *Beijing zhi chun* no. 1 (1979), and "Zizhi minzhu yu guojia xiaowang xueshuo" under the pseudonym Wen Qi in *Beijing zhi chun* no. 6 (1979). He had given the latter as a speech at the theoretical work conference. Personal conversation with Yan Jiaqi, New York, August 1, 1979.

10. Interview, New York, August 28, 1989.

11. Bao Tong, "Several Questions Concerning the Current Reform of the Political Structure," *Qiushi* No. 1, 1 July 1988, in FBIS-CHI-88-138, 19 July 1988, pp. 21–26.

12. *Zhengming* No. 140, 1 June 1989, in FBIS-CHI-89–103, p. 29.

13. Chen Xitong, "Report on Checking the Turmoil and Quelling the Counter-Revolutionary Rebellion," *Beijing Review* 32:29 (July 17–23, 1989), center section. More details of the charges against Zhao are contained in "Main Points of Yang Shangkun's Speech at Emergency Enlarged Meeting of Central Military Commission on 24 May 1989 (edited from transcript of speech)," Hong Kong *Ming Pao*, 29 May 1989, in FBIS-CHI-89-102, 30 May 1989, pp. 17–20.

14. A useful summary of ten years' of political reform is Liu Zheng, Cheng Xiangqing, and Du Xichuan, "Woguo jinshinian minzhu jianshe de zhuyao chengjiu he jingyan," *Zhonggong dangshi yanjiu*, 1988 No. 6 (November 25, 1988), pp. 28–36.

15. The demonstrations law enacted in July, on the contrary, makes autonomous demonstrations virtually impossible; "Zhonghua renmin gongheguo jihui youxing shiwei fa (cao'an)," *Renmin ribao, haiwaiban*, July 8, 1989, p. 4.

16. See Benedict Stavis, *China's Political Reforms: An Interim Report* (New York: Praeger, 1988); and Stavis, ed., *Reform of China's Political System*, special issue of *Chinese Law and Government* 20:1 (Spring 1987).

17. "Zhi you shehuizhuyi cai neng fazhan Zhongguo," *Renmin ribao, haiwaiban*, July 22, 1989, p. 1.

18. Chen Xitong, "Report on Checking the Turmoil and Quelling the Counter-Revolutionary Rebellion," *Beijing Review* 32:29 (July 17–23, 1989), center section.

19. See James D. Seymour, *China's Satellite Parties* (Armonk: M.E. Sharpe, Inc., 1987).

20. For the term desertion of the intellectuals, see Crane Brinton, *The Anatomy of Revolution*, paperback (New York: Vintage, 1956), pp. 41–52; for the general crisis, see Andrew J. Nathan, "Politics: Reform at the Crossroads" in Anthony Kane, ed., *China Briefing 1989* (Boulder: Westview, 1989), pp. 7–25.

21. *Jiushi niandai* no. 231, April 1989, pp. 20–27.

22. *New York Times*, May 5, 1989, p. 15.

23. *Huaqiao ribao* (New York), January 30, 1989, p. 2.

24. *Renmin ribao, haiwaiban*, April 11, 1989, p. 2.

25. See, e.g., *Renmin ribao, haiwaiban*, May 19, 1989, p. 4; Foreign Broadcast Information Service, *Daily Report: China*, FBIS-CHI-89–097, 22 May 1989, pp. 78–81.

26. *Renmin ribao, haiwaiban*, May 20, 1989, p. 1.

27. *Renmin ribao, haiwaiban*, May 4, 1989, p. 4.

28. This is quoted from the crucial April 26 editorial. The words are thought to have come from an internal talk by Deng the day before. *Renmin ribao, haiwaiban*, April 26, 1989, p. 1.

29. *Huaqiao ribao* (New York), June 1, 1989, p. 7.

30. "Li Peng, Yang Shangkun, Qiao Shi, Yao Yilin tongzhi zai 5 yue 22 ri huiyishang de jianghua yaodian," inner-party document, reprinted in *Huaqiao ribao* (New York), June 14, 1989, pp. 4–5.

31. Chen, "Report," passim.

32. See the denunciation of Liu in *Renmin ribao, haiwaiban* June 26, 1989, p. 4, reprinted from *Beijing ribao*, June 24, 1989.

33. Chen Zhixiong, "Cong Huang Debei shijian kan xinwen renyuan de 'zhiye lunli'," *Shibao zhoukan* (New York), No. 229 (July 15–21, 1989), p. 3; Chen Xitong, "Report," p. XVI.

34. Many reports, e.g., "Liu Binyan fang Xiangjiang [error for Xianggang] tan Beijing," *Huaqiao ribao*, June 19, 1989, p. 4.

35. See, e.g., "Zai Mei Tai Gang fandong shili de pihu zhichixia, pantao fenzi jinxing diandao Zhongguo zhengfu huodong," *Renmin ribao, haiwaiban*, August 2, 1989, p. 1.

36. Yan's June 4, 1989, statement in Paris; *Shibao zhoukan* No. 227 (July 1–7, 1989), p. 14.

37. "Chengli 'Minzhu Zhongguo zhenxian" changyishu," *Shijie ribao* (New York), July 21, 1989, p. 16.

38. Yan, speech at Columbia University, August 1, 1989.

39. *Shibao zhoukan*, no. 232 (August 5–11, 1989), pp. 8–10.

40. *Zhongguo zhi chun*, no. 75 (July 15, 1989), p. 23.

41. For example, New York-based dissident Ni Yuxian takes issue with Yan Jiaqi's stand of not opposing the communist party;

"Minzhu yundong yu Zhongguo gongchandang," *Shijie ribao*, August 21, 22, 23, 1989, all on p. 16.

42. Lloyd E. Eastman, *Seeds of Destruction: Nationalist China in War and Revolution, 1937–1949* (Stanford, Ca.: Stanford University Press, 1984), pp. 131–132; William Wei, *Counter-Revolution in China: The Nationalists in Jiangxi during the Soviet Period* (Ann Arbor: The University of Michigan Press, 1985), Ch. 2.

43. *Zhongguo zhi chun* no. 75 (July 15, 1989), p. 32.

44. Speech at Columbia University, August 1, 1989.

45. *Zhongguo zhi chun* no. 75 (July 15, 1989), p. 33.

46. *Zhongguo tongji nianjian 1984*, Guojia tongji ju, comp. (Beijing: Zhongguo tongji chubanshe, 1984), p. 492.

47. Speech at Columbia University, August 1, 1989.

48. Deng's June 9 speech, in *Beijing Review* 32:28 (July 10–16, 1989), p. 18.

49. Sima Qian in the *Historical Records*, quoted by Laurence A. Schneider, *A Madman of Ch'u: The Chinese Myth of Loyalty and Dissent* (Berkeley: University of California Press, 1980), p. 21.

11. Conclusion

1. These quotations come from *Selected Works of Deng Xiaoping (1975–1982)* (Beijing: Foreign Languages Press, 1984), pp. 171, 184, with a slight retranslation from the Chinese text, and "Deng Xiaoping on Upholding the Four Cardinal Principles and Combating Bourgeois Liberalization," *Beijing Review* 32:29 (July 17–23, 1989), p. 22.

2. Zhang Lin, "Women xuyao shemmeyang de minzhu," *Renmin ribao, haiwaiban*, July 24, 1989, p. 2.

3. Cf. Andrew J. Nathan, *Chinese Democracy*, paperback (Berkeley: University of California Press), chs. 3, 6.

4. P'eng-yüan Chang, "The Constitutionalists," in Mary Clabaugh Wright, ed., *China in Revolution : The First Phase, 1900–1913*, paperback (New Haven: Yale University Press, 1968), pp. 146–149; P'eng-yüan Chang, "Political Participation and Political Elites in Early Republican China: The Parliament of 1913–1914," trans. Andrew J. Nathan, *Journal of Asian Studies* 37:2 (February 1978), pp. 294–301; Andrew J. Nathan, *Peking Politics, 1918–1923: Factionalism and the Failure of Constitutionalism* (Berkeley: University of California Press, 1976), pp. 92–97.

5. Leo Ou-fan Lee and Andrew J. Nathan, "The Beginnings of Mass Culture: Journalism and Fiction in the Late Ch'ing and Beyond," in David Johnson, Andrew J. Nathan, and Evelyn S. Rawski, eds., *Popular Culture in Late Imperial China* (Berkeley, Ca.: University of California Press, 1985), pp. 368–373; *Statistical Yearbook of China 1983*, State Statistical Bureau, comp. (Hong Kong: Economic Information and Agency, 1983), pp. 299, 320.

6. *Statistical Yearbook*, p. 109.

7. I am using the 1972 figures reproduced in G. Bingham Powell, Jr., *Contemporary Democracies: Participation, Stability, and Violence*, paperback ed. (Cambridge, Mass.: Harvard University Press, 1982), p. 36, and also, for the purposes of illustration here, his list of what were at that time democratic regimes. And I am using the World Bank's evaluation of China's GNP per capita as standing at $300 in 1980 and aiming at $800 (in 1980 dollars) in 2000 in *China: Long-Term Development Issues and Options*, paperback ed. (Baltimore: The Johns Hopkins University Press, 1985), p. 21.

8. *World Development Report 1989* (New York: Oxford University Press for The World Bank, 1989), p. 168.

9. Guo Shutian and Liu Chunbin, "A Probe Into Urbanization in Rural Areas," *Beijing Review* 32:21 (May 22–26, 1989), p. 26.

10. *Statistical Yearbook 1988* (Paris: UNESCO, 1988), pp. 1–19 to 1–21.

11. Andrew J. Nathan, *Chinese Democracy*, paperback (Berkeley, Ca.: University of California Press, 1986), ch. 8.

12. Compare Seymour Martin Lipset, *Political Man: The Social Bases of Politics*, expanded and updated ed., paperback (Baltimore: The Johns Hopkins University Press, 1981), pp. 27–63; G. Bingham Powell, Jr., *Contemporary Democracies: Participation, Stability, and Violence*, paperback ed. (Cambridge: Harvard University Press, 1982), pp. 34–41.

13. Su Xiaokang and Wang Luxiang, chief writers, *Heshang* (Beijing: Xiandai chubanshe, 1988), quotations from pp. 103, 16, and 6.

14. Yi Jiayan [pseudonym], " 'Heshang' xuanyangle shemme?" *Renmin ribao, haiwaiban*, July 19, 1989, p. 4.

15. "On Questions of Party History," *Beijing Review* 24:27 (July 6, 1981), pp. 25–26.

16. J. Roland Pennock, *Democratic Political Theory*, paperback ed. (Princeton: Princeton University Press, 1979), pp. 239–253.

17. For the concept of civic culture, see Gabriel A. Almond and

Sidney Verba, *The Civic Culture: Political Attitudes and Democracy in Five Nations*, abridged, paperback ed. (Boston: Little, Brown and Co., 1965).

18. The project was supported by the U.S. National Science Foundation and designed in cooperation with the Opinion Research Center of China, a private research institute.

19. See, for example, Lester W. Milbrath and M. L. Goel, *Political Participation: How and Why Do People Get Involved in Politics?*, Second Ed., paperback (Chicago: Rand McNally, 1977).

20. Li Yiping, "Survey of the Political Psychology of Chinese Citizens," *Gaige* No. 6, 10 November 1988, in JPRS-CAR-89-023, 20 March 1989, pp. 1–6.

21. Almond and Verba, *Civic Culture*, ch. 12.

22. Interview with Zhao Fusan by Guy Sorman in *Le Figaro Magazine*, 27 May 1989, in FBIS-CHI-89-104, 1 June 1989, p. 32.

23. Adam Przeworski, "Some Problems in the Study of the Transition to Democracy," in Guillermo O'Donnell, Philippe C. Schmitter, and Laurence Whitehead, eds., *Transitions from Authoritarian Rule: Comparative Perspectives*, paperback (Baltimore: The Johns Hopkins University Press, 1986), p. 58, quotation slightly edited. Also see Douglas A. Chalmers and Craig H. Robinson, "Why Power Contenders Choose Liberalization: Perspectives from South America," *International Studies Quarterly* 26:1 (March 1982), pp. 3–36.

24. *Zhongyang ribao* (Taibei), December 26, 1985, p. 1.

25. "Main Points of Yang Shangkun's Speech at Emergency Enlarged Meeting of Central Military Commission on 24 May 1989 (edited from transcript of speech)," Hong Kong *Ming Pao*, 29 May 1989, in FBIS-CHI-89-102, 30 May 1989, p. 18.

26. *Renmin ribao, haiwaiban*, June 29, 1989, p. 1.

27. Deng's June 9 talk in *Beijing Review* 32:28 (July 10–16, 1989), p. 18.

28. Cf. Valerie Bunce, *Do New Leaders Make a Difference? Executive Succession and Public Policy Under Capitalism and Socialism* (Princeton: Princeton University Press, 1981).

29. For the concept of power deflation, see Chalmers Johnson, *Revolutionary Change*, 2d ed., paperback (Stanford: Stanford University Press, 1982), pp. 31–33.

30. Shang Rongguang, " 'We're Not Wrong, Mum!'—Report from the Hospital," *Beijing Review* 32:22 (May 29–June 4, 1989), p. 29.

INDEX

Studies of the East Asian Institute

The Ladders of Success in Imperial China, by Ping-ti Ho. New York: Columbia University Press, 1962.

The Chinese Inflation, 1937–1949, by Shun-hsin Chou. New York: Columbia University Press, 1963.

Reformer in Modern China: Chang Chien, 1853–1926, by Samuel Chu. New York: Columbia University Press, 1965.

Research in Japanese Sources: A Guide, by Herschel Webb with the assistance of Marleigh Ryan. New York: Columbia University Press, 1965.

Society and Education in Japan, by Herbert Passin. New York: Teachers College Press, 1965.

Agricultural Production and Economic Developments in Japan, 1873–1922, by James I. Nakamura. Princeton: Princeton University Press, 1967.

Japan's First Modern Novel: Ukigumo of Futabatei Shimei, by Marleigh Ryan. New York: Columbia University Press, 1967.

The Korean Communist Movement, 1918–1948, by Dae-Sook Suh. Princeton: Princeton University Press, 1967.

The First Vietnam Crisis, by Melvin Gurtov. New York: Columbia University Press, 1967.

Cadres, Bureaucracy, and Political Power in Communist China, by A. Doak Barnett. New York: Columbia University Press, 1968.

The Japanese Imperial Institution in the Tokugawa Period, by Herschel Webb. New York: Columbia University Press, 1968.

Higher Education and Business Recruitment in Japan, by Koya Azumi. New York: Teachers College Press, 1969.

The Communists and Peasant Rebellions: A Study in the Rewriting of Chinese History, by James P. Harrison, Jr. New York: Atheneum, 1969.

How the Conservatives Rule Japan, by Nathaniel B. Thayer. Princeton: Princeton University Press, 1969.

Aspects of Chinese Education, edited by C. T. Hu. New York: Teachers College Press, 1970.

Documents of Korean Communism, 1918–1948, by Dae-Sook Suh. Princeton: Princeton University Press, 1970.

Japanese Education: A Bibliography of Materials in the English Language, by Herbert Passin. New York: Teachers College Press, 1970.

Economic Development and the Labor Market in Japan, by Koji Taira. New York: Columbia University Press, 1970.

The Japanese Oligarchy and the Russo-Japanese War, by Shumpei Okamoto. New York: Columbia University Press, 1970.

Imperial Restoration in Medieval Japan, by H. Paul Varley. New York: Columbia University Press, 1971.

Japan's Postwar Defense Policy, 1947–1968, by Martin E. Weinstein. New York: Columbia University Press, 1971.

Election Campaigning Japanese Style, by Gerald L. Curtis. New York: Columbia University Press, 1971.

China and Russia: The "Great Game," by O. Edmund Clubb. New York: Columbia University Press, 1971.

Money and Monetary Policy in Communist China, by Katharine Huang Hsiao. New York: Columbia University Press, 1971.

The District Magistrate in Late Imperial China, by John R. Watt. New York: Columbia University Press, 1972.

Law and Policy in China's Foreign Relations: A Study of Attitude and Practice, by James C. Hsiung. New York: Columbia University Press, 1972.

Pearl Harbor as History: Japanese-American Relations, 1931–1941, edited by Dorothy Borg and Shumpei Okamoto, with the assistance of Dale K. A. Finlayson. New York: Columbia University Press, 1973.

Japanese Culture: A Short History, by H. Paul Varley. New York: Praeger, 1973.

Doctors in Politics: The Political Life of the Japan Medical Association, by William E. Steslicke. New York: Praeger, 1973.

The Japan Teachers Union: A Radical Interst Group in Japanese Politics, by Donald Ray Thurston. Princeton: Princeton University Press, 1973.

Japan's Foreign Policy, 1868–1941: A Research Guide, edited by James William Morley. New York: Columbia University Press, 1974.

Palace and Politics in Prewar Japan, by David Anson Titus. New York: Columbia University Press, 1974.

The Idea of China: Essays in Geographic Myth and Theory, by Andrew March. Devon, England: David and Charles, 1974.

Origins of the Cultural Revolution, by Roderick MacFarquhar. New York: Columbia University Press, 1974.

Shiba Kōkan: Artist, Innovator, and Pioneer in the Westernization of Japan, by Calvin L. French. Tokyo: Weatherhill, 1974.

Insei: Abdicated Sovereigns in the Politics of Late Heian Japan, by G. Cameron Hurst. New York: Columbia University Press, 1975.

Embassy at War, by Harold Joyce Noble. Edited with an introduction by Frank Baldwin, Jr. Seattle: University of Washington Press, 1975.

Rebels and Bureaucrats: China's December 9ers, by John Israel and Donald W. Klein. Berkeley: University of California Press, 1975.

Deterrent Diplomacy, edited by James William Morley. New York: Columbia University Press, 1976.

House United, House Divided: The Chinese Family in Taiwan, by Myron L. Cohen. New York: Columbia University Press, 1976.

Escape from Predicament: Neo-Confucianism and China's Evolving Political Culture, by Thomas A. Metzger. New York: Columbia University Press, 1976.

Cadres, Commanders, and Commissars: The Training of the Chinese Communist Leadership, 1920–45, by Jane L. Price. Boulder, Colo.: Westview Press, 1976.

Sun Yat-Sen: Frustrated Patriot, by C. Martin Wilbur. New York: Columbia University Press, 1977.

Japanese International Negotiating Style, by Michael Blaker. New York: Columbia University Press, 1977.

Contemporary Japanese Budget Politics, by John Creighton Campbell. Berkeley: University of California Press, 1977.

The Medieval Chinese Oligarchy, by David Johnson. Boulder, Colo.: Westview Press, 1977.

The Arms of Kiangnan: Modernization in the Chinese Ordnance Industry, 1860–1895, by Thomas L. Kennedy. Boulder, Colo.: Westview Press, 1978.

Patterns of Japanese Policymaking: Experiences from Higher Education, by T. J. Pempel. Boulder, Colo.: Westview Press, 1978.

The Chinese Connection: Roger S. Greene, Thomas W. Lamont, George E. Sokolsky, and American-East Asian Relations, by Warren I. Cohen. New York: Columbia University Press, 1978.

Militarism in Modern China: The Career of Wu P'ei-Fu, 1916–1939, by Odoric Y. K. Wou. Folkestone, England: Dawson, 1978.

A Chinese Pioneer Family: The Lins of Wu-Feng, by Johanna Meskill. Princeton University Press, 1979.

Perspectives on a Changing China, edited by Joshua A. Fogel and William T. Rowe. Boulder, Colo.: Westview Press, 1979.

The Memoirs of Li Tsung-Jen, by T. K. Tong and Li Tsung-jen. Boulder, Colo.: Westview Press, 1979.

Unwelcome Muse: Chinese Literature in Shanghai and Peking, 1937–1945, by Edward Gunn. New York: Columbia University Press, 1979.

Yenan and the Great Powers: The Origins of Chinese Communist Foreign Policy, by James Reardon-Anderson. New York: Columbia University Press, 1980.

Uncertain Years: Chinese-American Relations, 1947–1950, edited by Dorothy Borg and Waldo Heinrichs. New York: Columbia University Press, 1980.

The Fateful Choice: Japan's Advance Into Southeast Asia, edited by James William Morley, New York: Columbia University Press, 1980.

Tanaka Giichi and Japan's China Policy, by William F. Morton. Folkestone, England: Dawson, 1980; New York: St. Martin's Press, 1980.

The Origins of the Korean War: Liberation and the Emergence of Separate Regimes, 1945–1947, by Bruce Cumings. Princeton University Press, 1981.

Class Conflict in Chinese Socialism, by Richard Curt Kraus. New York: Columbia University Press, 1981.

Education Under Mao: Class and Competition in Canton Schools, by Jonathan Unger. New York: Columbia University Press, 1982.

Private Academies of Tokugawa Japan, by Richard Rubinger. Princeton: Princeton University Press, 1982.

Japan and the San Francisco Peace Settlement, by Michael M. Yoshitsu. New York: Columbia University Press, 1982.

New Frontiers in American-East Asian Relations: Essays Presented to Dorothy Borg, edited by Warren I. Cohen. New York: Columbia University Press, 1983.

The Origins of the Cultural Revolution: II, The Great Leap Forward, 1958–1960, by Roderick MacFarquhar. New York: Columbia University Press, 1983.

The China Quagmire: Japan's Expansion of the Asian Continent, 1933–1941, edited by James William Morley. New York: Columbia University Press, 1983.

Fragments of Rainbows: The Life and Poetry of Saito Mokichi, 1882–1953, by Amy Vladeck Heinrich. New York: Columbia University Press, 1983.

The U.S.-South Korean Alliance: Evolving Patterns of Security Relations, edited by Gerald L. Curtis and Sung-joo Han. Lexington, Mass.: Lexington Books, 1983.

Discovering History in China; American Historical Writing on the Recent Chinese Past, by Paul A. Cohen. New York: Columbia University Press, 1984.

The Foreign Policy of the Republic of Korea, edited by Youngnok Koo and Sungjoo Han. New York: Columbia University Press, 1984.

State and Diplomacy in Early Modern Japan, by Ronald Toby. Princeton: Princeton University Press, 1983.

Japan and the Asian Development Bank, by Dennis Yasutomo. New York: Praeger Publishers, 1983.

Japan Erupts: The London Naval Conference and the Manchurian Incident, edited by James W. Morley. New York: Columbia University Press, 1984.

Japanese Culture, third edition, revised, by Paul Varley. Honolulu: University of Hawaii Press, 1984.

Japan's Modern Myths: Ideology in the Late Meiji Period, by Carol Gluck. Princeton: Princeton University Press, 1985.

Shamans, Housewives, and Other Restless Spirits: Women in Korean Ritual Life, by Laurel Kendell. Honolulu: University of Hawaii Press, 1985.

Human Rights in Contemporary China, by R. Randle Edwards, Louis Henkin, and Andrew J. Nathan. New York: Columbia University Press, 1986.

The Pacific Basin: New Challenges for the United States, edited by James W. Morley. New York: Academy of Political Science, 1986.

The Manner of Giving: Strategic Aid and Japanese Foreign Policy, by Dennis T. Yasutomo. Lexington, Mass.: Lexington Books, 1986.

Security Interdependence in the Asia Pacific Region, James W. Morley, Ed., Lexington, MA-DC: Heath and Co, 1986.

China's Political Economy: The Quest for Development Since 1949, by Carl Riskin. Oxford: Oxford University Press, 1987.

Anvil of Victory: The Communist Revolution in Manchuria, by Steven I. Levine. New York: Columbia University Press, 1987.

Single Sparks: China's Rural Revolutions, edited by Kathleen Hartford and Steven M. Goldstein. Armonk, N.Y.: M.E. Sharpe, 1987.

Urban Japanese Housewives: At Home and in the Community, by Anne E. Imamura. Honolulu: University of Hawaii Press, 1987.

China's Satellite Parties, by James D. Seymour. Armonk, N.Y.: M.E. Sharpe, 1987.

The Japanese Way of Politics, by Gerald. L. Curtis. New York: Columbia University Press, 1988.

Border Crossings: Studies in International History, by Christopher Thorne. Oxford & New York: Basil Blackwell, 1988.

The Indochina Tangle: China's Vietnam Policy, 1975–1979, by Robert S. Ross. New York: Columbia University Press, 1988.

Remaking Japan: The American Occupation as New Deal, by Theodore Cohen, Herbert Passin, ed. New York: The Free Press, 1987.

Kim Il Sung: The North Korean Leader, by Dae-Sook Suh. New York: Columbia University Press, 1988.

Japan and the World, 1853–1952: A Bibliographic Guide to Recent Scholarship in Japanese Foreign Relations, by Sadao Asada. New York: Columbia University Press, 1988.

Contending Approaches to the Political Economy of Taiwan, edited by Edwin A. Winckler and Susan Greenhalgh. Armonk, NY: M. E. Sharpe, 1988.

Aftermath of War: Americans and the Remaking of Japan, 1945–1952, by Howard B. Schonberger. Kent: Kent State University Press, forthcoming.

Suicidal Narrative in Modern Japan: The Case of Dazai Osamu, by Alan Wolfe. Princeton: Princeton University Press, 1990.

Neighborhood Tokyo, by Theodore C. Bestor. Stanford: Stanford University Press, 1989.

Missionaries of the Reovlution: Soviet Advisers and Chinese Nationalism, by C. Martin Wilbur Julie Lien-ying How. Cambridge, MA: Harvard University Press, 1989.

Education in Japan, by Richard Rubinger and Beauchamp. Honolulu: University Hawaii, 1989.

Financial Politics in Contemporary Japan, by Frances Rosenbluth. Ithaca: Cornell University Press, 1989.

Thailand and the United States: Development, Security and Foreign Aid, by Robert Muscat. New York: Columbia University Press, 1990.

State Power, Finance and Industrialization of Korea, by Jung-Eun Woo. New York: Columbia University Press, 1990.

Anarchism and Chinese Political Culture, by Peter Zarrow. New York: Columbia University Press, 1990.

The Study of Change: Chemistry in China 1840–1949, by James Reardon-Anderson. New York: Cambridge University Press, 1990.

Competitive Ties: Subcontracting in the Japanese Automotive Industry, by Michael Smitka. New York: Columbia University Press, 1990.

China's Crisis: Dilemmas of Reform and Prospects of Democracy, by Andrew J. Nathan. New York: Columbia University Press.